D0927887

An American Transplant

THIS VOLUME IS SPONSORED BY

THE CENTER FOR CHINESE STUDIES

UNIVERSITY OF CALIFORNIA, BERKELEY

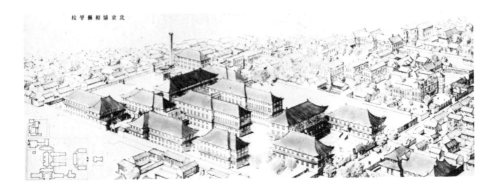

Architect's drawing of the proposed Peking Union Medical College complex, c. 1918.

An American Transplant

THE ROCKEFELLER FOUNDATION AND

PEKING UNION MEDICAL COLLEGE

Mary Brown Bullock

University of California Press

BERKELEY · LOS ANGELES · LONDON

University of California Press
Berkeley and Los Angeles, California
University of California Press, Ltd.
London, England
© 1980 by
The Regents of the University of California
Printed in the United States of America

Library of Congress Cataloging in Publication Data

Bullock, Mary Brown.
    An American transplant.

    Bibliography: p.
    Includes index.
    1. Medical colleges—China—Peking—History.
2. Rockefeller Foundation.   3. Peking. Union
Medical College.   I. Title. [DNLM: 1. History
of medicine, 20th century—China. 2. Public
health—History—China. 3. Research support—
China. WZ70 JC6 B9a]
R812.B84   610'.7'1151156   77-83098
ISBN 0-520-03559-3

1   2   3   4   5   6   7   8   9

To George

Contents

Illustrations

Tables and Maps

Preface

MY FIRST VISIT to the Rockefeller Foundation's Peking Union Medical College, today housing both the Capital Hospital and the Chinese Academy of Medical Sciences, took place very early on a hazy October morning in 1974. It was my first day in Peking, and not yet having adjusted to the time change, I awoke around 5:00 A.M. Dressing hurriedly, I descended through the lobby of the "old" Peking Hotel and out the front door to Ch'ang-an-chieh, the broad tree-lined avenue that leads directly to T'ien-an-men Square. Instead of turning west toward that famous site, I went east and then north on Wang-fu-ching, a shopping street at this hour almost deserted. Walking past the New China Book Store I turned right, a little uncertainly, at a narrow lane. After walking about one hundred yards past grey-walled courtyards where some life was beginning to stir, institution-like buildings with green-tiled roofs began to be evident behind a wall and through the morning mist. I had arrived!

Wishing desperately that I had brought one of the old campus maps from my files, I tried to remember if this first corner building had been Physiology, or maybe Anatomy where Davidson Black had studied the Peking Man bones. A few paces further, and I had no doubt of my location. To my left was the gate leading into the marble courtyard in front of the main administration building of

Peking Union Medical College. I knew that Roger Greene's office had been on the left as you entered the hallway, and that a long marble corridor connected this building with the hospital complex to the rear. Still standing in the quiet road I turned right to find the former Auditorium, which appeared newly restored. Here an organ once pealed on Sunday mornings. It was not difficult to picture graduation processions moving down the marble steps, through the elaborately carved and decorated gate, across the way to the Auditorium styled after a Confucian ancestral hall.

My reverie was broken when I turned to read the signs and *ta-tzu pao* (large character posters) scattered around. The main sign informed me that this was the Chinese Academy of Medical Sciences. A large placard hanging over the marble stairs read, "Long Life to Chairman Mao and the People's Republic of China." Smaller posters read, "Victory to the Proletarian Peoples of the World." The days when John D. Rockefeller, Jr., William Welch, Roger Greene, John Grant, J. Heng Liu, C. C. Ch'en, and Marian Yang had walked through this gate had long been gone. The posters were a reminder that six days earlier Peking had celebrated the twenty-fifth anniversary of the founding of the People's Republic of China.

During this and several subsequent visits to Peking,[1] I was never happier than roaming the lanes and streets which bordered the former PUMC. I gazed at the fading carved eaves which looked slightly out-of-place on clearly functional educational and medical buildings. I followed another road which led directly from Wang-fu-ching, past the Peking Duck Restaurant, to what is today the Capital Hospital. I located the former North and South Compounds where two-story brick residences in the style of the 1920s once housed the PUMC faculty. I was never quite sure I wanted to go *in* any of these buildings; for me they would always be inhabited by ghosts I had never personally met but had come to know through their articles, papers, letters, and friends.

On my second trip to China in April 1975 with a medical delegation, I did go into Capital Hospital. I walked through the wards and out into the compound area where lilac and forsythia were in bloom, and stacks of new green tiles suggested that some of the Chinese-style roofs were about to be repaired. This still renowned

1. As a member of the staff of the Committee on Scholarly Communication with the People's Republic of China, I have accompanied four scientific delegations to China, the American Seismology Delegation in 1974, the American Schistosomiasis Delegation in 1975, the CSCPRC Delegation in 1977, and the Earthquake Engineering Delegation in 1978.

hospital is an institutional reminder of the Rockefeller Foundation's presence in China. But it was elsewhere that I found a living legacy.

When the medical delegation I was accompanying arrived at Peking's Friendship Hospital, five or six white-coated doctors were waiting on the stairs to greet us. A balding doctor, barely five feet in height, led the others in welcoming us. Speaking in flawless English, with a slightly British accent, he introduced himself as Chung Huei-lan. Others informed us that he was Vice-Director of the hospital. We spent one day as Dr. Chung's guests, and he joined us for an evening discussion, a banquet, and waved us off at the Peking airport. During that time I watched and listened to him with rapt attention. Dr. Chung graduated from PUMC in 1929, pursued his medical studies in England and the United States, returned to PUMC's Department of Medicine where he authored many articles on parasitology, became editor of *The Chinese Medical Journal* after Liberation (a post he held until the Cultural Revolution), and was elected one of the few medical members of the prestigious Chinese Academy of Sciences. Judged by any standard, Chung Huei-lan was one of PUMC's most outstanding graduates.

Dr. Chung was eager to hear news of former colleagues and professors in the United States. He thoroughly enjoyed his several sessions with the American medical scientists. Occasionally he assisted a young Chinese medical translator with the appropriate English technical term. He was most impressive to me, however, when he briefed us at the Peking Friendship Hospital.

There was nothing especially unique about the information he provided about the hospital's department of pathology. The themes he stressed—"put prevention first" and "put the emphasis on the rural areas"—were to be repeated in all the medical institutions we visited. But knowing his research background, the slogans somehow seemed more powerful. Chung spoke with enthusiasm when he described a mass screening program for clonorchiasis, a disease caused by a liver fluke, in which his staff had instructed and then worked alongside barefoot doctors. There was unmistakable pride when he told of the eradication of kala-azar, a disfiguring parasitic disease affecting primarily children and adolescents which left untreated was usually fatal; and of the low incidence of paragonimiasis, an infection of the lungs caused by a trematode. Only a few decades earlier these parasitic diseases had ravaged North China. There was equal pride when he showed us the hospital's laboratories, and asked his much younger staff to describe their research.

Chung did not refer to his own research years earlier in PUMC's lavishly equipped laboratories when, as a young instructor, he contributed to the painstaking studies of kala-azar and paragonimiasis, research that years later had made possible the eradication campaigns. But I remembered the many articles published in *The Chinese Medical Journal* of the 1930s, and reflected on a career that spanned two very different eras, and on a medical scientist who had become a teacher and a leader for public health.

I had encountered a different kind of living legacy a year earlier on my first trip to China. It was about eight o'clock at night, and dark, when the train from Peking to Sian stopped briefly at Ting Hsien. A dimly-lit platform and a few street lights were all that I saw of this town made famous during the thirties as the center of Jimmy Yen's Mass Education Movement. The surrounding county of the same name had formed the experimental area for the MEM's educational, economic, and health programs. It was here that Ch'en Chih-ch'ien (C. C. Ch'en), a PUMC graduate in public health, hammered out a rural health organization strikingly similar to that of contemporary China, complete with lay village health workers, forerunners to today's barefoot doctors.

I did not have the opportunity to see what Ting Hsien is like today, but I did visit Hsing-t'ai, a rural village some one hundred miles due south. Hsing-t'ai is not on the beaten tourist track; but as the scene of a devastating earthquake in 1966, it was of special interest to the group of American seismologists I was accompanying. We were given a walking tour of the village, and at the dusty main intersection stood a nondescript, small brick building. Standing outside were a young man and woman who were barefoot doctors. Three other barefoot doctors served the commune, but they were on rotation that day, working in the fields. There were two rooms inside the health center, both with clay floors. One contained traditional and modern drugs, simple medical equipment, and public health brochures. The other had an obstetrical table. We were told that while most births took place at home, assisted by midwives who worked with the barefoot doctors, more complicated cases were brought to the center for delivery. I was immediately reminded of Marian Yang's midwifery program during the 1930s, funded in part by the Rockefeller Foundation's International Health Division, which pioneered the training of midwives for just such basic services as these.

These two barefoot doctors and the urbane Dr. Chung Huei-lan were, for me, far more tangible links between the Rockefeller Foundation and medicine in China today than the still-walled compound of the former PUMC. It was not until I met Dr. Chung and sensed his leadership in medical research and medical outreach that I, a

layman, began to understand the significance of quality training at
PUMC. And not until I talked with those two barefoot doctors, scarcely one hundred miles from Ting Hsien, did I become viscerally
convinced that the arduous decade of paramedical training by John
Grant, C. C. Ch'en, and Marian Yang had not been in vain.

Admittedly, Dr. Chung was only one man among many; and the
historical link between C. C. Ch'en and Marian Yang and China's
contemporary medical system is part of a broad process. This book
does explore one facet of the long-range influence of the Rockefeller
Foundation in China—the role of the PUMC graduates in the People's Republic. Studies which examine other aspects of the history
of modern medicine in China—missionary medicine, the Kuomintang's National Health Administration, war-time medical training
programs of both the KMT and the Chinese Communist Party,
medical services in Yenan, Soviet medical influence during the
1950s, the role of George Hatem (Ma Hai-teh)—are needed before
the Rockefeller Foundation's contributions to China's present medical system can be placed in proper perspective.

With Western medicine during the Republican period as a back-
drop, this study does examine the role of an American philanthropic
foundation in pre-Communist China. It is not a complete account
of the Rockefeller Foundation's China involvement, for its support
of the humanities, natural sciences, agriculture, and rural reconstruction in China are touched on only briefly. These efforts were,
however, financially and philosophically always secondary to the
Foundation's medical commitment to China. Nor is this a complete
history of Peking Union Medical College, the symbol of the Rockefeller Foundation not only in China, but throughout Asia. Two
earlier works have provided an introduction to PUMC. Mary Ferguson, former registrar of the medical college, has contributed an
authoritative account of the administrative relations between PUMC,
the Rockefeller Foundation, and the China Medical Board in her
*China Medical Board and Peking Union Medical College, A Chron-
icle of Fruitful Collaboration.* John Bowers' *Western Medicine in a
Chinese Palace; Peking Union Medical College, 1917–1951* is a de-
scriptive overview of the institution, which concentrates on the research and careers of the PUMC faculty, especially the western
contingent.[2]

This study differs from theirs substantively by focusing on the
careers of the PUMC students, and conceptually by its concern with

2. For a critique of these two books see the author's review in the *Journal of Asian
Studies*, 32 (August 1973): 689–691.

the appropriateness of the PUMC model. Also, I stray rather far from PUMC in focusing on the public health programs of one of its professors, John Grant, and in singling out the careers of two of his students. Topically, rather than comprehensively, this study depicts a Sino-American institution groping towards an accommodation with its Chinese environment.

There are few models or conceptual theories to serve as guidelines for this kind of a study. Traditionally, most studies of binational institutions and American cultural or intellectual activities abroad have concentrated on the sending side, the benefactors—their motives, funds, operations, and personnel. They have only given a side glance to the beneficiaries, much less the relationship between them. Explaining why he concentrated on the philanthropists, their goals and methods, rather than the receivers in his study, *American Philanthropy in the Near East*, Robert Daniel writes:

> The assessment of the impact of the American activities on the native culture, while of great importance, is most elusive. The material impact —the food, clothing, and funds—can be documented with a degree of precision.
>
> So can the introduction of new institutions—schools, presses, and dispensaries. The intellectual impact is less easy to evaluate.[3]

In this short paragraph the author used the word "impact" three times. It is a term frequently used in describing the influence of Western civilization in lesser-developed areas of the world. "Impact" is defined as "a striking together; collision" and further amplified as "the blow given by the striking body." There is something singular, instantaneous, and forceful about the word "impact." It is as aggressive as the word "response" is passive. Grants, programs, and personnel should have "impact"; and if this is not measurable, it should at least be discernible, and if not this year, then at least five years from now. The word "impact" leaves little room for the subtleties of time, process, diffusion, and reciprocation. It is a very final word.

In the past, we have commonly searched for an "impact" in foreign countries. This is partly due to our perception of philanthropy, or religion, or foreign aid as a one-way, or unilateral, transfer. It is also due in part to our assumption that the effects will be manifest in terms of a "response." Defined as "something said or done in answer," or in psychological terms as "any reaction to a stimu-

---

3. Robert Daniel, *American Philanthropy in the Near East* (Athens: Ohio University Press, 1970), p. x.

lus," this implies a single, causal relationship between "impact" and "response." There are several things wrong with utilizing this terminology in the arena of intercultural relations. First, it suggests that the nature of the "impact" determines the nature of the "response." Secondly, it implies that it is possible for a country to have a single, unified response to outside influences. Thirdly, it relegates the role of recipients to a passive stimulus-response reaction. And finally, it ignores the evolving dimensions of time and change. The underlying problem with the "impact-response" syndrome, as it defines both sender and receiver, is that it is singular and one-dimensional.

It is, of course, far easier to point out these conceptual flaws than it is to offer a new approach to intercultural programs. In the pages which follow, three different components of the Rockefeller Foundation's China presence are considered—ideology, institutions, and individuals. The ideology is that of Western, particularly American, medicine. The institutions are educational—Peking Union Medical College and the distinct standards of medical training it embodied. The individuals are Chinese and Americans, interpreters of both the ideology and the institutions. The crucial issues are not impact, but *adaptation*; not response, but *assimilation*.

These latter concepts offer no systematic guideline for analysis: they are fluid and open-ended. Adapt means: "to make suitable, especially by changing." In this context, adaptation suggests that the American input, either institutionally or individually, has the potential to respond to a foreign environment, through change and creativity. Assimilate means: "to take up and make part of itself, or oneself." Assimilation suggests that, through modification and selective absorption, a culture or an individual itself determines the nature of the impact. Both adaptation and assimilation suggest an on-going process, a temporal evolution.

In this study I am primarily concerned with both whether and how an ideology and its institutions were *adapted* to China. I am also interested in assimilation, but that is a far more complex process, especially when it involves something as enmeshed in the cultural and institutional fabric of a society as medicine. More research into the interaction between traditional and modern medicine, and a broader treatment of the Chinese medical profession, is needed before the problems of assimilating "Rockefeller" medicine in China can be fully explored. Here the focus is more narrow. The protagonists are only the American and Chinese middlemen associated with the Rockefeller Foundation's programs in China. And by far the greatest attention is focused on one distinct group—

the graduates of Peking Union Medical College. They are not un-
important, for like the two-faced Janus of old they looked both east
and west, and could become involved or not involved in both the
adaptation and the assimilation.

Today there is no better spot to ponder America's cultural involvement in China, both past and future, than from the roof of the old
Grand Hotel de Pekin. During the period James Thomson has so
poignantly called "while China faced west," this roof served as a
summer dance floor for the foreign community in Peking. Many
old China hands as well as passing tourists, including John D.
Rockefeller, Jr., enjoyed its panoramic view. It is only partially
changed today.

Looking directly south, you will see a tree-filled residential section, while looking southwest toward T'ien-an-men Square you will
see the roofs of Mao's mausoleum and the monumental Great Hall
of the People. Those edifices, the greatly enlarged square, and its
central cenotaph dedicated to the "Heroes of the Chinese Revolution," are new. So too in the distance is the row of ten-story apart-
ment buildings along the southern perimeter of where Peking's
city wall once stood. However, the nearby peaceful residential area
with its graceful compounds dates from the early part of the century and is the former Legation Quarter. Today much of it seems
deserted or converted to political purposes. The buildings of Peking's Revolutionary Committee, for example, are in this section.
Twin spires, with their crosses still attached, soar over what was
once a Catholic Church and is now a kindergarten. Buildings that
clearly once were banks stand in disrepair. The former American
Marine barracks today houses People's Liberation Army troops.

If you look to the northwest, a hazy golden glow emanates from
the hundreds of curved tiled roofs of the once Forbidden City. Their
stylized harmony still presides over the comings-and-goings in
T'ien-an-men Square. Turning to the northeast, the green-tiled
roofs of the twenty-odd buildings of the PUMC complex are clearly
visible. In the shadow of the Forbidden City, and under Chinese
roofs, Rockefeller medicine was brought to China.

Although the dance floor remains closed, the refurbished Peking
Hotel with its modern multi-story addition once again is a central
gathering place for tourists, diplomats, businessmen, and scholars
from all over the world. Since President Richard Nixon's 1971 trip
to China, the hotel has welcomed scores of prestigious American
scientific delegations, who, not unlike the Rockefeller Foundation's
early medical commissions, have sought to evaluate the state of
China's science. These foreign specialists have once more raised

questions of standards, and today this issue is again being debated in Chinese journals and newspapers.

New Chinese-American scientific and medical projects are rising from the ashes of the great interregnum in American-Chinese relations. Once more the Rockefeller Foundation is involved with China. With Tsinghua University, Peking Union Medical College was the most influential model of Sino-American scientific cooperation during an earlier era. It is now nearly thirty years since PUMC ceased to exist as an American institution, and more than half a century since John D. Rockefeller, Jr., came to China for its dedication. Both countries have changed enormously since that time, and both have learned some painful lessons about the pitfalls of what has been called "cultural imperialism." But PUMC has a living legacy, and much can still be learned from its history.

Acknowledgments

THIS STUDY of the Rockefeller Foundation and Peking Union Medical College began as research for a Ph.D. dissertation at Stanford University in 1970. At that time the Rockefeller Foundation Archives were not open for scholarly research, and it was problematical whether or not enough primary materials could be gleaned to provide details on the inner workings of the Foundation and its China activities. I am, therefore, especially grateful to the late Dr. Raymond B. Fosdick, President of the Rockefeller Foundation from 1936–1948, who not only shared his memories but also assisted me in gaining critical access to the Rockefeller Family Archives. This collection, located in the Rockefeller Center, New York City, includes the personal letters of the Rockefeller family and policy documents pertaining to their business and charitable ventures. It not only provided insight into the personal roles and views of three generations of Rockefellers, but it also included the most important policy documents for the period under discussion in this book. Dr. Joseph Ernst, Curator of the Rockefeller Family Archives and Director of the Rockefeller Archive Center, was exceedingly helpful in locating letters and documents for my perusal.

In my early search for materials, I was especially fortunate in that the papers of several individuals prominently involved in the

Rockefeller Foundation and Peking Union Medical College were open to the public. These included the Simon Flexner and Victor Heiser Papers in the American Philosophical Association Library, Philadelphia, Pennsylvania; the William Welch Papers, William Welch Medical Library, The Johns Hopkins University School of Medicine, Baltimore, Maryland; and the Roger Greene Papers at the Houghton Library, Harvard University, Cambridge, Massachusetts. I am grateful to the staff of each of these libraries for assistance. The China Medical Board, Inc., of New York also allowed me to use its library, which included copies of all the articles published by PUMC faculty and graduates.

Since 1973, the Rockefeller Foundation has slowly been opening its archives for scholarly use. Today these archives are located at the Rockefeller Archive Center, Hillcrest, Pocantico Hills, North Tarrytown, New York. The China-related materials that are open and processed include the China Medical Board Collection, the PUMC Papers (processed as the China Medical Board, Inc., Collection), and various segments of the Rockefeller Foundation records, especially those relating to the activities of the International Health Board and the China Program of the mid-1930s. During many visits to the Foundation archives, first located in a warehouse in New York City and now in a first-rate research facility in North Tarrytown, Dr. William Hess, Assistant Director, guided me through processed and unprocessed collections. His personal interest and flexibility greatly eased the final stage of research for this book. I wish to thank the Rockefeller Archive Center for providing eleven of the twelve photographs in this volume.

I worked in several libraries, including the Hoover Institution and the Library of Congress. However, it was the extensive but relatively unknown collection on Chinese medicine and medical education in the National Library of Medicine, Bethesda, Maryland, which provided the most valuable repository of journals and secondary materials.

An enjoyable aspect of studying Peking Union Medical College has been the opportunity to meet individuals who were associated with its history. I owe special gratitude to Miss Mary E. Ferguson, long-time registrar of PUMC and herself a chronicler of its administrative history. An earlier version of this manuscript benefited from her careful reading. During our many conversations over several years, PUMC came alive to me. I also especially appreciate the time and assistance provided by Mrs. John Grant, Dr. Harold Loucks, Dr. Francis Dieuaide, and the late Dr. Marshall Balfour. A list of the individuals who were formally interviewed is included in the Bibliography. I am grateful to each for sharing time and memories.

Over the past years I have also met informally literally scores of individuals who were involved with, or had special knowledge of, the Rockefeller Foundation and Peking Union Medical College. These include some PUMC graduates and professors living in the People's Republic of China. Each encounter enriched my understanding of the character of PUMC.

I am aware that many associated with PUMC, on both sides of the Pacific, will not agree with all my views. But I hope that those with whom I talked will feel that this portrayal is more accurate because of their assistance. Because of them, I came to realize the significance of quality training at PUMC.

I owe far more than perfunctory gratitude to Professor Lyman P. Van Slyke, my dissertation advisor at Stanford University. From across a continent he guided my research and writing with detailed letters of criticism and encouragement. And he first believed that my study would become a book.

Anne Keatley, former Staff Director of the Committee on Scholarly Communication with the People's Republic of China, provided me with the opportunity to become involved personally in the renewal of Chinese-American scholarly relations and also urged me to take a leave of absence to complete this book. The Rockefeller Foundation's Bellagio Study and Conference Center at Lake Como, Italy, provided gracious hospitality for a quiet month of writing. Dr. Huang Kun-yen, Professor of Microbiology, George Washington University, assisted me in understanding PUMC's kala-azar research, and reviewed the medically-oriented sections of this book. John Service made helpful suggestions at several stages in the preparation of this manuscript and his careful reading caught many errors.

Most importantly, my husband, George D. Bullock, has been a part of this endeavor from the beginning. He read and commented in detail on all drafts and provided a happy mix of prodding and support that brought it to completion.

I, alone, am responsible for errors, and I, most of all, realize how many more stories Peking Union Medical College has to tell.

Abbreviations

ABMAC	American Bureau for Medical Aid to China
CMB	China Medical Board
CMBC	China Medical Board Collection
CMB Inc.	China Medical Board, Incorporated
CMJ	*Chinese Medical Journal*
CMMA	China Medical Missionary Association
EMSTS	Emergency Medical Service Training School
FA	Rockefeller Foundation Archives
IHB	International Health Board
KMT	Kuomintang
MEM	Mass Education Movement
MMFB	*Milbank Memorial Fund Quarterly Bulletin*
MRC	Medical Relief Corps
NA	National Archives
NCNA	*New China News Agency*
NEPB	National Epidemic Prevention Bureau
NHA	National Health Administration
NMA	National Medical Association
NMJC	*National Medical Journal of China*
PRC	People's Republic of China
PUMC	Peking Union Medical College
RCA	Red Cross Archives
RF	Rockefeller Foundation
RFA	Rockefeller Family Archives
RGP	Roger Greene Papers
SCMP	*Survey of China Mainland Press*
SFP	Simon Flexner Papers
UNRRA	United Nations Relief and Rehabilitation Administration
VHP	Victor Heiser Papers
WWP	William Welch Papers
YMCA	Young Men's Christian Association

ONE The Dedication

The influence of this medical school is going to be much more far reaching than we had dreamed. It is already setting the standards for China and its influence is extending even now beyond the boundaries of that country.

John D. Rockefeller, Jr., to
John D. Rockefeller, Sr.,
September 19, 1921, Peking

CHRISTIANITY, Western education, and American commerce were all exported to the Orient on the *Empress of Asia* which sailed on August 18, 1921, from Vancouver, Canada, for Yokohama, Japan. Among the usual assortment of missionaries, lesser diplomats, and individual entrepreneurs on that particular trans-Pacific passage were several prominent representatives of American involvement in China.[1]

John D. Rockefeller, Jr., only son of the Standard Oil tycoon, and George Vincent, President of the Rockefeller Foundation (RF), led a group of over twenty-five scientists, professors, and trustees to the dedication of Peking Union Medical College (PUMC), the center of the Foundation's work in Asia. Dr. Ernest DeWitt Burton, professor of theology at the University of Chicago, headed the China Education Commission, an ecumenical committee appointed to study the educational work of all mission societies in China. J. P. Morgan and Company, the largest Wall Street financial institution of its day, was represented by a five-man delegation headed for China to further American investment opportunities under the new consortium agreements of 1920.

1. *New York Times*, 7 August 1921, II, 1:4. This article has an extensive passenger list.

I

These passengers, and those on other ships plying the Pacific in the early twentieth century, were quite different from their counterparts on the North Atlantic crossings of roughly the same era. While travellers to Europe were eager to identify with the culture of the Old World lands,[2] the Pacific voyagers' vague awareness of the Asian cultural heritage was dimmed by the prevailing conviction that the Far East was backward, illiterate, impoverished, and heathen. The motives of these passengers to the Orient undoubtedly spanned a spectrum from genuine religious obligation to individual aggrandizement, but most believed deeply in the superiority of Western civilization.

Of all the groups aboard the *Empress of Asia*, none represented the ambiguities of American participation in China's twentieth century so dramatically as the one led by John D. Rockefeller, Jr. His entourage was travelling almost ten thousand miles to dedicate an institution which symbolized the Rockefeller Foundation's sophisticated commitment to Western scientific and medical education in China. Designed to train medical leaders for the "sick man of Asia," Peking Union Medical College was a quintessentially American institution being transplanted to China. It was to be sustained financially by funds furnished from the monopolistic growth of the Rockefeller family's Standard Oil Company, nurtured intellectually by the leading medical scientists of the day, and blessed morally by a tacit alliance with evangelical missionary societies. With these warranties, it would have seemed naive to question whether the fledgling college would flourish in a foreign land. And travellers on the *Empress of Asia* would have smiled gently at the age-old Chinese admonition to those who would uproot themselves from their native land: "Will you adapt to the soil and water [*Shui-t'u fu-pu-fu*]?"

On this trip John D. Rockefeller, Jr., was the philanthropic symbol of this fusion of religious dedication, educational affirmation, and commercial exploitation. Still, the image of his billionaire father was never far away. The Chinese had already named Peking Union Medical College the "Yu Wang Fu"—the "Oil Prince's Palace." And his son would write to him from Peking: "Of course as is both natural and proper, you are the central figure of this whole enterprise."[3]

2. See, among others, John M. Brinnin, *The Sway of the Grand Saloon: A Social History of the North Atlantic* (New York: Delacorte, 1971), pp. 305–411.

3. John D. Rockefeller, Jr., to John D. Rockefeller, Sr., September 19, 1921. This letter is located in Record Group 3 of the Rockefeller Family Archives, New York City. All subsequent material cited from these archives is contained in this record group, and the collection will be referred to as *RFA*. The nickname "Yu Wang Fu" was a Chinese pun. Part of the PUMC property bought by the Rockefeller Foundation

But Junior's presence was more than a token gesture. Years earlier John D. Rockefeller, Sr., had turned the family's charitable responsibilities over to his enthusiastic son. As chairman of both the board of trustees of the Rockefeller Foundation and its executive committee, John D., Jr., was a powerful representative of his octogenarian father. And in the course of two months in Asia, Rockefeller would find himself courted and entertained by the leading scientists, educators, politicians, missionaries, and businessmen of both China and Japan.

John D. Rockefeller, Jr.'s personal interest in China had preceded the Foundation's formal activities there by nearly twenty years. Evidence of his early acquaintance with China and things Chinese include his systematic teenage tithes in the early 1890s to a Chinese Sunday School in New York City, and the many hours he spent contemplating Benjamin Altman's Chinese porcelain collection. His admiration of Chinese porcelain was to grow into an amateur collector's knowledge of and search for valuable specimens. He himself attributes the beginning of his own collection to several fortuitous circumstances. An English dealer by chance in 1913 showed him "Black Hawthornes" from the K'ang Hsi period. In 1915 the death of J. P. Morgan, Sr., brought his valuable personal collection of Chinese vases up for sale. Although Rockefeller was 39 years old at the time, he had to borrow money from his father in order to make the purchases, primarily of the *famille noir, verte* and *jaune* of the K'ang Hsi era, for the price came to well over one million dollars. Raymond Fosdick, Rockefeller's biographer, gives this insight into Junior's preoccupation with vases of the early Ch'ing dynasty:

> A great admirer of craftsmanship, he would find the ancient skill of the Chinese potter brought to its peak in the K'ang Hsi porcelains. . . . There was, in addition, a certain impersonality about the porcelains which must have appealed to Mr. Rockefeller. Centuries of tradition had gone into their elaborate animal and flower symbolism, and the passions of their human figurines had been refined and simplified by legend. Here was none of the "self-expressionism" which he found so objectionable in modern art.[4]

Rockefeller's admiration of Chinese porcelain reflected that of the leading collectors of his time—a preoccupation with "craftsman-

---

had once belonged to a Prince Yü. The Chinese word for oil [*yu*] was similar in pronunciation to the Prince's name, although a different Chinese character. Thus, "Prince Yü's Palace" was quickly corrupted into "The Oil Prince's Palace."

4. Raymond Fosdick, *John D. Rockefeller, Jr., A Portrait* (New York: Harper and Brothers, 1956), p. 335; see also pp. 22–24. These vases are now on permanent display at the Metropolitan Museum of Art, New York.

ship" and the very ornate Ch'ing art. These art forms were those to which Europe had been exposed in the days when seventeenth-century Jesuits sent "chinoiserie" to the courts of Europe. Their elaborate, decorative forms came to symbolize for the West, including twentieth-century America, the stylized and impersonal exoticism that must be Asia.

By 1921, Rockefeller's interest in China had gone considerably beyond a mere passion for Chinese porcelain. As first president of the Rockefeller Foundation (1913–1917), he had chaired the initial discussions regarding the possible inclusion of China in plans for the Foundation. Through correspondence and regular attendance at the major planning sessions of the Foundation, John D., Jr., became familiar with the detailed reports of the three survey commissions which had been sent to explore the needs of China.[5] In 1914, the Foundation created the China Medical Board (CMB) as an internal division to handle the planning and administration of medical education in China. In 1915, the CMB decided to create and sustain two major centers of education, one in Peking and one in Shanghai.

The Shanghai plan was later abandoned, but in Peking the Foundation bought the property and buildings of the Union Medical College, a joint venture of six missionary societies. Plans were made to expand, strengthen, and up-grade that medical institution. In the course of the next six years the RF built fourteen educational buildings and thirty-six faculty residences on the Union Medical College site. By 1921, the full-time faculty numbered over fifty, drawn largely from the United States.[6] The internationally recognized caliber of the faculty, the impressive outlay of over eight million dollars for capital improvements alone, and the prominence of the Rockefeller name created an aura of expectance and promise at the Peking Union Medical College.

The formal dedication of the school, planned for September of 1921, was designed to induce the American trustees of both the Rockefeller Foundation and PUMC, as well as the executive members of the China Medical Board, to visit Peking. Some in Peking had thought the plans for the occasion too elaborate, but the opportunity for a convocation of medical science in Asia was not to be

---

5. These commissions were: The Burton Commission, 1909; the First China Medical Commission, 1914; The Second China Medical Commission, 1915.

6. "The Buildings of Peking Union Medical College," in *Addresses and Papers, Dedication Ceremonies and Medical Conference, Peking Union Medical College* (Concord, N.H.: Rumford Press, 1922), pp. 14–15; Peking Union Medical College, *Annual Announcement*, 1921, pp. 1–15.

missed. John D. Rockefeller, Jr., wholeheartedly supported plans for the gala opening and personally urged the various trustees to attend.[7] He and his wife, Abby Aldrich Rockefeller, and their daughter Abby left New York for China on August 11, 1921, travelling by special train to Vancouver. Their private entourage included secretaries, valets, a nurse, and two important representatives of the Foundation, George Vincent, its President, and William Henry Welch.

Now over seventy years old and Director of the School of Hygiene and Public Health at The Johns Hopkins University, Welch had for some time been known as the "dean of American medicine." As professor of pathology and later dean of The Johns Hopkins University School of Medicine during its formative years, Welch had been prominent among those responsible for integrating scientific research, clinical treatment, university and medical education into the "Johns Hopkins model" which greatly influenced the course of American medical education.

It was not surprising that John D. Rockefeller, Jr., had chosen Welch as one of his companions for the long trip to China. Through years of close association, primarily in medical endeavors, the younger man developed a filial affection for the genial scientist-educator, who was informally known as "Popsy." This feeling was evinced somewhat later in a letter of unusual warmth from Rockefeller to Welch: "Next to my own father, I think there is no man for whom I have the same deep feeling that I have for you."[8] Furthermore, this was not Welch's first trip to China on behalf of the Rockefellers. In 1915 he had been a member of the Rockefeller Foundation's exploratory Second Medical Commission. Now, six years later, Welch was to attend the dedication of the institution he had been instrumental in designing. His daily diary provides an intimate picture of that 1921 journey.

The Rockefellers journeyed in comfort by rail across the United States and Canada. Welch observed that *The Pioneer*, their private railroad car, "has 5 private rooms, kitchen, dining room, sitting

7. Mary E. Ferguson, *China Medical Board and Peking Union Medical College: A Chronicle of Fruitful Collaboration, 1914–1951* (New York: China Medical Board, Inc., 1970), p. 50. This reference is hereinafter cited as *CMB and PUMC*. See also correspondence between Rockefeller, Jr., and Simon Flexner, June, 1921, Simon Flexner Papers (*SFP*), American Philosophical Society Library, Philadelphia, Pennsylvania.

8. Rockefeller Jr. to Welch, February 27, 1933. William Welch Papers (*WWP*), William H. Welch Medical Library, The Johns Hopkins Medical School, Baltimore, Maryland. For biographical information on Welch, see Simon Flexner and James Thomas Flexner, *William Henry Welch and the Heroic Age of American Medicine* (New York: Viking, 1941); Donald H. Fleming, *William H. Welch and the Rise of Modern Medicine* (Boston: Little, Brown, and Co., 1954).

room at rear and observation platform, shower, bath, and is most comfortable." Aboard the *Empress of Asia*, the Rockefellers had one of the more luxurious suites, "three rooms and a bath." Later, while travelling through China when luggage was perhaps more visible, Welch stated that the Rockefellers had sixty bags for a two-month tour of Asia. The train ride and the subsequent sea voyage provided many days for reading: "Mr. and Mrs. Rockefeller most hospitable, considerate, and agreeable. We all read a good deal. I read 'Peking Dust,' by Miss [Florence] La Motte, 'The Lost Girl,' an unpleasant sexual novel by [D. H.] Lawrence, belonging to Mrs. Rockefeller, and began [J. O. P.] Bland's 'China, Japan and Korea,' belonging to Mr. Rockefeller who has brought a large bag full of books."[9]

The presence of the Rockefeller group aboard the *Empress of Asia* undoubtedly aroused much passenger interest. Welch himself was asked to give one of the periodic shipboard lectures on either China or Japan. Titling his talk "Medical Education in China," Welch noted with some satisfaction: "Good audience (including Mr. Rockefeller and Vincent)." Welch's themes, such as "the value of developing scientific spirit," and "what Western medicine can contribute to the Chinese civilization," illustrate the then-current American civilizing mission. But he also mentioned "studying sanitary problems of China" and, even more importantly, "adapting medical education and work to special environment and needs of China."[10] Although Welch offered no special suggestions for adapting American medical education, his diary briefly mentions Dr. J. B. Grant, a fellow passenger bound for Peking. A product of Welch's own School of Hygiene and Public Health, Grant would eventually design not only an internationally emulated public health curriculum for PUMC, but a health care delivery system for urban China.

From time to time Welch noted discussions on contemporary politics with missionaries who had spent years in China. Favorable opinions of the warlord Yen Hsi-shan and a rather futile attempt to learn more about the President of China, Hsü Shih-ch'ang, were mentioned. For some reason Welch missed the lecture given by the Chinese secretary of the Shanghai YMCA on "The New Thought Movement among the Student Body in China," but he did borrow another passenger's notes on these remarks. These included a description of the wave of student protests following the imposition of Japan's Twenty-one Demands. The demonstrations and debates

9. William Welch, *Diary #15*, (WWP), pp. 5, 35, 12.
10. *Ibid.*, pp. 27, 28.

which began on May 4, 1919, involved far more than foreign policy: the Confucian tradition and its Western counterpart, Christianity, were widely attacked.[11]

These notes did not mention, nor did Welch or any Rockefeller Foundation official ever seem cognizant of, the depth to which the basic values of Western civilization, such as the "scientific spirit" mentioned by Welch in his own talk, were also items of major controversy during what came to be called the "May Fourth" intellectual revolution. Nor did Welch's attempts to learn more about China's changing society give any indication that he understood the complexity of "adapting medical education and work to [the] special environment and needs of China."

There was a certain euphoria about the exciting trip to Peking in 1921. Welch arranged for the Rockefellers to entertain a number of Chinese students in their stateroom lounge. These were the proverbial "returning" Chinese students, travelling back to their homeland after years of graduate study abroad. Tea and other refreshments were served, and all seemed well pleased with the brief and perfunctory occasion.[12] Young Chinese intellectuals carrying back to China Western education and civilization met with John D. Rockefeller, Jr., scion of wealth and noted American philanthropist, who was heading a delegation to participate in the opening of a great medical institution aimed at strengthening Western scientific medicine in China. It seemed most fitting.

Neither group could then have perceived that Western-trained intellectuals would find it difficult to make an impact on the Middle Kingdom, even in the twentieth century. And Welch and Rockefeller could hardly have foreseen a time when the West might look to China for insight into medical techniques, education, and public health.

Standard Oil representatives met Rockefeller's ship in Yokohama for a tour of Japan's historic cities. Dr. Welch, however, departed immediately for Peking where he was to supervise a round of discussions with PUMC's staff. Six years earlier he had travelled extensively in China studying existing medical schools and drawing up guidelines for the Rockefeller institution in Peking. Now, from his suite in the Grand Hotel de Pekin, he saw the physical realization of this enormous undertaking: "Looking to the North, I see from my window to the right the green tiled roofs of the Rockefeller Hospital, and to the left the yellow roofs of the Forbidden City."[13]

The parallel between the architecture of the American enterprise

11. *Ibid.*, pp. 23, 29.   12. *Ibid.*, p. 32.   13. *Ibid.*, p. 47.

and the Forbidden City, which for centuries had been the symbolic focus of Chinese political authority and cultural superiority, was intentional. The decision to design the buildings of PUMC in the Chinese style of architecture involved much expense, consultation, and controversy.[14] For most participants in the Rockefeller work, the result was well worth the effort. Davidson Black, who was to discover the prehistoric Peking Man in 1926, included the following description in his 1924 report on the PUMC Department of Anatomy:

> An attempt has been made to harmonize the buildings with the great architectural monuments of Peking by adapting as nearly as possible Chinese forms for the exteriors. . . . The most striking feature of this treatment are the curved roofs of green tile, with conventional decorations on the eaves in colors, and the entrance courts designed after the model of the old temples and palaces.[15]

The motive seems to have been more than just visual effect. The Rockefeller Foundation *Annual Report* presents an insight into the purpose of PUMC's architectural design: "[the buildings] thus symbolize the purpose to make the College not something foreign to China's best ideals and aspirations, but an organism which will become part of a developing Chinese civilization."[16] In no other foreign country did the Rockefeller Foundation expend such effort to synthesize the physical surroundings of an institution with its cultural milieu.[17] PUMC stood both as tribute to the durability of Chinese culture and as monument to an American effort to change it. Much as the Jesuits of the seventeenth century donned Confucian scholars' robes to gain respect for their Christian message, the Rockefeller Foundation raised a Chinese roof to foster admiration for their mission of scientific education. But there was a difference in the attitude: the seventeenth-century Westerners appear to have been genuinely admiring, whereas their modern successors were perhaps more patronizing.

On September 4, two days before the anticipated arrival of the Rockefeller party, Welch accompanied Roger S. Greene, at that time the Resident Director of the China Medical Board and who

---

14. Ferguson, *CMB and PUMC*, pp. 30–34; see the architect's forty-page report, Charles Coolidge to China Medical Board, October 20, 1916, *SFP*.

15. Davidson Black, "Peking Union Medical College Department of Anatomy," *Methods and Problems of Medical Education*, First Series (New York: The Rockefeller Foundation, 1924), p. 25.

16. Rockefeller Foundation, *Annual Report*, 1917, p. 224.

17. French medical educators, in fact, balked at the Foundation's functional and economic approach to architecture in their country. See Wilder Penfield, *The Difficult Art of Giving: The Epic of Alan Gregg* (Boston: Little, Brown, & Co., 1967), p. 161.

Rooflines of Peking Union Medical College. View of College Court to Gatehouse and Auditorium, 1926.

later directed PUMC for many years, to "a house in Chinese style . . . which is to be occupied by the Rockefellers, situated in a north and south street, not very far from [the] Southern wall and within the Imperial City. Here the ladies . . . were putting down rugs and fixing up for the Rockefellers. An attractive place with small courtyard, rock gardens, courts, etc. They should be most comfortable."[18]

The Rockefellers arrived on the 6th, and on the next day Rockefeller was taken on his first visit of the PUMC campus. On this first day he seems to have spent most of his time thoroughly examining the anatomical laboratory which was presided over by Davidson Black. The laboratories and scientific equipment were the best that money could buy. Rockefeller conveyed his enthusiastic approval of the equipment and buildings in a letter to his father: "We are delighted beyond expression at the Peking Union Medical College buildings, which are perfectly adapted to the purposes and a great contribution not only to science but to architecture."[19]

The Rockefellers spent their first days in Peking largely as tourists. This city, which has stirred visitors for centuries, strongly impressed them. Welch's comments, however, are somewhat laconic:

18. Welch, *Diary #15*, p. 51.
19. Rockefeller Jr. to Rockefeller Sr., September 12, 1921, *RFA*.

"Drove with Mr. Rockefeller, Vincent and Embree [Secretary of the RF and CMB] to Hato Gate and walked to Chien Men gate. Saw sunset." He did not accompany them on their two-day trek to the Great Wall and Ming Tombs. But he does recount escorting the Rockefellers to the top of the Grand Hotel de Pekin for dancing on a Saturday night: "The roof garden and dancing floor of the Hotel de Pekin at least on Saturday nights, are gay and filled with people, evidently the rendezvous for all the fashions of Peking of every race."[20] That evening the crowd was indeed a diverse group including the Manchu Princess Der Ling, Wu Lien-teh, an eminent Chinese physician, many Japanese businessmen, and Rockefeller dancing with his teenage daughter Abby.

The formal business of the visiting Rockefeller Foundation representatives began with a series of meetings on September 13. It is perhaps fitting that the main item on the agenda was the PUMC budget, for this was to be a topic which caused discord and friction throughout the entire history of this American foundation's involvement in China. Costs of the physical plant had already skyrocketed from an estimated US$1 million in 1915 to an actual expenditure of nearly US$8 million by 1921. Now the annual budget appeared to be moving in exactly the same direction. In the first year of operation (1919–1920), the budget for PUMC had been Mex. $493,000, whereas the proposed budget for 1921–1922 had more than doubled, coming to a total of Mex.$1,065,000.[21]

These budgetary figures were vastly higher than originally calculated by the Rockefeller Foundation and had already caused some consternation. Dr. Simon Flexner, Director of the Rockefeller Institute in New York, and an RF and PUMC Trustee, wrote in 1919 of his concern to George Vincent: "I was and still am staggered by the Peking budget. . . . I cannot help asking myself whether such prodigious expenditures in China are necessary and will justify themselves, and whether they may not act as a deterrent on desirable developments by the Chinese themselves."[22] Flexner's words were prophetic, and his concern was shared by others in the Foundation. But sustained by the roseate glow of the dedication, the visiting Rockefeller officials voted to approve the 1921–

20. Welch, *Diary #15*, pp. 62, 79.

21. "Peking Union Medical College—Comparison of Budgets, 1919–1920 and 1920–1921," *SFP*; Ferguson, *CMB and PUMC*, p. 51. Since both American currency and Chinese currency were utilized by PUMC and the CMB, whenever there is a possibility of confusion, monetary figures will be designated either US$ or Mex.$, the silver currency used in China. Throughout most of this period, Mexican currency was valued at about Mex.$2 to US$1.

22. Simon Flexner to George Vincent, November 25, 1919, *SFP*.

1922 budget in its entirety. Rockefeller justified their action in a letter to his tight-fisted billionaire father: "The expenditure is a modest one in comparison with the expenditures in similar institutions in America . . . the danger of extravagance and undue haste in the development of the institution has been reduced to a minimum."[23] The trustees' vote of confidence was in part sustained by the ebullience which surrounded PUMC at the time of the dedication, and in part by the knowledge that the Rockefeller Foundation, unlike missionary boards, did in fact have funds to cover this undertaking. In subsequent years it would be difficult to practice economy at PUMC, for the recipients, both Chinese and Americans, viewed Rockefeller resources as virtually unlimited.

The festive atmosphere which surrounded dedication week in Peking was heightened by the number of receptions and dinners held in honor of the guests and the occasion. The hosts ranged from chiefs of diplomatic missions living in the Legation Quarter to the Peking Chamber of Commerce, and events included a reception with the President of the Republic of China, Hsü Shih-ch'ang. For that latter ceremony the visiting Americans dressed in morning coats and high hats and were taken by barge to the Winter Palace where they "wandered through rock gardens, zig-zag bridges, pavilions, buildings, courtyards until we came to the President's reception room—large, not handsome, with striking, rather ugly modern silk rug." Rockefeller and his wife were entertained by the President while the approximately 150 other guests waited: "At last we crowded forward and the President appeared, an elderly, rather sad looking, kindly gentleman who read a speech in Chinese."[24] It was as though Welch sensed, if he did not in fact know, that Hsu's position as President of China was a titular and temporary one, based on his amiability and flexibility toward the rival warlord factions that had dominated Chinese politics since the death of Yuan Shih-k'ai in 1916.

Two years later a letter from Hsü's secretary to a Dr. Beebe, President of the China Medical Missionary Association, appeared in *The China Medical Journal*. It stated that commemorative medals which President Hsu had ordered struck on the occasion of the PUMC dedication had just been completed. The Chinese Missionary Medical Association was asked to distribute the medals to those who attended the dedication since President Hsu had been forced to resign from the Presidency in 1922 and no longer held the preroga-

23. Rockefeller Jr. to Rockefeller Sr., September 19, 1921, *RFA*.
24. Welch, *Diary #15*, p. 97.

John D. Rockefeller, Jr., and party in Presidential Palace, Peking, 1921. Foreground, from left to right: Mrs. Rockefeller, Miss Abigail Rockefeller, President of the Republic of China Hsü Shih-ch'ang, Mr. Rockefeller.

tives of that office.[25] Such delay was typical, but the erratic nature of Chinese politics in the 1920s both masked and expressed the more profound and enduring problems of Chinese society.

Several days prior to President Hsü's reception, the Chinese Chamber of Commerce had honored the new medical college by sending a memorial plaque to the PUMC campus. The gift was dispatched with much ritual, and the Oriental trappings of its arrival must have heightened a pageantry somewhat antic in Western eyes:

About 4 there appeared the President's band accompanying a delegation from the Peking Chamber of Commerce (Chinese) with a gaily decorated chair or palanquin on which rested a memorial tablet, which was borne into the pavilion by tasselled servants, and placed over [the] door opposite the entrance with the inscription, "Your kindness (or benevolence or

25. Archibald P. Chien to Dr. Beebe, *China Medical Journal* 28 (1923): 199. The *China Medical Journal* became the *Chinese Medical Journal* in 1932: both journals will be cited as *CMJ*.

grace) extends far and near, or has no bounds, or universal benevolence." It is curious that no two translated it exactly the same.[26]

The spectacle of such a beautiful campus and so many
wealthy foreigners also impressed the "tasselled" Chinese coolies
who delivered the gift. Surely some of the "universal benevolence"
would descend upon them. They stood around waiting for payment
from the PUMC staff who accepted the gift. L. Carrington Goodrich,
at that time Assistant Resident Director of PUMC, tipped them with
Mex.$5.00. Welch, in an uncharacteristic outburst, recorded: "They
were not satisfied but kept after him for more. Graft. Graft. What
a picture of the country, these bearers of a gift clamoring for
squeeze. Also the intention to squeeze the Rockefeller undertaking
to the limit. Recently the papers had a paragraph intimating the
Government might ask Mr. R. for a loan!"[27]

"Squeeze," "graft"—how often these two words were to appear
in Western descriptions of China during the first half of the century.[28] Begging was to be a constant irritant, underlining the economic disparity between China and America, made obvious by the
presence of Westerners in China. It was inevitable that foreigners
and their institutions, with the Rockefeller enterprise possessed of
seemingly unlimited resources at the apex, constantly reminded
all Chinese of their own poverty. And though it seemed incredible
to Welch that the Chinese government would ask Rockefeller himself for a loan, in the years ahead various Chinese ministries would
in fact receive support from the Rockefeller Foundation.

This incident may have marred the occasion for Welch, but it
also seemed to open his eyes to some of the realities of China and
the Peking Union Medical College. While attending a Trustee meeting he watched groups touring the new campus: "I could see from
window large numbers of Chinese, men and women, well dressed,
a few Japanese and a considerable number of foreigners being conducted through the buildings." Welch then mused on the absence
of ordinary Chinese: "the crowds were not very large and I should
not say the interest on the part of the people of Peking was much
aroused."[29] It had become obvious to Welch that the name "Rockefeller" prompted lavish entertaining and a warm response from the
official Chinese community, but the whole question of the impact

26. Welch, *Diary #15*, p. 92.
27. *Ibid.*, p. 94.
28. George N. Kates, *The Years that Were Fat: Peking, 1933–1940* (New York: Harper and Brothers, 1952), pp. 51–52.
29. Welch, *Diary #15*, p. 94.

of its institution on the some four hundred million people of China remained moot.

Peking's *lao-pai-hsing*—the common people—may have been indifferent to PUMC in 1921, but the missionary community had been enthusiastic ever since the first hint of Rockefeller involvement in China. Visions of Rockefeller support to individual hospitals and medical schools throughout China first captured the attention of the missionary groups. Some grants to missionary medical schools and fellowships to missionary doctors were forthcoming, but at the time of the dedication the missionary community focused on the unique role of PUMC. Over a hundred medical missionaries from fifteen provinces flocked to Peking to attend the ceremonies. The appeal was not the dedication itself, but rather the series of lectures, clinical demonstrations, and scientific symposiums scheduled for the week-long celebration.

One of these was a symposium on kala-azar, a parasitic disease endemic in China. At that time, the reports concerned experiments with various means of treating kala-azar.[30] In the future, kala-azar research at PUMC included a search for the cause and prevention of that disease. Dr. Theodore Tuffier, Professor of Clinical Surgery at the University of Paris, gave a lecture on "Osteomyelitis," which explored the surgical procedures to correct that bone disease.[31] During the 1920s and 1930s PUMC faculty and students undertook to discover the cause of osteomyelitis in North China women, concluding eventually that nutritional defects were responsible. These and other scientific reports and discussions established from the very opening day the pre-eminent role that Peking Union Medical College was to play in medical research in Republican China.

For some at that Conference, however, it was not the need for medical research which seemed of paramount importance. It was the need for doctors. In his evening lecture, Dr. Edward Hume, Dean of the Yale-in-China Medical College in Hunan, sought to dramatize China's medical crisis in human terms.[32] He cited the fact that in the China of 1921, one medical student existed for every 175,000 people, whereas in the same year the United States enrolled one medical student for every 8,000 people. Moreover, in America there was already one physician for every 720 persons, while in China there was only one modern-trained doctor for every

---

30. *Addresses and Papers*, pp. 270–272.
31. *Ibid.*, pp. 247–250.
32. See especially Jonathan Spence's chapter on Hume in his *To Change China: Western Advisers in China, 1620–1960* (Boston: Little, Brown, & Co., 1969), pp. 161–183.

120,000 persons. Recitals of statistics such as these always seemed to point to a stark impossibility of training enough doctors for China's millions. But in apparent self-contradiction, Hume moved quickly from the dearth of doctors to urge that the stress on high standards being set by PUMC be extended to medical institutions throughout China.[33]

This new Rockefeller emphasis on higher "standards" seemed— then and throughout the period—to numb Westerners, and most of the Chinese they trained, to any feasible alternative for hastening the day when medical services for China would be adequate. Higher standards inevitably entailed larger expenditures for fewer students, and thus created a vicious cycle, especially for less well-endowed institutions such as Hume's own. Twenty-five years later, in 1946, Hume attended a conference of the American Bureau for Medical Aid to China in New York City, which included prominent Chinese and foreign representatives of Western medicine in China. Questions of "standards" still dominated planning for post-war Chinese medical education. Dr. James K. Shen, Assistant Director of the National Health Administration of the Nationalist Government, concluded: "If we hope to produce doctors to staff the necessary health program, it will be fifteen years or maybe *one hundred years* before we can reach the number required."[34]

Hume, beset with the problems of meagre resources and inadequate staff, was unavoidably impressed by the PUMC model. But he also expected much from the prestigious institution. In his talk, Hume stressed that the average PUMC doctor, freed from administrative problems and financial worries, would have the time to learn "how" to teach and "what" to teach. Instead of merely transplanting Western didactics to China, the teacher at PUMC should learn "to modify his curriculum" to the exigencies of the Chinese situation. The research should focus on the primary medical problems of China, such as trachoma of the eye and parasitic diseases, as well as conducting investigations into the possible uses of the historical Chinese pharmacopoeia. Studies should be made of ways in which to adapt the structure of Western hospitals to the needs of the Orient.[35]

Edward Hume clearly saw potential success for PUMC only if it adapted its entire program and resources to the unique demands

33. *Addresses and Papers*, pp. 85–87.
34. The American Bureau for Medical Aid to China, Inc., "Conference on the Present Medical Situation in China," (June 15, 1946), New York City, p. 33. Emphasis added.
35. *Addresses and Papers*, pp. 85–87.

of China. But he implied that it *must adapt*. The medical milieu of PUMC was at the outset radically different from the American one which spawned it, and forthcoming events were to continue to alter it. The need for "adaptability" was recognized by many observers. But medical institutions, perhaps like institutions of any nature, possess a certain rigidity. PUMC, as things turned out, was no exception.

The actual dedication ceremony of PUMC was eulogized by on-the-spot observers, and later in histories of the Rockefeller Foundation or PUMC. One contemporary account described the striking contrasts between the Western academic procession and its urban Peking surroundings. The medical scientists passed "beneath the great overhanging roofs of green tile, past modern laboratories, and age-old water carts, through rows of students of Western medicine and past groups of wondering coolies and ever-present beggars."[36] Far away in America, the *New York Times* included vivid descriptions of the buildings, the ceremonies, and the lavish reception of the junior Rockefeller by the Chinese.[37] A recent brief history emphasizes the scientific prestige of the international group assembled: "There has never been a comparable assemblage of intellectual might."[38] This may be overdrawn, but the occasion was a notable convocation of internationally renowned medical scientists—assembled as much to do honor to the Rockefellers as to benefit the people of China.

Speeches at such festivities are usually polite, perfunctory, and boring. It is doubtful whether many of those packed into the PUMC auditorium on that sunny day in September listened carefully for nuances intermingled with customary trite phrases. The presentations were mostly in English, and the few in Chinese were translated into English. Most guests were probably relieved when it was over. A close reading of these talks, however, reveals a wide spectrum of attitudes toward the purpose of PUMC and the benefits to be derived from Western scientific medicine.

It is almost uncanny that the remarks from the speaker's platform that day reflected so well the ambiguous position of this American philanthropic institution in China. Speech after speech juxtaposed the merits of Western science with the traditions of Chinese civilization, and the personal benevolence of the international phil-

---

36. The quote is from Edwin Embree, cited in Ferguson, *CMB and PUMC*, pp. 52–53.
37. *New York Times*, 19 September 1921, 14:3 and 21 September 1921, 14:7.
38. John Bowers, "The Founding of Peking Union Medical College," Part II, *Bulletin of the History of Medicine* 45 (1971): 424.

anthropist with the racial prejudice of his countrymen. The very nature of PUMC ultimately seemed to augur against the realization of its founder's goals. And if those present soon forgot the proceedings, forty years later Roger Greene's speech was to be resurrected to demonstrate the cultural arrogance and self-serving motivation of the Rockefeller Foundation in China.

The service in the auditorium, which in outward appearance resembled a Confucian temple, began with an invocation by John Leighton Stuart, then the President of Yenching University and later American Ambassador to China. Stuart's prayer tried to reconcile the spiritual aims of the missionaries with the scientific aims of the Rockefeller Foundation—"because we believe that all the finer urgings are from Thee."[39] George Vincent, in a brief statement as President of the RF, presented the institution as a gift from the Foundation. Dr. Henry Houghton, Director of the PUMC, affirmed, in a short speech of acceptance, that the "primary function of this institution is to teach."[40] The act of presentation in itself was a kind of fiction, for no transfer of funds or property was taking place in China. The buildings and grounds were owned by the Rockefeller Foundation; the PUMC was funded and operated by a division of the Rockefeller Foundation, the China Medical Board; and the Peking Union Medical College Trustees, whose authority was frequently rebuffed anyway, did not include a single Chinese representative. From a legal standpoint, the affair could just as well have taken place in the Rockefeller Foundation offices at 61 Broadway, New York City.

Following Houghton's remarks, four representatives of the Chinese government made brief welcoming comments. A recent history of PUMC dismisses their words with the misleading observation: "They also acknowledged the supremacy of Western medicine over the indigenous system."[41] Though technically correct, this assertion overlooks the qualifying phrases in these speeches which in fact reflected a wide diversity of Chinese opinion regarding the supposed "supremacy of Western medicine."

The first statement from the Chinese community was given by W. W. Yen (Yen Hui-ch'ing), the American-educated Minister of Foreign Affairs, speaking on behalf of President Hsü Shih-ch'ang. Yen spoke with an enthusiasm typical of his peers in the Western-trained Chinese elite. Warmly accepting the new medical institution, he joined with others of his generation in deprecating Chi-

39. *Addresses and Papers*, p. 41.
40. *Ibid.*, p. 43.
41. Bowers, "The Founding of PUMC," Part II, p. 425.

nese medical traditions: "Unaccustomed to scientific thought, China has been slow in adopting Western medicine and surgery." He went on to predict that "with such a magnificent seat of medical learning . . . the time will soon arrive when a truer understanding and better appreciation will dawn upon the masses, so that they will not hesitate to trust themselves to scientific treatment."[42]

The emphasis here is important. Yen, a diplomat who would have been loathe under any circumstances to slap the hand of American givers, blamed the difficulty of China's medical modernization on the ignorance of the masses. Speaking in English, he optimistically asserted that understanding will somehow mystically "dawn" upon the people. How the "magnificent seat of medical learning" might communicate with the impoverished masses was not explored.

The second Chinese speaker, Chi Yao-san, the Minister of Interior, was probably a more typical representative of the transitional government official of the early 1920s. Speaking in Chinese, Chi took care to include in his speech reference to the Chinese medical system in the Han and Sung Dynasties. Although affirming the strength of China's medical tradition, Minister Chi was reluctant to probe more deeply into the relative merits of Western and Chinese medicine in the 1920s. He concluded on a welcoming note: "Long Live the Republics of China and of the United States! Long Live the Peking Union Medical College."[43]

The Ministry of Interior was also represented by S. P. Chen (Chen Ssu-pang), a British-trained medical doctor. Not unexpectedly, he depicted "Western medicine steadily gaining the upper hand" over the old Chinese system, and applauded the Rockefeller Foundation's commitment to quality rather than quantity in medical education.[44]

Of these first three Chinese speakers, W. W. Yen and S. P. Chen unequivocally accepted the pre-eminence of Western medicine while Chi Yao-san tentatively introduced the subject of China's own medical traditions. It remained for the final Chinese speaker, Ma Lin-yi, the Minister of Education, to suggest a synthesis between Chinese and Western medicine. Born in 1870 in the interior province of Honan, far from the early incursions of Western commerce, Ma's educational background was quite different from either S. P. Chen or W. W. Yen. Attaining the *chü-jen* degree within China's traditional examination system, Ma had held several educational positions within Honan, and then, during the educational re-

42. *Addresses and Papers*, p. 46.
43. *Ibid.*, p. 47.
44. *Ibid.*, p. 49.

forms of the early twentieth century, served as the Commissioner of Education for Kansu, Anhui, and Chihli provinces before becoming the Minister of Education in 1921.[45]

Ma Lin-yi's experience was grounded in China's, rather than a Western, educational milieu. He thus seemed more willing—if not compelled—to urge that some *modus vivendi* be encouraged between the two systems. Speaking to eminent Western scientists at this dedication, Ma was remarkable for his forthrightness and his dogged refusal to let China's traditions be submerged totally under the avalanche of Western scientific thought:

> It is needless to say that much progress has been made in Western nations, and that when it was introduced into China, it caused great surprise because of its new methods of treatment. In my opinion there was in olden times no difference between the medical theories and practices of the East and the West, for in those days there were similar methods of determining the cause of a disease and attempting to find a cure for it.[46]

Instead of going on to say, as Western histories of Chinese intellectual thought tend to do, that medicine in China withered because of the absence of scientific thought, Ma affirms that it merely went in another direction: "Later Chinese medical study became more philosophical, while Western medicine followed the progress of modern science. . . . We hope that this college, using both Chinese philosophy and Western science may be able to discover new theories and make great contributions to medical history."[47]

For most sitting in that auditorium even the vaguest intimation of simultaneous utilization of Western science and Chinese philosophy was inconceivable. The implications of Ma's speech probably passed over their collective heads. With regard to medicine, Chinese philosophy and Chinese medicine were irrelevant. And not only Westerners had come to this conclusion. Many Chinese intellectuals of the 1920s had by-and-large repudiated any synthesis between the two systems. Ch'en Tu-hsiu, the leading iconoclast of the May Fourth Movement and later a founder of the Communist Party, himself described Chinese medical philosophy as consisting of "nonsensical ideas and reasonless beliefs."[48] Lu Hsün, a popular left-wing satirist, used his background in Western medicine to cast

45. *China Year Book, 1921–22*, p. 923.
46. *Addresses and Papers*, p. 51.
47. *Ibid.*
48. Ch'en Tu-hsiu, *Hsin ch'ing-nien*, I, 1:6, quoted in Ralph C. Crozier, *Traditional Medicine in Modern China: Science, Nationalism, and the Tensions of Cultural Change* (Cambridge, Mass.: Harvard University Press, 1968), p. 71.

aspersion on Chinese folk medicine in numerous short stories. Western observers, even those inclined to be charitable, saw the "philosophical" direction of Chinese medicine as so much folderol and "superstition." Victor Heiser, a member of the Rockefeller Foundation's International Health Board, is not untypical of Occidentals who in one breath could cite the discovery of anesthesiology by Hua T'o, a Chinese surgeon in the 2nd century A.D., and in the next exclaim: "Or, how would you like to be a Chinese child who, instead of castor oil, is forced to swallow an infusion of ground cockroach."[49]

During its more than thirty years of existence as an American institution in China, a few serious attempts were made by PUMC scientists to examine the therapeutic value of traditional drugs. The discovery of ephedrine, internationally used in respiratory diseases today, came from synthesizing the active chemicals of the Chinese drug, *ma-huang*. The work of Professor Bernard Read in cataloguing the Chinese pharmacopoeia was another significant step in exploring the value of Chinese medicine. These attempts, however, do not represent the main thrust of PUMC's leadership in medical research. For most of those associated with the Peking Union Medical College, the supremacy of Western science also convincingly established the supremacy of Western medicine.

The passing comments at the dedication ceremonies by Chi Yao-san and especially Ma Lin-yi concerning the question of comparative medical history did not represent any pronounced trend in Chinese thinking of that period. But their remarks are significant because they are so unusual in the record of Rockefeller involvement in China. They reflect a refusal to succumb to expressions of inferiority before that formidable foreign assemblage. Few others ever tried to express anything to the representatives of the Rockefeller Foundation except China's inferior medical status and crying need.

From the perspective of the 1970s, these comments are noteworthy because a time eventually did come when Chinese philosophy, Western science, *and* Chinese medicine would be synthesized into an impressive indigenous medical system. However, the conviction that there is no creative tension between scientific medicine and folk medicine, that modern medicine is necessarily Western medicine, dies slowly. As late as 1970, Raymond Fosdick,

49. Victor Heiser, "China," pp. 35, 10. This is an unpublished manuscript of 100 pages apparently intended as part of a book. Victor Heiser Papers (*VHP*), American Philosophical Library, Philadelphia, Pennsylvania.

President of the Rockefeller Foundation from 1935 to 1946, reminisced about the wisdom of introducing modern medicine into China, and concluded: "The conflict of ideologies . . . does not relate to medicine."[50]

Roger Greene's speech at the dedication certainly provided fuel for future ideological debate, for he addressed himself in a peculiar way to the larger question of motivation for American international philanthropy. Much of his speech concerned intellectual cooperation, but he also suggested the degree to which he believed Chinese immigration to be the crucial problem in Sino-American relations: "Either those who have little or nothing must be enabled to improve their conditions at home, or they will eventually go to the country of those who have, and in such numbers as to cause a violent upheaval in the country which they invade."[51] Even though "yellow peril" sentiment was not uncommon in his day, it seems incredible that a fear of multitudes of poor Chinese invading rich America should be in Greene's eyes a primary reason for American philanthropic work in China. This concern with the difference between peoples as races was developed even further by his suggestion that eugenic research be undertaken by the scientists at PUMC to determine whether or not there was a valid biological difference between the Chinese and Westerners.[52] Greene himself seemed to indicate that he firmly believed there is no significant difference; but his inclusion of these kinds of gratuitous remarks concerning racial traits seems hardly appropriate at such a gathering.

Greene died in 1947, but in 1951 his dedication speech furnished provocative material for at least two attacks on the American "imperialists" who had previously directed PUMC. For a short while after the Communist victory, PUMC students published a pamphlet titled "The New PUMC." In their February 1951 issue, Greene's speech was quoted extensively to reveal the ulterior motives of American philanthropy.[53] And in March of the same year, the Hong Kong *Ta Kung Pao* ran an article which also included incriminating ex-

50. Raymond Fosdick, "Foreword," in Ferguson, *CMB and PUMC*, p. 5.

51. *Addresses and Papers*, p. 54. Greene repeatedly addressed himself to the subject of immigration, see Greene to Buttrick, April 11, 1917, *SFP*; Greene to Nelson Johnson, November 26, 1928, Nelson Johnson Papers (*NJP*), Library of Congress, Washington, D.C.

52. *Addresses and Papers*, p. 55.

53. *Hsin Hsieh Ho* [The new PUMC], 2 February 1951, pp. 9–10. This copy and one dated 20 April 1951 are in the papers of Peking Union Medical College located at the Rockefeller Foundation Archives, North Tarrytown, New York. This is a collection which was maintained by the China Medical Board, Inc. until 1971, and will be referred to as the *PUMC Papers*.

cerpts from Greene's talk and concluded: "What an obnoxious insult it was."[54]

Of all the speeches that September day in Peking, none revealed PUMC's inherent contradictions so clearly as the earnest effort of John D. Rockefeller, Jr., himself. One cannot read his remarks without a sense of admiration, for more directly than any of the other speakers, Rockefeller addressed himself to the problem of PUMC's role within China. He recognized the limits of an American solution to China's educational problems by stating: "For the China Medical Board recognized from the outset that only the Chinese nation itself could cope with a task so colossal as the establishment of modern scientific medical education throughout the Republic and all that Western civilization could do would be to point the way."[55]

Rockefeller through his speech tried to keep in mind this function of PUMC "to point the way" for medical education in China. Recognizing the twin pitfalls of prolonged Western control and soaring financial costs, Rockefeller seemed to sense the need to adapt PUMC to the conditions of China. Although he himself had acquiesced in PUMC's spiralling costs, he prophetically observed that for the institution to become a viable model "it is essential that the current cost of operating should always be kept on the conservative level." He also committed the Rockefeller Foundation to steadily increasing Chinese representation on the Board of Trustees and Faculty: "So we must look forward to the day when most, if not all, of the positions on the Faculty . . . will be held by Chinese, when the Board of Trustees . . . will include leading Chinese."[56]

These remarks were foresighted. But Rockefeller's espousal of an institution "of a standard comparable with that of the leading institutions known to Western civilization"[57] augured against the adaptability of the PUMC model. The PUMC administration believed that for the college to be in fact equal to American and European institutions, the escalating costs of the Peking plant were unavoidable. And, during the college's formative years, the Foundation reluctantly agreed. Rockefeller had also stated that the school should not be more expensive than a similar school in Europe or America. This reflected the admirable goal of not treating China as a second-class nation. But it also revealed a profoundly oversimplified under-

54. *Ta Kung Pao*, 18 March 1951, p. 2. A translated copy of this article was sent by a former PUMC graduate, Stephen Chang, to the CMB and it will be found in the *PUMC Papers*.

55. *Addresses and Papers*, p. 59.   56. *Ibid.*, p. 65.   57. *Ibid.*, p. 59.

standing of Chinese economic conditions if he indeed assumed that costs equal to those of the foremost American medical schools, such as Johns Hopkins, could be sustained by China's limited educational budget. Even more significantly, a school designed to be the equal of the best in Europe and the United States would always suggest an institution *similar* to Western medical colleges. The appropriateness of the PUMC model was not questioned.

After the dedication ceremonies, the Rockefellers remained in Peking for several more days of special banquets and receptions. They then proceeded south on a tour arranged for them by the officials of the Standard Oil Company in China. Travelling first by rail in a private car sealed off from the rest of the Chinese train, and then by Standard Oil river launches, they made their way to Shanghai, the major Western commercial entrepôt in Asia.

It does not appear to have occurred to the Rockefellers—or to Welch, the chronicler of their China journey—that there was any inconsistency in Rockefeller's simultaneous identification with the PUMC and the Standard Oil Company while he was in China. Political and medical leaders in Peking had entertained the Rockefellers; so, too, did the commercial and business community of Shanghai:

> The warehouses, tanks, and docks of Mei-foo (Standard Oil) are about 6 miles below Shanghai on the left bank of the Whangpoo. In honor of Mr. Rockefeller the boats were gaily decorated with a large number of flags of all nations, and the officials and the local company were on hand to greet the party.[58]

After several days of entertainment in Shanghai and "tired from these strenuous days," the Rockefellers left China on October 1. Reflecting on the various activities of the past month in China, Welch wrote:

> Mr. R. has made a splendid impression on everybody by his fine address, his simple, democratic, courteous, obliging disposition and ways, and what he stands for. His coming will do a great deal of good not only for our Rockefeller medical undertakings but for America.[59]

There were many questions raised by Rockefeller's trip to China, but the one that shall concern us first is the American origins of the Rockefeller Foundation's China venture.

58. Welch, *Diary #15*, p. 115.
59. *Ibid.*, p. 139.

TWO "A Johns Hopkins for China"

Though Dr. [Timothy] Richard did not himself throw his
thoughts into that form, what he really suggests is a Johns
Hopkins for China. . . .

Ernest Burton, "Journal," 1909

F ORTY-FIVE YEARS before he accompanied the
Rockefellers to the dedication of Peking Union Medical College,
William Henry Welch had travelled to Germany to study in the laboratory of a renowned medical scientist, Carl Ludwig. At that time,
in 1876, medical discoveries in Europe were completing the transformation of Western medicine into scientific medicine. Welch's
future institution, The Johns Hopkins University School of Medicine, was destined to be the principal vehicle for transmitting German scientific standards to American medical education; it later
also became the model for PUMC. The scientific revolution in medicine was thus linked with the advent of Rockefeller Foundation
medical work in China. That the nature of the resulting educational
revolution was elitist, not populist, was to have profound effects on
the medical modernization of China.

Before describing the impact of Johns Hopkins on American
medicine, a brief sketch of the history of American medical education is required. Prior to the twentieth century, American medicine
had experienced periods of both elitism and populism in training
medical practitioners. During the early colonial period, decentralized apprenticeships provided a practical and expedient medical
education. But by the time of the Revolution a more aristocratic
concept, which included a college degree and European training,

prevailed. With the rise of Jacksonian democracy in the 1820s, elitism and rigid professionalism came under heavy attack. Migrations from the eastern seaboard to the western frontier demanded social and educational institutions which could meet the exigencies of pioneer life. Proprietary medical schools which were not associated with colleges and universities proliferated: between 1800 and 1900 over 400 medical schools were created. Although most had a relatively short life, there were still approximately 160 medical schools in the United States in 1900.

The result was not an absence of standards, but a variety of standards. To the degree that the graduates responded to the social needs of rapid population growth, the waves of westward migration, and the continuing European immigration, they performed valuable medical services. Inevitably, laxity of standards also produced its share of malpractice and quackery. Furthermore, as rapid scientific discoveries in Europe completely altered the basic premises of Western medicine, the egalitarian movement which had spawned these schools was unable to survive.

The second half of the nineteenth century was so critical in the development of modern medicine that one author has labelled the years 1850–1900 as "the gestation and birth of scientific medicine."[1] Mechanical inventions such as the stethoscope, the ophthalmoscope and the laryngoscope were transforming the clinical diagnosis of disease. Now, utilization of the microscope prompted research into the origin of disease, necessitating the study of medicine in a purely scientific form. Knowledge of European discoveries, especially in the fields of bacteriology, parasitology, and pathology, slowly filtered through the American medical profession. Thousands of students flocked to the German laboratories, and the need for change in American medical education became glaringly obvious.

Training in the basic sciences, especially chemistry, biology, and physics, was an absolute prerequisite to understanding the new medicine. But it was not offered in American medical schools. Instruction heretofore had only provided a few rudimental techniques: actual laboratory experience was almost non-existent. American medical education was at this low ebb when Welch began his stud-

1. Lester J. Evans, *The Crisis in Medical Education* (Ann Arbor: University of Michigan Press, 1964), p. 7. This discussion of American medical education is drawn from the following additional sources: Rosemary Stevens, *American Medicine and the Public Interest* (New Haven: Yale University Press, 1971), pp. 1–88; C. Sidney Burwell. "The Evolution of Medical Education in Nineteenth Century America," *Journal of Medical Education* 37 (1962): 1157–1165; Richard Shryock, *The Development of Modern Medicine* (New York: Alfred A. Knopf, 1947).

ies in 1872 at Yale's School of Medicine. Years later he remembered "the inadequate preliminary requirements, the short courses, the faulty arrangement of the curriculum, the dominance of the didactic lecture, the meagre appliances for demonstrative and practical instruction."[2]

By the last decades of the nineteenth century, there were a number of reforms underway, such as curriculum innovation at Harvard Medical School, the growth of both the American Medical Association and local medical societies, and an increasing number of professional journals. But the most important development was heralded in 1874 when a Baltimore merchant, Johns Hopkins, bequeathed seven million dollars to create a graduate university combined with a medical school and a modern hospital. The Johns Hopkins University opened in 1876, the hospital in 1889, and the medical school in 1893.

The Johns Hopkins University Medical School coalesced into one institution the varying European influences on American medicine.[3] The university pattern of medical education which the colonists inherited from England had been renewed by contact with German universities which dominated the latter part of the nineteenth century. During the first half of that century, the French system of hospitals and clinics had, however, also exercised an important role in American medical thinking. Now, at Johns Hopkins, the Medical School was a graduate institution affiliated with a major university and Johns Hopkins Hospital an integral part of the teaching facilities. Clearly, however, the German influence was strongest in shaping its curriculum, teaching, and scientific orientation.

The German model for American medical education included higher entrance standards, more emphasis on laboratories and demonstration techniques than on lecturing, and a faculty whose full-time commitment was to the university. At Johns Hopkins, for the first time since the American Revolution, a four-year liberal arts college education was required before admittance to the medical school. The faculty during the formative years included the most important medical educators of that period. In addition to Welch

2. William Welch, "Some of the Conditions Which Have Influenced the Development of American Medicine," *Addresses and Papers by William Henry Welch*, 3 (Baltimore: Johns Hopkins University Press, 1920), p. 289.

3. The best discussion of Johns Hopkins is Richard Shryock, *The Unique Influence of the Johns Hopkins University on American Medicine* (Cophenhagen: Ejmar Murnsbsgoard, Ltd., 1953). A more informal account is Bertram Bernheim, *The Story of the Johns Hopkins* (New York: McGraw Hill, 1948). For a more recent evaluation see Robert A. Moore, "The Social and Cultural Background of Medical Education in the United States," *Journal of Medical Education* 36 (1961): 1218–1227.

in pathology, there were William Osler in medicine, Frederick Mall in anatomy, and William Halsted in Surgery. It is important to stress that these men were biomedical scientists, and their teaching and research pioneered the introduction of medical science into American medical education.

As professor of pathology and first dean of the Medical School, Welch was instrumental in creating the academic atmosphere of the institution. In the years before he attained national prominence as a medical educator, his laboratory at Hopkins produced pioneering research in bacteriology and infectious diseases. Many of the well-known medical leaders of the early twentieth century had passed under his tutelage. His influence extended beyond that of laboratory instruction. One recent biographer, Donald Fleming, has aptly stressed his mark on the modern hospital: "He more than anyone else had made Johns Hopkins a new kind of hospital in American experience—the home not of charity, but of science."[4]

As the twentieth century and the Progressive Era dawned, the scientific revolution in American medical education which was epitomized by Johns Hopkins was just beginning. The problems of too many poorly trained physicians were becoming widely evident. In 1904, the American Medical Association established a Council on Medical Education, which sought higher educational standards and investigated the conditions of many medical schools. Many states revised and upgraded their licensing requirements. But the catalyst for reform came in 1910 when Abraham Flexner—younger brother of RF Trustee Simon Flexner—burst on the scene with a relentless exposé of American medical colleges.

Innocuously presented as *Bulletin Number Four of the Carnegie Foundation for the Advancement of Teaching*,[5] Flexner's survey revealed the woeful inadequacies of nearly all the existing American institutions of medical education. Wasting no diplomacy or pleasantries, Flexner not only castigated the proprietary colleges, but even blasted the pretensions of such esteemed university-affiliated medical schools as Harvard and Yale. Only Johns Hopkins Medical School was immune from attack. Although other schools had good

4. Donald H. Fleming, *William H. Welch and the Rise of Modern Medicine* (Boston: Little, Brown, & Co., 1954), p. 95.

5. Abraham Flexner, *Medical Education in the United States and Canada* (New York: Carnegie Foundation, 1910). For a recent re-evaluation of Flexner's influence see Robert P. Hudson, "Abraham Flexner in Perspective: American Medical Education, 1865–1910," *Bulletin of the History of Medicine* 46 (Nov.–Dec., 1972): 545–561; also, James G. Burrow, *Organized Medicine in the Progressive Era: The Move Toward Monopoly* (Baltimore: Johns Hopkins University Press, 1977), pp. 15–35.

points, Flexner recommended that Johns Hopkins become the prototype for American medical education.

Flexner's report capped a reform movement which had been brewing for several decades. But it dramatized such a watershed in medical annals that the major periodization of American medical history continues to be pre-Flexner and post-Flexner. This is not because his report was unique, but because it brought the national publicity required to translate reform into reality. Almost half of the medical schools in the country closed in the ten years following Flexner's report. In 1905, only five schools had required any college education; by 1915 nearly all medical colleges required one or two years of college training. Proprietary schools disappeared, and medical colleges increasingly revolved around university education.

Ever since the rigorous intellectual demands of German scientific medicine had filtered into the American medical milieu, a crisis over standards had been smoldering in the medical profession. But the success of the Flexner Report cannot be simply seen as the culmination of a reform movement. Funded by the Carnegie Foundation, Flexner's report caught the attention of leading American philanthropists. As Rosemary Stevens succinctly states in her provocative study, *American Medicine and the Public Interest*: "Much of the achievement of reform . . . was less the result of the stick of sanction than of the carrot of foundation subsidy implicit in the Flexner visits. Foundation money enabled the better schools to make the suggested improvements—and left the worse schools out in the cold."[6]

The Rockefellers led the way in funding Flexner's reforms. Their involvement in medical education can probably best be traced through Frederick T. Gates, who has aptly been called "the externalized conscience of Rockefellers."[7] An erstwhile Baptist fundraiser, Gates was the philanthropic advisor to John D. Rockefeller, Sr., and is largely responsible for organizing Rockefeller's random charities into boards, institutes, memorials, and foundations. In 1897, Gates took William Osler's monumental *Principles and Practices of Medicine* on a vacation and returned to Rockefeller's New York office convinced that scientific medicine held, if not the keys to the kingdom, at least the keys to the worldly future. As he himself recollects: "I brought my Osler into the office at 26 Broadway and there I dictated for Mr. Rockefeller's eye a memorandum. It enumerated the infectious diseases and pointed out how few of the

6. Stevens, *American Medicine*, p. 68.
7. Fleming, *Welch*, p. 153.

germs had yet been discovered and how great the field of discovery, how few specifics had yet been found and how appalling was the unremedied suffering."[8] Heretofore Gates, a Baptist minister, had primarily directed the charities of Rockefeller towards religious organizations, but as one writer put it: "At a time when dogmatic theology had already begun to sink toward its low-water mark in America, Gates as a clergyman persuaded himself that scientific medicine was a kind of theological research."[9]

Gates' memorandum to Rockefeller lay dormant for several years. Then, in 1901, with the backing of John D. Rockefeller, Jr., a committee was organized to create an institute for medical research. William Welch, by then dean of Johns Hopkins Medical School, was asked to serve as chairman and thus began his long association with Gates and the Rockefellers. The Rockefeller Institute, caricatured as the McGurk Institute by Sinclair Lewis in *Arrowsmith*, opened in 1905 as an independent medical research laboratory. Designed to attract advanced medical scientists, it was patterned after the Koch Institute in Germany and the Pasteur Institute in France. Rockefeller Sr.'s financial contribution to this institution during his lifetime was about sixty million dollars.

With this background, it is not surprising that Gates, and through him the Rockefellers, would have been impressed and influenced by Flexner's report. In fact, Gates was so excited upon reading the survey that he arranged to have lunch with Flexner shortly after it was published. Upon asking Flexner what he would do with a million dollars, Flexner gave the oft-quoted reply, "I would give it to Dr. Welch at Johns Hopkins."[10] Thus began a series of financial contributions from one of the Rockefeller trusts, the General Education Board, to Johns Hopkins that eventually totalled not one million but ten million dollars.

Flexner's recommendations were hailed at the time by progressive leaders in American medicine. In comparison with other professional fields of the times, especially law and theology, medical practitioners were woefully uneducated. Furthermore, Flexner documented his demand that many schools be closed by demonstrating that the American medical profession was overpopulated, with a ratio of 1 doctor for every 568 persons in 1910. The closure of schools and the elevation of standards raised the quality of the pro-

8. Frederick T. Gates, "The Memoirs of Frederick T. Gates," *American Heritage* 6 (April 1955): 73.

9. Fleming, *Welch*, p. 153.

10. Abraham Flexner, *An Autobiography* (New York: Simon and Schuster, 1960), pp. 109.

fession and enabled it to become an international leader in medical research.

But the social consequences of Flexner's reforms narrowed the base of the profession and in the decades to come greatly restricted its numbers. Between 1890 and 1910 eight black medical schools had produced some 2,000 doctors. All but two were closed as a result of the Flexner revolution. Since white medical colleges were slow to admit black students, a shortage of black doctors, especially those willing to work in Southern rural areas, ensued. The same phenomenon was true of lower-class white students, who found it difficult to make the financial commitment to medical education necessitated by increased expense, the demise of night schools, and a greatly lengthened curriculum. The American medical profession became a highly specialized, upper-middle-class elite heavily concentrated in urban centers.

It is only in recent years that American medical educators have perceived that the Flexnerian reforms resulted in a rigid educational system which seriously mitigated against the application of medical care to all levels of society. Dr. John Knowles, who became president of the Rockefeller Foundation in 1972, once wrote:

> The Flexner report accentuated, crystallized, and established the place of science in medicine and medical education, and no one would question the necessity, the value, or the benefit of this establishment. . . . [But] As the pace of science accelerates in all walks of life . . . who can solve some of the resultant problems so that the benefits are more readily available to society? [11]

The years in which Frederick Gates was directing Rockefeller funds toward American medical education were also notable for an increasing national awareness of China. The Boxer Rebellion and the loss of American missionary lives in China dramatized for the people at home the heroic nature of American involvement. The Open Door Policy of Secretary of State John Hay reinforced an idealized image of America's self-conceived mission in the Middle Kingdom. Rumblings of reform within the Ch'ing dynasty, later shown by the abandoning of the examination system and the tentative introduction of Western education, suggested to many that America's specific contribution to the reform of China should be through education. The early twentieth century was marked by a great outpouring of missionaries through the enthusiastic recruit-

---

11. John Knowles, "The Balanced Biology of the Teaching Hospital," in Knowles, ed., *Hospitals, Doctors, and the Public Interest* (Cambridge, Mass.: Harvard University Press, 1966), p. 40.

ment policies of the Student Volunteer Movement for Foreign Missions. But at the same time, more secular institutions such as Yale, Princeton, and Harvard began to establish affiliates in China (at Changsha, Peking, and Shanghai, respectively).

All these crusades were reflected in miscellaneous correspondence to Gates and John D. Rockefeller, Sr.[12] Rockefeller himself responded by donating large random sums to China missionaries and was constantly besieged by individual requests. John R. Mott, popularizer of the YMCA and leader of the activist Student Volunteer Movement, is known to have been in frequent communication with the senior Rockefeller, and Mott's first trip to China in 1896 undoubtedly brought requests for financial assistance.[13] The patronage by John D. Rockefeller, Jr., of a Chinese Sunday school in New York exemplifies some of the "home missions" approach that characterized the Rockefeller family. Gates himself seems to have had some latent interest in China, apparently having attended a college lecture on Asia shortly after the Civil War.[14] He certainly thereafter had constant contact with Baptist missionaries.

At any rate, requests to aid programs in China proliferated. Gates and Rockefeller, Jr., began planning a charitable foundation with an international outreach, and Gates decided that conditions in China warranted further investigation. He was especially impressed by a 1906 letter which proposed that an American university be created in China. Co-authored by Harry P. Judson, president of the University of Chicago, and Ernest Burton, professor of theology there, it noted that "we have become deeply impressed with the desirability that there should be established in China as early as possible a University, distinctly Christian, but wholly undenominational in character, and of the highest ideals and broadest catholicity."[15] Since, under Gates' tutelage, the elder Rockefeller had founded the University of Chicago, the Chicago educators were especially persuasive. Gates decided that an educational commission led by Ernest Burton should be sent to China. This proposal was conveyed by Rockefeller Jr. to his father, who, after some

12. See, for example, H. P. Parker to Gates, October 23, 1907; M. O. Eubank to Gates, 1907; Henry C. Mabie to Gates, January 29, 1908, *RFA*.

13. Shirley S. Garrett, *Social Reformers in Urban China: The Chinese YMCA, 1895–1926* (Cambridge: Harvard University Press, 1970), pp. 65, 87.

14. Mary Ferguson, "The PUMC from 1914–1950: A Study in Administrative Relationships," pp. 1–2. This is an unabridged version of her published *CMB and PUMC* which will hereinafter be referred to as "The PUMC." Typed copies are in the possession of Mary Ferguson, Sandy Spring, Maryland, and in the office of the China Medical Board, Inc., New York.

15. Burton and Judson to Gates, December 31, 1906, *RFA*.

demurring, agreed to fund the survey by providing the $20,000 needed.[16]

Shortly before Burton left for China, Rockefeller Jr. clearly outlined the purpose of the mission and connected it with the Rockefeller Foundation, then on the drawing boards. In a letter to his father he stated: "We should have fuller and more accurate data regarding educational and religious conditions in these distant lands before undertaking to inaugurate any such educational or civilizing works as are possible under the new and broad charter."[17] Gates himself instructed Burton as to the main focus of his trip, which had expanded to include several other Asian countries: "I regard the question of the study of the value of scientific education of the Chinese and the best means of inculcating it as the very bullseye of your mission."[18]

Before turning to examine Burton's survey, it is well to consider the evolution up to that time of Western education in China. In the nineteenth century, evangelical missionaries recognized the appeal that Western schools offered for Chinese at many social levels. The educational efforts which resulted began tenuously with the rudiments of Western knowledge, but expanded in the late nineteenth century to include middle schools and a few colleges. Following the T'ung Chih Restoration in 1860, the Chinese government made a few attempts to introduce Western knowledge through specialized schools. These had primarily included technical training connected with shipping, arsenals, mining, and language instruction. After the defeat of China by Japan in 1895, progressive officials began to open up Western-style schools in their local provinces.

The real impetus for Westernized reforms, however, came with the abolition of the traditional examination system in 1905. It became mandatory that a new educational system replace the old. Missionary colleges, such as the University of Nanking, Shantung Christian University, and Yenching University, although not officially recognized within the Chinese system, date their real growth from this time. Middle and higher schools under Chinese auspices began to proliferate, culminating in the creation of major universities such as Nankai University in Tientsin and Peking University in Peking. The Chinese government initially adopted a Japanese

16. Gates to Rockefeller Jr., August 26 and August 31, 1907; also multiple correspondence between Rockefeller Jr. and Rockefeller Sr., August–September, 1907, RFA.

17. Rockefeller Jr. to Rockefeller Sr., March 10, 1908, RFA.

18. Gates to Burton, May 22, 1908, RFA.

curriculum; but, in the decentralized condition of the country, many schools were also patterned after German, French, and American models.

Thus when Burton surveyed the educational scene in 1908–1909, Western education was simultaneously embryonic and evolutionary. Burton was accompanied by University of Chicago chemistry professor Thomas C. Chamberlain. The survey became known publicly as the Chicago Commission and the Oriental Education Commission. It was not announced as a Rockefeller project, although many in China seemed to be aware of the Rockefeller financial support. Burton always minimized his connection with the oil magnate, and repeatedly emphasized the exploratory nature of his investigation. His report, however, was subsequently distributed to all who attended the first China Conference of the Rockefeller Foundation in 1914, and it became required reading for the official Rockefeller medical commissions to China in 1914 and 1915.[19] Burton's conclusions regarding education for the upper class and the potential for medical education greatly influenced the educational philosophy and program of the Rockefeller Foundation in China.

The utility of elite education and the corresponding need for excellence in any new American institution in China had already been stressed by two very different educators in China, Timothy Richard and Chang Chih-tung. Early in his missionary career, Richard had broken with the nineteenth century Protestant appeal to the poor and ignorant masses of China. Dressing in Chinese clothes and teaching physics and chemistry, Richard, like the Jesuit predecessors whom he resembled, was convinced that the only way to influence China was through the gentry. Burton spent long hours in conversations with Richard, and included in his personal diary many verbatim records of Richard's ideas:

> Missionaries in past times had done the best they could, but to pursue further the policy of educating from the bottom up is foolish in the extreme. Educate at the top, at the very top, and the rest will take

19. Burton records that Dr. F. L. Hawks Pott of St. John's College, Shanghai, publicly rejected any Rockefeller money. Also, when W. A. P. Martin welcomed Burton as "Mr. Rockefeller's representative," Burton said this "called for explanations on my part." See Ernest D. Burton, "Journal and Record of Interviews and Observations, University of Chicago, Oriental Education Investigation, 1909," typed mimeographed copy, Missionary Research Library, New York, pp. 571 and 513. The official report of this mission was Burton and Chamberlain, "Report of the Oriental Commission of the University of Chicago, Part VI, China," December 1909, typed mimeographed copy located at the Missionary Research Library, New York.

care of itself. The highly educated will educate others a little lower down, these again those still further down and so on.[20]

Burton also sought an interview with Chang Chih-tung, elder statesman of the late Ch'ing educational reforms. He felt that Chang's attitude toward American educational efforts would reflect that of Chinese officialdom. His interview came on February 28, 1909, but Chang's querulous opinion of American educators left Burton uncertain as to government enthusiasm for his project. Although he was unable to determine Chang's real disposition toward Americans, he did record that Chang was worried about the credentials of Americans teaching in China. Chang stated: "Best teachers do not like to come to China. What we have are second class teachers. Very few good well-qualified teachers are in our Chinese schools." Burton tried to reassure him that any new venture would send men of quality: "We are anxious not to send many, but to send those that will serve China well."[21]

While discussions with Timothy Richard and Chang Chih-tung were suggesting the wisdom of quality training, a memorandum from Josiah C. McCracken, a medical doctor affiliated with the Canton Christian College, and conversations with John Fryer in Shanghai, presented a case for scientific and medical education.

McCracken prepared for the Oriental Education Commission by drawing up a proposal for a well-equipped medical school in Canton. The distinguishing features of this school vis-à-vis those already in existence would be that the students would be better prepared than in other schools, enabling them to become the future medical educators of China. McCracken estimated that with an initial US$120,000 for capital expenses this school could become a reality.[22]

Medical education, as well as science in general, were topics of conversation with John Fryer, perhaps the most influential Westerner in teaching science to the Chinese since the Jesuits. Fryer was wholeheartedly in favor of a scientific or medical university, but he warned Burton on the question of teaching in the English language: "NO: it's fooling the Chinese to try to tell them that by a smattering of English they can learn the sciences. It ought to

20. Burton, "Journal," p. 503. For Richard, see Garrett, *Chinese YMCA.*, pp. 19–22.

21. Burton, "Journal," p. 588. For Chang, see William Ayers, *Chang Chih-tung and Educational Reform in China* (Cambridge, Mass.: Harvard University Press, 1971).

22. Burton, "Journal," pp. 453–455.

be a matter of accomplishment, but not used as the medium of instruction."[23]

Burton's final report predicted that political conditions were not propitious for an immediate educational mission to China. His recommendations were focused on the future. Several of these mark a new departure for American educational efforts in China. Any new work should be initiated only with the approval and support of the Chinese government. And Confucianism, as well as Christianity, should be taught on a volunteer basis. The potential for science and medical education, as well as the need for standards of excellence, were epitomized in Burton's pregnant comment following a discussion with Timothy Richard: "Though Dr. Richard did not himself throw his thoughts into that form, what he really suggests is a Johns Hopkins for China."[24]

Two years after the Burton Oriental Commission and a year after Flexner's report, Frederick Gates synthesized reform at home and mission abroad in a typically effusive vision: "Might we not do in medicine in China what we had failed in our attempt to do in University education? Might we not indeed at once attempt scientific medicine in China?"[25] He and John D., Jr., designed the internationally-oriented Rockefeller Foundation with both China and scientific medicine as its focus.

The Rockefeller Foundation was incorporated in July of 1913, and Gates took the initiative in formulating the medical direction of this new foundation. At the first meeting of the Trustees, he stated:

> If science and education are the brain and nervous system of civilization, health is its heart. It is the organ that pushes the vital fluid into every part of the social organism, enabling every organ to function. . . . Disease is the supreme ill of human life, and it is the main source of almost all other human ills—poverty, crime, ignorance, vice, inefficiency, hereditary trait, and many other evils.[26]

The early medical orientation of the Foundation was evidenced both domestically and internationally. The hookworm eradication cam-

23. *Ibid.*, p. 494. For Fryer, see Adrian A. Bennett, *John Fryer: The Introduction of Western Science and Technology into Nineteenth Century China* (Cambridge, Mass.: Harvard University Press, 1967), and Spence, *To Change China*, pp. 140–160.

24. Burton, "Journal," p. 514.

25. Quoted in Ferguson, *CMB and PUMC*, p. 14.

26. Quoted in Raymond B. Fosdick, *The Story of the Rockefeller Foundation* (New York: Harper and Brothers, 1952), pp. 23–24. The incorporation of the RF involved

paign in the American South was the first notable domestic program. The International Health Board was the first international division of the RF.

In January of 1914, the Foundation's first China Conference was held. This brought together the Rockefeller trustees; educators such as Burton and Charles Eliot, former president of Harvard University; missionary enthusiasts such as Robert Speer and John R. Mott; and a number of medical missionaries.[27] Eliot's presence was especially significant, for he had travelled to China in 1912 on behalf of the Carnegie Endowment and had returned with fervor: "Here, then is a great gift that the West can make to China— scientific medicine and surgery."[28] During the seven years between this first China Conference and the dedication of PUMC in 1921, there were numerous conferences, meetings, and two major Rockefeller Foundation commissions which explored and subsequently defined the nature of Rockefeller involvement in China. What is of interest here is the philosophy of medical education for China which evolved during this period.

The major determinant of this philosophy clearly was an inexorable link with American medical education. The first blush of enthusiasm for higher standards was upon those most closely associated with the educational programming of the Rockefeller Foundation—Charles Eliot, William Welch, Abraham and Simon Flexner.[29] Not once does the RF record, public or private, suggest any reservation about the appropriateness of transferring the Johns Hopkins model to China. Not only were Flexner's educational standards carried to China; specific parallels can be drawn between the *process* of Flexnerian reforms in America and the evolving Rockefeller program in China.

Abraham Flexner had surveyed the existing American medical institutions and found them wanting. In 1914, the RF's First Medical Commission to China similarly surveyed the missionary and Chinese medical schools and found their standards abysmally low.

---

much controversy. For a fuller discussion of its beginnings and organizational structure, see the author's doctoral dissertation.

27. "China Conference of the Rockefeller Foundation, Held at No. 26 Broadway, New York City, on January 19th and 20th, 1914," p. 10, *RFA*. Typed stenographic record of about 100 pages. Pagination my own.

28. Charles W. Eliot, *Some Roads Toward Peace: A Report to the Trustees of the Carnegie Endowment on Observations Made in China and Japan in 1912* (Washington, D.C.: Carnegie Endowment, 1913), p. 22.

29. Abraham Flexner was not as directly involved as the others, but he frequently served as a consultant. See Flexner, *Autobiography*, pp. 141–142; Greene to Buttrick, June 21, 1915; Greene to Flexner, June 30, 1915; both in Roger Greene Papers (*RGP*), Houghton Library, Harvard University, Cambridge, Mass.

The detailed program of the China Medical Board, designed by the Second Medical Commission in 1915, was to administer a first-rate medical college and also raise scientific standards in other institutions.[30] Just as the Rockefeller-supported General Education Board had only backed the best of the American medical colleges, so too the China Medical Board only contributed to the best existing medical schools and hospitals. As late as 1922, seven years after its first grants to China, it was reported that "as yet no schools under Chinese auspices had reached a standard which warranted aid from the China Medical Board."[31]

An excess of doctors in the United States, coupled with the increasing sophistication of medical science, had justified Flexner's attack on American educational standards. This same procedure was blindly applied to China, a country of 400 million persons and considerably fewer than 500 trained physicians. Although the Rockefeller Foundation's medical philosophy was primarily influenced by these American domestic educational currents, it was also shaped by the state of Western medicine in China.

From the beginning of Rockefeller interest in China, the eyes of missionaries had been the lens through which the philanthropists viewed China. The early missionaries to China were personally overwhelmed by the crowds of impoverished people, many of them suffering from diseases or physical impairments for which Western medicine had an immediate cure. When Peter Parker formulated goals for Canton Hospital in 1834, his hope was "to make a contribution towards the relief of human suffering."[32] This sense of personal responsibility continued even in the late nineteenth century when institutional efforts through hospitals and medical schools began to supplement the personal role of the missionary as healer. The conviction continued that the individual missionary doctor could make a difference—*now*. The immediacy which was a part of the conversion message was also a part of the medical mission.

30. Members of the First Medical Commission were: Harry Pratt Judson, Francis W. Peabody, Roger S. Greene and George B. McKibbin (Secretary). Their official report is China Medical Commission of the Rockefeller Foundation, *Medicine in China* (New York: University of Chicago Press, 1914). Members of the Second Medical Commission were: Wallace Buttrick, William H. Welch, Simon Flexner, Frederick L. Gates (son of Frederick T. Gates), and Roger Greene. For a detailed discussion of these two commissions see John Bowers, *Western Medicine in a Chinese Palace; Peking Union Medical College, 1917–1951* (New York: The Josiah Macy, Jr. Foundation), pp. 29–61.

31. "History of the CMB," 1931, p. 41, *RGP*. No author is indicated for this lengthy early history of the CMB.

32. Harold Balme, *China and Modern Medicine: A Study in Medical Missionary Development* (London: United Council for Missionary Education, 1921), p. 42.

The American medical missionaries of the late nineteenth and early twentieth centuries were akin to the frontier physicians of the American West. While many were graduates of the better Eastern schools, their concept of medical practice was altered by the social environment in which they found themselves. In both instances, the relative dearth of medical facilities and doctors necessitated improvisation. They were participants in a populist concept of medicine which sought, with varying degrees of scientific expertise, to bring quick relief to as many as possible: results were more important than standards. And in China, this was also because medical activities were closely related to proselytizing: results lured converts.

By the 1920s, when isolation wards, window screens, latrines, and modern bathing facilities had become the watchwords for hospitals, there were few in either China or the United States who could view with equanimity the earlier make-do tradition. Harold Balme, a perceptive Englishman, tentatively observed that the mud huts of the first missionary hospitals had served at least some purpose:

> A hospital which looked like their own Chinese house and in which they could live and eat and sleep very much as they did at home could not after all be such an uncomfortable or foreign place.[33]

As knowledge of reforms in American medical education filtered into the missionary community in China, new principles for medical missions were formulated. These included greater attention to training Chinese doctors. By 1910 there were eight medical colleges for men and three for women, and the near doubling of the missionary population between 1905 and 1915 (from over 3,000 to over 5,000) suggested that even more schools might be started.

This then was the fortuitous moment at which the Rockefeller Foundation entered the scene—a time at which Western medicine had become sufficiently established to be evaluated, and education sufficiently in flux to be malleable. The fact that the China Medical Board's programs evolved in reaction to missionary medical education is closely associated with the wider scientific revolution in medicine. It also bears some resemblance to the elitist rejection of populist education in the United States. The unfolding of a Rockefeller Foundation philosophy for Chinese medical education is especially well illustrated by the reactions and suggestions of

33. *Ibid.*, p. 88.

William Welch during his three-month tour of China as a member of the Second Medical Commission in 1915.

Welch recognized that a background factor for modern medicine in China was the tenacious strength of traditional Chinese medicine. In a Baltimore talk shortly after returning from China, he described the herbal treatises of the legendary emperor Shen-nung and the exploratory surgery of Hua T'o in A.D. 200. Welch then went on to characterize Chinese views of anatomy, physiology, and the nature of disease as "fantastic and absurd" inasmuch as bans on human dissection had precluded experimental verification. He thought that their methods of diagnosis and numerous pulse countings were "more enlightened," although he deplored the absence of clinical questioning. Welch saved his praise for the sophisticated compendiums of herbal and drug remedies: "A great distinctive feature of Chinese medicine is its *materia medica*. . . . The Chinese surpass the world in their empirical *materia medica*."[34]

This understanding of at least some aspects of the strength of traditional medicine led Welch to discern the inadequacy of Western medicine as heretofore practiced in China. After just a week in China, he reflected on a disturbing characteristic, the primary emphasis on surgery. A lifetime spent promoting biomedical research is reflected in Welch's diary notation: "The Chinese appreciate Western surgery, but do not seem to consider Western drugs superior to their own. Query: Has Western medicine, in contrast to surgery been in [a] position or so represented as to demonstrate its superiority to Chinese medicine."[35] Welch was not alone in the recognition of the singular importance of surgery in the missionary medical repertoire. Balme, in his history of medical missions, noted how simple operations performed over and over with success inspired confidence in Western medicine. Additionally, the procedures were easily taught to assistants, even if they lacked scientific background.[36]

For Welch, the pathologist, it was the discoveries and probings of Western medicine into the causation of disease which had earned it worldwide acceptance. That the Chinese had not responded to

34. William Welch, "Medicine in the Orient," in *Addresses and Papers by William Henry Welch*, 3 (Baltimore: Johns Hopkins University Press, 1928), p. 181.

35. Welch, *Diary #2*, p. 24. Welch also emphasized this in talks in America, see "Medicine in Orient," p. 185.

36. Balme, *China and Modern Medicine*, p. 90. Kenneth Scott Latourette, *A History of Christian Missions in China* (New York: Macmillan, 1929), p. 452, also emphasizes the importance of surgery.

Western medicine because of the strength of their indigenous *materia medica* was only a partial answer. Welch's observations of pathology classes at the Union Medical College suggested another:

> ... [they teach] by giving students a series of mounted sections, to be later returned—students do not cut, stain, or mount their own sections, no autopsies, and only surgical material available for some gross pathological anatomy—1 microscope for four students—deficiencies in equipment.[37]

In the guise of missionary education, scientific medicine heretofore had simply not put its best foot forward.

The first step in transforming Western medicine in China was to enlist better-trained teachers. With regard to selecting faculty for the new PUMC, Welch insisted: "In the choice of teachers especial emphasis should be laid upon their capacity as investigators or to stimulate investigation, as such men are generally the best teachers."[38] Not only would the staff of the Rockefeller college need to be upgraded, so would the students. When Frederick L. Gates described the students at Yale-in-China in Changsha, he noted that they seemed to reflect quality, "unlike many of the other missionary schools with their coolie constituency."[39] Welch was not so condescending, suggesting more gently that the Rockefeller students should reflect "higher social positions" than the missionary students. It became generally recognized that the CMB desired to attract the elite of China, not the *declassé* who had been drawn to the missionary schools.

The missionary community welcomed financial contributions from the Rockefeller Foundation, but they reacted strongly against some aspects of the Foundation's "model" for medical education in China. Symbolic of the divergent approaches was the question of language. Should instruction be given in Chinese or English? Almost from the very beginning, plans for Rockefeller education had included teaching in English. In spite of his conversations with John Fryer, Ernest Burton had recommended English as the medium of instruction. During the various discussions in New York on this issue, Simon Flexner seems to have been the only one who ever argued against using English. When the question of language and standards arose at the very first China Conference in 1914, Flexner observed: "An immense amount of medical treatment can

37. Welch, *Diary* #2, p. 21.

38. William H. Welch, "North China," January, 1916, p. 19, *WWP*. This is Welch's formal report, and copies are also located in *RFA* and *SFP*.

39. Frederick L. Gates, "Hankow and Changsha," January, 1916, p. 7, *SFP*.

perhaps be practiced with a very limited knowledge—or perhaps, no knowledge, in a wide sense—of chemistry, physics or biology."[40] He then concluded that it would be a "waste of time" to teach a foreign language. Before he travelled to China in 1915, Flexner apparently retained some flexibility on this subject, but after arrival he told the missionary community:

> As a historical point, you might be interested to know that I at first supposed that of course teaching would be in Chinese. It is since I have come over here and have seen the attempts and their results, and have faced the problem from the point of view of education in general, that my view has radically changed.[41]

The Rockefeller commitment to teaching in English became closely joined with their primary educational aims. As Welch put it: "The *essential* thing is to raise Chinese to be first class medical men, and every proposition must be considered from that point of view."[42] In order to prepare Chinese for this role, Welch felt it axiomatic that they be taught in English. While translations of some medical works existed in Chinese, they were meagre. In a day in which medicine was internationally focused, and even Americans continued to travel to Germany and France, an international language such as English was indispensable for scientific communication.

The missionary faculty of the former Union Medical College, as well as most of the missionary community in general, almost unanimously favored teaching in Chinese. As one member of that faculty put it in a dinner conversation with Welch: "Chinese students taught medicine in English are likely to be out of touch with the people and will not advance Chinese medicine."[43] Not until the mid-1930s, however, did the Rockefeller Foundation ever seriously consider teaching in Chinese at PUMC. They spent some funds in translating services, and in aid to schools where instruction was in Mandarin, notably Shantung Christian College's Medical School in Tsinan. But their tendency to view teaching in English as a universal "standard" for China continued for some time. George Vincent, writing in 1919, was convinced that the language question was settled: "Tsinanfu remains practically the sole center for instruction in Mandarin. There is a good deal of doubt as to whether

40. "China Conference of the Rockefeller Foundation," 1914; also quoted in Ferguson, "The PUMC," p. 13.

41. Quoted in Ferguson, "The PUMC," p. 47.

42. *Ibid.*, p. 49. Emphasis in original.

43. Welch, *Diary #1*, p. 83.

this Mandarin-speaking group will be able to successfully perpetuate itself."[44]

This emphasis on instruction in English, scientific excellence for professors, and social standing of students was predicated on the assumed intellectual and social requirements for establishing scientific medicine in China. It was also related to the hope that PUMC would produce the medical elite of China. In explaining the purpose of their mission to the Minister of Foreign Affairs, Lu Cheng-hsiang, Welch stated: "Our ultimate aim, though years ahead, was to train Chinese as medical teachers and leaders who would eventually take over the work."[45]

Having surveyed the existing state of Western medicine in China, and having determined that it had been "applied but not absorbed," Welch previewed the Rockefeller medical school: "The aim should be to create as good a medical college as can be found anywhere in Europe or America."[46] How frequently those oft-repeated words would echo in future years! PUMC's entrance requirements were based on Welch's vision: a high school degree and two years of college with a premedical emphasis in physics, chemistry and biology. As might have been expected, these standards were considerably removed from reality. Welch and Flexner considered that *no* college in China offered adequate instruction in the basic sciences. There was no choice except to go one step further and establish the PUMC's own premedical school!

The standards set by PUMC not only matched the standards of better American schools, they surpassed them in many ways. Many of the first students at the premedical school had attended college prior to their premedical training of three years. After 1926, when PUMC's premedical school closed, nearly all students received B.A. degrees prior to attending PUMC. In contrast, as late as 1932, most medical institutions in the United States only required two years of college.[47]

The timing of cultural collision is accidental. It was by chance that just when the cycle of elitist versus populist medical education had resolved itself in America in favor of restricted professional training, the Rockefeller Foundation began to implant scientific medicine in China. Furthermore, scientific medicine had become very nearly synonymous for the Rockefeller educators with "stan-

44. George Vincent to Simon Flexner, August 13, 1919, *SFP*.
45. Welch, *Diary #2*, p. 30.
46. Welch, "North China," p. 17.
47. Stevens, *American Medicine*, p. 68.

dards," American Flexnerian standards. PUMC intentionally became the model for Western medicine in China. The educational pendulum of one country, one civilization, was swinging over one that was very different.

The Rockefeller commissioners appear to have given more consideration to their role as modernizers than to the transferability of their medical model. They were firmly convinced that Americans should be instructors, not participants, in the extension of modern medicine. Wisely eschewing individual participation and accepting the fact that assimilation had to come from the Chinese, the Rockefeller educators concentrated on teaching up-to-date scientific medicine. There is no doubt that they inculcated the best in medical knowledge that the West had to offer. But, in so doing, they inevitably removed themselves from the mundane and day-to-day poignancy of China itself.

This is not to say that Welch and his colleagues were unmindful of efforts being made by Chinese to teach and integrate modern medicine into their society. Both commissions visited all the modern Chinese medical schools, as well as those run by the French and Germans. In visiting the Peking Medical Special College, Welch remarked: "I apprehend that the groups at this school must regard with some jealousy and apprehension the expected development of the Union Medical College."[48]

The "jealousy and apprehension" of struggling Chinese medical educators were not echoed in official contacts with the Chinese government. Never, perhaps, had China's officialdom welcomed American aid so much. The Minister of Foreign Affairs, Lu Chenghsiang, upon hearing that the RF hoped to be able quickly to turn its college over to Chinese leadership, urged "that before relinquishing control we must be sure that his countrymen really could be entrusted with carrying the work forward and that much time would be required."[49]

These, and other comments of self-abasement, were made in the full knowledge of the wealth of Rockefeller and with great expectation from his munificence. A Hankow newspaper reported:

> The American Medical Commissioners are passing through Wuhu. Mr. Rockefeller, the most wealthiest man in the United States (famous as the Great King of Oil) has donated $70,000,000 gold—each dollar is equal to $2 Mexican—for promoting the sanitary conditions of the world.

48. Welch, *Diary #1*, p. 123.
49. *Ibid.*, p. 30.

Most of this sum will be devoted to the educating of Chinese medical students and for assisting the hospitals.[50]

In the face of such generosity, Chinese government leaders could afford to be passive and let the American educators impose their own philosophy of medical modernization. Roger Greene's recapitulation of his conversation with Li Yuan-hung, titular President of the new Republic, exemplifies this attitude:

And when I told him that we were not expecting to turn out a very large number of doctors, but rather to prepare a few Chinese who might become the leaders themselves in medical work in China, he said he thought that was a very wise and farseeing plan of action.[51]

In essence, there was very little dialogue between the American modernizers and the Chinese leaders of the early Republican period. Meetings and banquets, yes; dialogues, no. Yet, if there had been, it is unlikely that there would have been serious objections to the nature of the RF program. In her study of the YMCA during this period, Shirley Garrett notes that there was a reason that the period 1911–1925 constituted a high point for Sino-American institutions. Education was a mutual value, and the role of elite groups as reformers was not foreign to the Chinese tradition: "Basic to both traditions was a faith in the power of education to work miracles in transforming man and through him society at large."[52]

The few Chinese with whom extended discussions did occur certainly corroborated the views of the Foundation. Ernest Burton had lavished praise on the work of Chang Po-ling at Nankai University in Tientsin, and every other Rockefeller report reiterated it. A moderate reformer, once called the father of private education in modern China, Chang had done an outstanding job in developing one of the first middle schools into one of the best Chinese universities. Adopting a Western curriculum, he too hoped to train the new leaders of modern China.

Wu Lien-teh, Director of the Manchurian Plague Prevention Administration, antedated the reports of the RF commissions in his espousal of English as the medium of instruction in Chinese medical schools.[53] Constantly cited as a source in the RF reports, it did not occur to them that Wu himself was the kind of marginal man

50. T. M. Chu to Roger Greene, June 26, 1914, *RGP.*

51. Roger Greene, "Interview with Li Yuan-hung, 1916," May 8, 1916, *SFP.*

52. Garrett, *Chinese YMCA.*, p. 122.

53. Wu Lien-teh, "Memorandum of Medical Education in China," *CMJ* 28 (1914): 116; Wu, *Plague Fighter: Autobiography of a Chinese Physician* (Cambridge, England: W. Heffer, 1959), p. 468.

that those advocating instruction in Chinese hoped to avoid. Born in Singapore, trained in Japan—and undoubtedly the most important medical person in China at the time—Wu himself nonetheless spoke Chinese only haltingly.[54]

The closest to a real exchange of opinions came when Welch and Flexner visited Yale-in-China. Edward Hume had been a student of Welch's, and there had been some correspondence between them in the earliest years of Hume's work. Thus Welch was well aware of his unique cooperation with the Hunanese gentry. A dinner in honor of the Rockefeller Commission was given by the local gentry. Welch himself seemed duly impressed with the proud traditions of the area, commenting that the banquet was being held in the family hall of Tseng Kuo-fan, a nineteenth century governor-general well-known for his role in putting down the Taíping Rebellion.

In this assemblage, even though the band played "Yankee Doodle," the dignity of Chinese participation in modern medical activities became apparent. The Commissioner of Police stressed to Welch the need for cooperation between the medical profession and the police in municipal sanitation. Mr. H. Y. Liang, local manager of the Wah Chong Mining and Smelting Company, talked of intellectual cooperation—"not charity which might pauperize China."[55] At this encounter which heralded Chinese participation, the educational goals of the Rockefeller Foundation were not questioned. The gentry of Changsha, themselves elite modernizers, were in full accord with the "educate at the top, and the rest will take care of itself" philosophy of the Rockefeller Foundation. The educational approach of the RF was clearly not dissimilar from the educational philosophy of the Chinese elite during this period.

The conviction that scientific knowledge was needed to reform the attitudes of traditional China was also not new to the generation of the May Fourth Movement. Chinese intelligentsia of the times—including Liang Ch'i-ch'ao, Chang Chih-tung, Ting Wen-chiang, Wu Chih-hui, Hu Shih, Li Ta-chao, and Ch'en Tu-hsiu—to varying degrees also found in Western science a panacea for China's backwardness. Nonetheless, there existed a great divergence between the scientific vision of the Rockefeller scientists and the Chinese

54. "The Reminiscences of Doctor John B. Grant," Columbia University Oral History Research Project conducted by Dr. Saul Benison, 1961, p. 190. Hereinafter "Grant Reminiscences."

55. Welch, *Diary #1*, p. 160; Edward Hume, "Recollections of Dr. William Henry Welch—A Great Teacher," *New York State Journal of Medicine* 52 (15 February 1952): 309–314. Reprint in Edward Hume Papers, Missionary Research Library, New York.

educated elite. For the Chinese, who for the most part were not scientists, science became scientism, an expansive philosophy which applied the prestigious cachet of science to all spheres—economics, politics, and sociology.[56]

This broad concept of science was not characteristic only of politicized intellectuals, who used the principles of science to buttress changes in Chinese society, but was also embraced by those thoroughly grounded in scientific subjects. Ting Wen-chiang, the noted geologist, wrote: "The omnipotence of science . . . lies not in its subject matter, but in its method."[57] Using scientific analysis, Ting was able to construct theories about Chinese society, family relations, and government.

But for most Americans connected with the scientific revolution in medicine, scientific thinking became involuted, not expansive. Enshrined in the standards required of scientific technology, medicine, the most applied of all sciences, became valued for its content, not its applicability. Since the discovery of a "cure" was inherently applicable, it was relatively easy to forget that efficacy was also determined by social, educational, and economic factors. For China's new intelligentsia, science became the telescope with which to focus on the rest of society; for American medical scientists of the same period, science had become a microscope with which to probe more deeply the medical ills of individual man, individual disease.

The need was for both, but this was difficult at Peking Union Medical College, a medical school whose standards had been set in defiance of the social and economic conditions of the country. The discrepancy bears some resemblance to the *t'i–yung* dichotomy, which the earliest advocates of change in traditional China had recognized, and which continues, albeit in a different context, in the "red versus expert" conflict in Maoist China: substance versus utility, Eastern ethics versus Western knowledge, ideology versus technology, medical knowledge versus medical application, and also Rockefeller scientists versus barefoot doctors.

For the moment, the Rockefeller educators had resolved this dichotomy in favor of the substance, medical knowledge, with apparent disregard for the *yung*, its function. They were not totally unaware of the need for *yung*, for as Welch repeatedly reminded: "Our purpose is not to impose something foreign on the Chinese,

56. D. W. Y. Kwok, *Scientism in Chinese Thought, 1900–1950* (New Haven, Conn.: Yale University Press, 1965), see chapter 1 especially.

57. Quoted in Charlotte Furth, *Ting Wen-chiang: Science and China's New Culture* (Cambridge, Mass.: Harvard University Press, 1970), pp. 113–114.

but to train up a truly Chinese medical profession. . . . The rapidity with which they accept scientific medicine as their own, and the rapidity with which our importance in the field diminishes, and their importance increases, will be the measure of our success."[58] But, for the time being, with priority assigned in this instance to a Western *t'i*, the harmonizing *yung* and the application of this knowledge, as well as its Sinification, remained for the future.

At the time of its dedication, Peking Union Medical College was very obviously an American institution, a Johns Hopkins implanted in China. Since the donor and recipient nations were so basically diverse, there was always the potential prognosis that the Chinese body might reject parts, or all, of its Western transplant. In order to become compatible with its Chinese host, PUMC would necessarily undergo considerable modification. The pressures came from within and without, and in the beginning the process was slow and at times almost imperceptible.

The remaining chapters explore various facets of the attempts to change PUMC from a foreign implant to a viable transplant. Chapters 3, 4 and 5 examine the major components of the medical college—the administration, the faculty, the curriculum, and the students. Chapters 6 and 7 focus on the individual careers of a PUMC professor and several of his Chinese students. Chapter 8 and the Epilogue trace the history of the institution and its graduates from World War II until the mid-1970s. Throughout, the central issue is whether and how Peking Union Medical College and its progeny took root in the Middle Kingdom.

58. Quoted in "The Rockefeller Foundation in China," *CMJ* 30 (1916): 45.

THREE Roger Greene, Peking Middleman

*So we must look forward to the day when most, if not all, of
the positions on the faculty . . . will be held by Chinese; when
the Board of Trustees . . . will include leading Chinese. . . .
Let us then go forward with one accord towards the
attainment of this objective which will make permanent the
establishment on Chinese soil.*

John D. Rockefeller, Jr.,
PUMC Dedication, 1921

TRANSFERRING power from one person to another,
from one institution to another, from one country to another, is a
wrenching task. For the Rockefeller Foundation this entailed relinquishing legal and financial control over PUMC. For PUMC this entailed relinquishing administrative and faculty positions to Chinese
nationals. That this was the goal of the entire enterprise was never
in question. The succinct statement of John D. Rockefeller, Jr.,
at the PUMC dedication had made this abundantly clear. And yet,
devolution of authority became the crucial administrative problem
which faced the Rockefeller Foundation in China.

There were many middlemen involved in this weaning process,
both Americans and Chinese. None of them is more representative,
more symbolic, than Roger Sherman Greene. Greene's tenure with
the Rockefeller Foundation and Peking Union Medical College
extended over more than twenty years. He held a variety of positions, including Director of the China Medical Board, Vice-President of the Rockefeller Foundation in the Far East, and *de facto*
Director of PUMC. The son of missionary parents to Japan and a
graduate of Harvard, Greene came in contact with the Rockefeller
Foundation while serving as American Consul-General in Hankow,
and through his brother, Jerome Greene, then the Secretary of the
Foundation. In 1914, Greene was asked to serve as a member of

the first Rockefeller Foundation Commission to China. Although only in his early thirties, Greene so impressed Foundation officials that he was offered the position of Resident Director in China for the CMB. In accepting, he turned down a promotion by the State Department to Consul General-at-large for the Far East.[1]

Since he had no medical background, Greene spent several months observing the administration of Johns Hopkins Hospital before assuming his first position with the Rockefeller Foundation. Throughout his tenure in China, Greene energetically promoted the work of the China Medical Board and Peking Union Medical College, and became well-known throughout China for his numerous articles on the work of the Foundation and the need for scientific medicine in China.[2] Because of his diplomatic experience, Greene also became active in a variety of non-PUMC matters. From being an advisor to such groups as the China Foundation and the Mass Education Movement, he was probably better informed on Chinese conditions than any of the other Rockefeller Foundation officials.

In spite of his loyalty and competence, Roger Greene's relationship with the Rockefeller Foundation was a controversial one which ended in his abrupt dismissal in 1934. "Dismissal" is the appropriate euphemism: in reality Greene was fired by John D. Rockefeller, Jr. Were Greene's imbroglio with Rockefeller only a personal matter, it would have had no lasting importance. What is significant is that the issues involved—finances, religion, the relationship between the China Medical Board and the PUMC Trustees, and the intervention of the Rockefeller family—symbolize three decades of conflict between New York and Peking. And, directly or indirectly, each of these problems was related to the ultimate difficulty—transferring authority from New York to Peking.

Mary Ferguson has provided a detailed administrative history of the RF, the CMB, and PUMC.[3] The focus here, however, is on the conflicts of authority between New York and Peking. These are well illustrated by viewing Roger Greene as a broker between America and China, especially during the years 1927–1935, a time of institutional crisis and change. As an intermediary, Greene consistently

---

1. Roger Greene to Secretary of State William Jennings Bryan, August 8, 1914, *RGP*. For an excellent new biography of Greene, see Warren I. Cohen, *The Chinese Connection; Roger Greene, Thomas W. Lamont, George E. Sokolsky and American-East Asian Relations* (New York: Columbia University Press, 1978).

2. For example, see Roger S. Greene, "Medical Needs of the Chinese," *Chinese Recorder* 49 (April 1918): 224–230; "The China Medical Board, 1918–1919," *The China Mission Year Book*, 1919, pp. 184–189.

3. Ferguson, *CMB and PUMC*.

advocated more autonomy for those exercising authority in Peking, both Americans and Chinese. The players were mostly Americans, but that was really not his fault. Nor, however, was Greene a latter-day saint during this era of extraterritorial prerogative. While he had no patience with Rockefeller paternalism, he was not immune from its spirit. In Peking he favored an American presence, and, perhaps unconsciously, became indispensable himself. But before plunging into the momentous years which brought a surge of Chinese nationalism, the Great Depression, and the firing of Roger Greene, the institutional stage must be set.

From the inception of the Foundation to its first major reorganization in 1927, the most important aspect of the administrative structure was the interlocking membership between the Rockefeller Foundation, the China Medical Board, and the PUMC Trustees. The Trustees, ironically, do not appear to have had any real jurisdiction over PUMC. Although Mary Ferguson affirms that legally "the Trustees assumed responsibility for the internal administration of the College,"[4] their location in New York and their dependence on the RF indicates that they did little more than rubber-stamp decisions made elsewhere.

There was a substantial overlapping and duplication of membership on these boards. Until 1927, it was also difficult to discern differences in their responsibilities. For example, the CMB assumed jurisdiction over non-PUMC fellowships and grants to China, but also shared responsibility with the Trustees for faculty appointments at PUMC. This same confusion existed in Peking. As the representative of the China Medical Board, Greene was accountable for non-PUMC grants to missionary colleges, surveys of scientific education in China, and disbursal of fellowships. He was also responsible for recruitment of American professors for PUMC and transmission of the PUMC budget to New York. In these matters his authority often overlapped that of Franklin McLean and Henry Houghton, directors of PUMC during those years.

The first director of PUMC, Franklin McLean, was only twenty-eight years old at the time of his appointment in 1916. A graduate of the University of Chicago and Rush Medical College (Chicago), McLean had subsequently spent some time at the University of Oregon Medical School, in Europe, and at the Rockefeller Institute. Instrumental in building the first faculty, McLean resigned his position as director to become professor of medicine at PUMC. In 1922 he left Peking for a distinguished medical and administrative career

4. *Ibid.*, p. 23.

at the University of Chicago.[5] The second director of PUMC, Henry S. Houghton, had received his M.D. from Johns Hopkins in 1905 and then travelled to China where he served as professor and dean át the Harvard Medical School in Shanghai. Director of PUMC from 1921–1928, Houghton presided over PUMC during its years of growth and consolidation. He left China for the University of Iowa and later the University of Chicago, but maintained close ties with the Rockefeller Foundation and returned to Peking in 1934 as the Foundation's envoy during the institutional crisis brought on by the firing of Roger Greene.

The relative youth of Greene, McLean, and Houghton was one factor in the lines of authority which were drawn during the early years. At the outset, policy flowed from New York to Peking, from an inner coterie of senior Rockefeller advisors to a younger cadre of Foundation officers. Channels of authority were not rationalized, but were rather geographic and personal. Responsibilities were further confused by the presence of the Foundation's "old guard" (Simon Flexner, William Welch, Wallace Buttrick, George Vincent, and Rockefeller Jr. himself) on all three boards—the Rockefeller Foundation, the China Medical Board, and PUMC. The following organizational chart illustrates the geographic and personal determinants of authority.

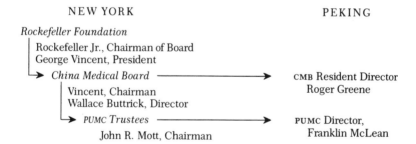

NEW YORK   PEKING

Rockefeller Foundation
  Rockefeller Jr., Chairman of Board
  George Vincent, President
  → *China Medical Board* ⟶ CMB Resident Director
    Vincent, Chairman   Roger Greene
    Wallace Buttrick, Director
    → *PUMC Trustees* ⟶ PUMC Director,
      John R. Mott, Chairman   Franklin McLean

During the early years, relationships between the Rockefeller Foundation and PUMC were analogous to that of a parent and child. Neither Roger Greene, CMB representative in China, nor Franklin McLean, PUMC director, were invested with enough authority to administer decisively CMB and PUMC affairs in Peking. The fiasco which surrounded construction costs occurred partly because of the absence of local supervision. Official histories of the RF do not men-

5. For recent biographical information on McLean, see Marshall R. Urist, "Phoenix of Physiology and Medicine: Franklin Chambers McLean," *Perspectives in Biology and Medicine*, 1975, Autumn, pp. 23–58.

tion graft in association with the skyrocketing construction costs of PUMC, but a contemporary participant and RF official, Victor Heiser, reported: "Am hearing many complaints about Rock Hospital. Also stories about graft. Hussey [Harry H., architect] reported to have been given $300,000 to cancel his contract after he had been caught grafting."[6]

Whatever the truth of corruption, the building committee during the early years was too far away to be of assistance: Wallace Buttrick, George Vincent, and Starr J. Murphy, all of New York, were the representatives. In 1919, Vincent travelled to China to investigate the mounting construction and administrative difficulties. In a cable to the New York office, he wired: "Long distance control now serious impediment."[7] So in 1919, three years after construction had begun, New York authorized a Peking building committee.

When the institution became fully operative in the early twenties, there was some decline in New York's passion for detailed supervision. Still, as Acting Director of PUMC during the interim between McLean's resignation and Houghton's subsequent appointment, Richard Pearce (Director of the RF's Division of Medical Education) personally experienced many of the difficulties which continued to plague Greene. In December 1920, Pearce wrote candidly of his frustrations: "I am forced to the conclusion that the chief difficulty is in the management of China Medical Board affairs in the New York office."[8] Writing again several months later and urging greater autonomy for PUMC, Pearce observed that "the control of policies has in the past centered largely in the New York office, which has not had a very adequate conception of the extent of the interests it has been trying to handle."[9]

Some minor changes resulted from Pearce's recommendations. Inordinate supervision, however, continued by the China Medical Board as well as by the Manhattan-based RF Trustees. Five years after Pearce's review, Dr. David Edsall, Dean of Harvard Medical School, was a visiting professor at PUMC. His survey of the teaching and administrative problems of PUMC echoed many of Pearce's earlier complaints about the role of the home office. After detailing the tedious trans-Pacific process by which departmental promotions

6. Victor Heiser, Notes #16, p. 5116, VHP. This is Heiser's daily diary which he kept throughout his years as an RF official.

7. "Statement of Actions of the Board in Relation to the Construction of Peking Union Medical College," n.d., p. 7, RFA.

8. Pearce to Vincent, December 9, 1920, SFP.

9. Quoted in Ferguson, "The PUMC," p. 138.

took place, Edsall went on to make the apt comment: "The methods in question here are more like those of a business organization than an academic one."[10]

Unfortunately, the business analogy was not relevant to the financial management of the College. New York's concern over the rising PUMC budget dated almost from the institution's inception, yet the Foundation continued to acquiesce in the spiralling expansion of PUMC. In 1914, the trustees estimated that by 1920 PUMC's annual budget would rise to the US$150,000–200,000 range and then stabilize at that level. In actuality the budget for the first year, 1916, was US$225,000 and it continued to grow relentlessly, reaching US$900,000 by 1927. Additionally, the staff became enormous. As early as 1922 it had reached 177 foreigners and 700 Chinese. The trustees were alarmed at the "fungus-like" development: "It rivals Minerva in springing into existence full-grown. The budget proposed for next year . . . is much more extensive than that of many of the medical schools in this country."[11]

And yet, if the plant had become too unwieldy, only the Foundation itself could be faulted. In a discussion paper prepared for a confidential reassessment of PUMC in 1921, Richard Pearce squarely laid the blame: "Would any one or any group of the Trustees handle a business involving an expenditure of approximately $10,000,000 in the same casual way as the P.U.M.C. has been handled?" While critical of the financial planning, Pearce also justified the expanse and expense of the institution: "Have they [the trustees] always appreciated the fact that the plan they were developing is not merely a medical school, but in reality a university with a hospital for both the Chinese and foreign community?"[12] For a while this argument was persuasive and the Foundation continued to grant annual budget increases to PUMC. Predictably, those in Peking came to rely on the Foundation's ever-expanding purse.

As long as the CMB and PUMC remained under the control of the Rockefeller Foundation, the transfer of authority from New York to Peking was mostly a wistful dream. However, in the late twenties as a result of the reorganization of the Foundation, the parent institution appeared to release its offspring, the CMB and PUMC, from

10. David L. Edsall, "Memorandum Concerning Peking Union Medical College," December, 1926, p. 20, *SFP.*

11. "Conference on Matters Concerning the Peking Union Medical College and China Medical Board," Gedney Farms Hotel, White Plains, New York, May 16 and 17, 1921, Exhibit A (Embree to Pearce, February 1, 1921), *RFA.*

12. *Ibid.,* Exhibit D (Questions by Dr. Pearce), p. 1.

the nest. In fact, this reshuffling only tangled the reins of authority and aroused expectations which were never met.

The Rockefeller Foundation's reorganization spelled the end of an era in which it had pioneered philanthropic activities in medicine and public health. The broadening of Foundation responsibilities into the natural sciences, social sciences, humanities and arts, agriculture, and forestry resulted in a decrease of attention to former priority items. Moreover, years of experience had brought substantial changes in concepts of philanthropic management. Thus, the China Medical Board and PUMC, two of the earliest activities of the Foundation, came under special scrutiny.

As the Rockefeller Foundation sought to diversify its interests, it is quite evident that PUMC had become something of an embarrassment and, to a few, even an albatross. By the mid-twenties it had become stated Foundation policy to give institutional grants only on a matching basis, *and* in decreasing amounts. In contrast, not only did PUMC receive all of its funds from the RF, the Foundation was the legal owner of this international school. Never again did the Rockefeller Foundation consider that outright control was the most effective means to disburse funds for international medical education.[13]

Accordingly, a persistent theme in the thinking of the RF Trustees during the time of the reorganization was that PUMC should become independent of the Foundation. In a memorandum titled, "P.U.M.C. Future Organization," from the Board Minutes of November 4, 1927, the *aim* of the reorganization was spelled out:

a. Progressive autonomy of PUMC, including responsibility for plant, maintenance, budget and control.
b. Disappearance from Foundation's financial statement of the value of the Peking plant, and the amount of capital funds.
c. Steady increase of Chinese staff.
d. Utilization of foreigners as visiting professors rather than permanent staff.
e. Consequent reduction of the budget by elimination of foreign salaries from the yearly expenses.[14]

While that was the formal goal, it was hard to let go. The official reorganization committee had earlier recommended that an American corporation, independent of the Foundation, be created as an

13. Fosdick, *Rockefeller Foundation*, pp. 135–138; Rockefeller Foundation, *Annual Report, 1925*, pp. 38–43.
14. "P.U.M.C. Future Organization," November 4, 1927, from Board Meeting Minutes, *SFP*.

"endowment-holding body" for PUMC.[15] It should be recalled that the New York-based PUMC Trustees had never exercised independent authority over the institution. No consideration seems to have been given to strengthening that group by making it the endowment-holding body. Only fleeting mention was made of actually transferring the funds to China, although that supposedly was the final intent.

Having decided to make PUMC independent by giving it an endowment, two questions remained: the nature of the endowment-holding body, and the size of the endowment. Although the reorganization committee had merely specified that this corporation was "to receive from the Rockefeller Foundation, and hold sufficient funds to yield the income needed by the institution,"[16] the prerogatives of that body gradually expanded in the years which followed. The first indication of this is in a letter in late 1926 from the RF counsel, Thomas M. Debevoise, to Raymond Fosdick, one of the most active trustees and future president of the Foundation:

> With the funds providing the income for the maintenance of the College held by another American corporation . . . there would be in this country a healthy practical control of the College which would be fully justified by the fact that it owed its existence, its property and its maintenance to the Foundation.[17]

"Healthy practical control of the College" was further provided for by Roger Greene, the man who in future years was to suffer the most from it. He had originally opposed the reorganization, instead preferring that the Foundation retain full financial responsibility for PUMC until such time as the institution could be completely turned over to the Chinese. Faced with a fait accompli, Greene sought assurance that access to the Foundation's largess would not be jeopardized. He suggested that the membership of the new independent corporation "be selected exclusively from the membership of the Foundation," and that its name be the China Medical Board, Incorporated, to facilitate registration with the Chinese government.[18] (The original CMB, a division of the RF, was being disbanded. This was a logical step in that the non-PUMC activities of

15. "Report of the Committee on Reorganization of the Rockefeller Foundation," November 5, 1926, *RFA*, p. 7.

16. *Ibid.*

17. Debevoise to Fosdick, December 18, 1926, *RFA*.

18. Greene to Fosdick, January 29, 1927, *RFA*. Greene wrote a number of letters concerning the reorganization: to Pearce, January 29, 1926; October 12, 1927; November 5, 1927, *RGP*; to Fosdick, April 14, 1926, *SFP*.

the CMB—namely, financial support to missionary and Chinese institutions—had greatly declined.)

Utilization of the same name, coupled with RF members serving
on the board of the new "independent" organization, are but two
illustrations of the incomplete separation of powers—primarily a
bookkeeping change—which took place at the time of the reorganization. Even so, devolution of financial liability for PUMC from the
Rockefeller Foundation to a separate organization might have succeeded had the initial endowment been sufficient for the yearly
budgets of PUMC.

On both sides of the Pacific it was insisted that the changes would
be meaningless unless the new CMB Inc. had sufficient funds.
Greene stressed that a partial endowment, forcing PUMC and the
new CMB Inc. to apply annually to the Foundation for supplemental
sums, would be self-defeating and exceedingly complicated.[19]
Simon Flexner put it more cogently: "If the College should ever
be in a position to make a reasonable request once, the separation
of the two institutions [RF and PUMC] from that time on would be
incomplete."[20]

The endowment requested for PUMC was US$18 million. Yearly
interest on that sum, calculated at five percent, would yield US
$900,000, PUMC's current operating budget. When in May 1928
the final decision was made, however, the CMB Inc. was given an
endowment of only US$12 million, the income from which all rec-
ognized to be inadequate. The Rockefeller Foundation agreed to
supplement the budget for the following five years, 1928–1933,
by US$1,500,000 in a series of decreasing grants. In 1933, the
Rockefeller Foundation would examine long-range funding for
PUMC.[21]

In retrospect it appears that the Rockefeller Foundation did *exactly* what those intimately involved thought would be most disas-
trous: it perpetuated the financial dependence of PUMC, via the
CMB Inc., on the Rockefeller Foundation. Reorganization meant
that the entire PUMC annual budget would have to be approved
by the China Medical Board, Inc., and the Trustees of the Rockefeller Foundation. In order to be apprised fully of the financial needs
of PUMC in 1933, the Foundation had retained this right of review.
Since involvement in the budget was synonymous with involve-

19. Greene to Pearce, December 27, 1926, *SFP*.

20. Quoted in Margery Eggleston [Secretary of the China Medical Board]
to Greene, January 13, 1928, *RGP*.

21. "Report on Reorganization of the Rockefeller Boards," May 22, 1928, p. 7,
RFA; Ferguson, *CMB and PUMC*, pp. 59–60.

ment in the affairs of the College, the RF trustees remained an integral part of the interlocking boards which continued to oversee PUMC.

In the document, "P.U.M.C. Future Organization," mention was made of a "steady increase in Chinese staff," but there was no reference to present or potential Chinese administrative leadership. Where were the advocates for Chinese participation? There appear to have been few. In fact, Roger Greene argued *against* including Chinese on the new CMB Inc.: "The Chinese public and officials will regard it as perfectly natural that the endowment be held by a purely American body so long as it is thought desirable to keep control of the funds in American hands."[22]

In the discussion of these new institutional relationships, no mention has been made of any Chinese participants, so nominal were their roles. Since the devolution of authority from New York to Peking claimed that the ultimate recipient would be Chinese leadership, this is a telling indictment. Later chapters will explore faculty recruiting and promotion policies as well as the relative passivity of Chinese nationalism at PUMC. Here we will trace the efforts which were made to involve Chinese at the administrative level, from the first abortive "managerial" group to a Peking-based Board of PUMC Trustees, a majority of whom were Chinese.

In 1922, an advisory committee of distinguished leaders was appointed "to interpret to the people the purposes and policies of the institution as well as to advise the officers in matters requiring special knowledge of local conditions."[23] The group was a curious blend of well-known educators, such as Ts'ai Yuan-p'ei and Chang Po-ling, Presidents of Peking and Nankai Universities respectively, and political officials, such as T'sai T'ing-kan, Assistant Director of Customs. Undoubtedly its original purpose was to prepare a group in China to become a local board of managers, the type of administrative vehicle used by missionary institutions to simulate local leadership.

Whatever its intended function, the group does not appear to have been used to any great extent. Minutes of the occasional meetings suggest that the primary purpose was to acquaint Chinese leaders with PUMC's programs, not to elicit their advice. Sessions were held on the functions of a hospital, the public health activities of the College, and the problems of women nurses. From time to time, one of the advisors would intercede with government

22. Greene to Pearce, October 12, 1927, *RGP*.
23. K. Chimin Wong and Wu Lien-teh, *History of Chinese Medicine* (Tientsin: Tientsin Press, 1932), p. 551.

authorities—customs and the police most frequently—on an administrative problem.[24]

In 1926, Houghton made it quite clear that this group wielded no authority: "The longer I think about that Committee as an ultimate directing body, the more sure I am becoming that we should not take any important steps in building up their responsibility."[25] Later, three Chinese members of the PUMC Trustees were drawn from that group, but the Chinese advisory committee, *per se*, appears to have been a truncated move in the direction of Chinese managerial involvement in PUMC. The only tangible evidence of some transfer of administrative authority from Westerners to Chinese was the appointment of J. Heng Liu (Liu Jui-heng) as superintendent of the hospital in 1925.

Born in Tientsin in 1890, Liu had studied at Anglo-Chinese and Peiyang Colleges before enrolling at Harvard, where he received his B.S. in 1908. He subsequently received his M.D. *cum laude* from Harvard Medical School in 1913. After several years of teaching surgery at the Harvard Medical School of China in Shanghai, Liu joined the staff of PUMC in 1918 as an associate in surgery. Subsequent training in the early 1920s at the Rockefeller Institute and Johns Hopkins, coupled with his considerable administrative ability, made Liu an obvious candidate for the first Chinese appointment to a senior administrative position. As Houghton observed in a letter to Greene: "He discovers that he can do this thing, and likes it. He is restive; his colleagues applaud him. . . . Do we want him in administration?"[26] Liu displaced an American, Dwight Sloan. Thus began the difficult personnel task of replacing foreigners by Chinese that was to tax the varying national loyalties of the College.

Until 1927, pressure to increase Chinese managerial responsibility had to come either from New York or from within the institution. While the early 1920s spawned a number of nationalistic movements, such as the anti-Christian movement of 1921 and the student strikes of 1925, these did not result in effective regulations governing foreign institutions operating in China. To be sure the various warlord governments, which had controlled Peking until June of 1928, had required local managerial boards. But since PUMC

24. For copies of the minutes of this Committee, see China Medical Board Collection (*CMBC*), Rockefeller Foundation Archives, Box 67.

25. Houghton to Greene, October 31, 1926, *RGP*.

26. Houghton to Greene, February 21, 1925, *RGP*. For biographical information on Liu, see Howard Boorman, ed., *Biographical Dictionary of Republican China* (New York: Columbia University Press, 1968), 3:402–403.

(as the old Union Medical College) had been officially recognized by the Ch'ing Dynasty, the institution had taken no steps to conform to this newer regulation.

This situation quickly changed when Chiang Kai-shek's Kuomintang became the official government in Nanking. As the Rockefeller Foundation's reorganization was taking place, the Nationalist government's Ministry of Education moved quickly to promulgate regulations concerning Western-owned educational institutions. The two ordinances which were to affect PUMC drastically were the requirements that all institutions must have a Chinese director, and a local managerial body whose composition included a majority of Chinese.

As a first response to edicts requiring Chinese leadership, F. C. Yen (Yen Fu-ching) was appointed PUMC's vice-director for the academic year 1927–1928. This was admittedly a stop-gap measure because Yen intended to return to Hsiang-Ya [Yale-in-China] Medical School in Hunan the following year. In 1928, J. Heng Liu was appointed vice-director and Roger Greene himself as acting director of PUMC. Greene at that time had also been named vice-president of the RF in Asia, a new position created during the Foundation's reorganization.

It soon became evident that the Nanking government required a Chinese director, not just a vice-director. Liu was the obvious candidate, but his administrative success had not gone unnoticed by the Chinese government. Appointed Vice-Minister of Health in 1928, Liu was actively involved in building a national health organization in Nanking, *in absentia* from his Peking post. Through consultation with political leaders, Greene ascertained that the appointment of Liu as director, even though his role in Nanking insured that his involvement in PUMC affairs would be nominal, would nonetheless satisfy the authorities. Accordingly, the positions were reversed, and Liu was appointed director, and Roger Greene vice-director. Liu held the title of PUMC Director for the next ten years, until 1938, even though his national responsibilities continued and he lived in Nanking.[27]

Roger Greene's attitude toward the edict requiring a Chinese director reflected that of most of the Westerners at PUMC. In correspondence with Richard Pearce he made it evident that he believed the time was not ripe for Chinese leadership. As director of the Division of Medical Education, Pearce was in charge of PUMC affairs while the final organization of the CMB Inc. was pending. In

27. Ferguson, *CMB and PUMC*, pp. 60–62.

this capacity, Pearce repeatedly urged Greene to consider Chinese appointees for *both* the position of director and vice-director, but Greene responded that the institution was not yet ready for a complete transfer to Chinese management.[28] When Liu was appointed director, Greene made it quite clear that he himself would be running the show. His candid, personal letter to Liu discussing their future relationship is a most revealing document, and a portion needs to be quoted in full:

> On the other hand it is necessary to face frankly the fact that my special relation to the Trustees and the Rockefeller Foundation would give me greater power in reality than would literally and legally rest with the office of Vice Director, especially since I should be expected to continue to correspond with them. A good many members of the staff, especially the foreigners, would continue to look to me. This situation would provide ample room for friction between two men who did not thoroughly understand each other. . . .[29]

Given Liu's active and far-removed participation in government affairs in Nanking, it was obvious that the compliance with official regulations was merely symbolic. This sham of adherence occurred within the continuing existence of extraterritorial prerogatives for Americans in China and was by no means confined to PUMC. Yenching University, for example, operated under two separate constitutions in the years 1929–1937, one in Chinese and one in English. The latter softened for the American church board the secular and nationalistic concessions to the Chinese. In explaining why the Nationalist government accepted token Chinese administrations, Philip West, in his study of Yenching University, concludes: "The Kuomintang never enforced its own regulations, because, it might be argued, it couldn't. It might also be argued that it didn't want to, for it deeply believed in maintaining strong political and cultural ties with the West."[30]

The second aspect of the Chinese educational ordinances was the securing of a Chinese managerial body. The PUMC Trustees and Rockefeller Foundation considered several options, which included ignoring the edict or establishing a shadow board in China. From China, Greene warned them "that the open statement of any . . . limitations of the power of the local board would render its con-

28. Pearce to Greene, June 30, 1927; Greene to Pearce, July 23, 1927, *RGP*.
29. Greene to Liu, January 24, 1929, *RGP*.
30. Philip West, "Yenching University and Chinese-American Relations, 1917–1937" (Ph.D. Dissertation, Harvard University, 1971), p. 265.

stitution unacceptable to the Ministry of Education."[31] Since the former PUMC Trustees had never been an active body, and since CMB Inc. was being constituted as an American-based holding board for PUMC anyway, it was not too difficult for the former trustees to agree "to change the membership of the present PUMC Trustees to include a majority of Chinese permitting meetings in China."[32]

Accordingly, in April 1929, a number of the original PUMC trustees, including Simon Flexner, William Welch, and John D. Rockefeller, Jr., resigned. The original sole Chinese representative Y. T. Tsur, (Chou I-ch'un) was joined by six more, to make a total of seven Chinese and six Americans. The new Chinese members were distinguished political and educational leaders: Alfred Sao-ke Sze (Shih Chao-chi), Chang Po-ling, C. C. Wu (Wu Ch'ao-shu), J. Heng Liu, Hu Shih, and Wong Wen-hao. Several months later, in order to conform to further regulations that Chinese constitute a two-thirds majority, W. W. Yen (Yen Hui-ch'ing) and Sohtsu G. King replaced two Americans as trustees.[33]

These new trustees were among China's most prominent Western-oriented political and educational leaders. All but one, Chang Po-ling, had received their formal college or graduate training in the United States or Europe, and even Chang had studied for a short time at Teacher's College of Columbia University. Yen, Wu, and Sze were well-known diplomats, equally at home in Washington, London, Paris, or Moscow. Chang Po-ling was president of Nankai University in Tientsin. Y. T. Tsur had served as the first president of Tsinghua University. Wong Wen-hao, a Belgium-trained geologist, was director of the China Geological Survey and Hu Shih, professor of philosophy at Peking University, was the internationally known disciple of John Dewey and prominent spokesman for Chinese language reform.

In the past the PUMC Trustees had been a nominal body, dominated by the CMB, an inner organization of the Foundation. There had been no particular difficulty in transferring that body to China, but its role in actually governing PUMC had yet to be defined. Furthermore, while no one could doubt the eminence of the new trustees, they were a widely scattered and extremely active group of individuals. Only J. Heng Liu had any background in operating

31. "Exhibit F, Registration of the College," document prepared by Roger Greene for Trustee meeting of April 10, 1929, *WWP*, p. 4.

32. *Ibid.*, p. 2.

33. Ferguson, "The PUMC," p. 184; *CMB and PUMC*, pp. 63–64.

a medical college. These group characteristics did not augur well for the new PUMC Trustees' ability to function as a cohesive, managerial body.

There is no question that the reorganization of the Rockefeller Foundation and the PUMC Trustees brought a measure of autonomy to PUMC, and that some authority was passed from Westerners to Chinese. In both cases, however, devolution of authority was incomplete. During the next decade this resulted in more tension and international misunderstanding than had existed during the earlier period of unilateral authority.

The central protagonist in the ensuing years of growing controversy between the Rockefeller Foundation, China Medical Board, Inc., and PUMC was Roger Greene. It was perhaps inevitable that Greene encountered difficulties, for he was simultaneously responsible to the three separate systems of authority which governed PUMC. The following diagram indicates the structural changes following the reorganization. Most noticeable are the legal independence of the CMB and the transfer of PUMC authority to China.

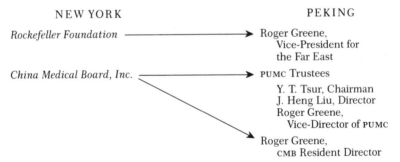

As Vice-President of the Rockefeller Foundation for the Far East, Resident Director in China for the China Medical Board, Inc., and Vice-Director of PUMC, it is no wonder that Greene should write of "the anomaly of my position *vis-à-vis* the Rockefeller Foundation."[34]

Greene's was not the only anomalous position. The role of the China-based PUMC Trustees was untried, and the function of the new CMB was unclear. Furthermore, the ambivalence of the Rockefeller Foundation with regard to insuring an independent PUMC was clearly revealed in a clause in the final charter of CMB Inc. It stipulated that the CMB would be empowered to transfer the PUMC property and endowment to the PUMC Trustees in China "when convinced that this institution has reached a basis of stability and

34. Greene to Gregg, May 9, 1930, *RGP.*

permanence."[35] It is difficult to conceive a more subjective and temporizing criterion.

What is clear is that from 1929 to 1933 the internal separation of the CMB Inc. from the RF became progressively more fiction than fact. By 1933 the membership of the CMB had become dominated by RF personnel, including George Vincent, John D. Rockefeller III, and Alan Gregg (Richard Pearce's successor as director of the RF's Division of Medical Education). An even more obvious step was the selection of Vincent as chairman in 1934.[36] It will be recalled that Vincent had been President of the Rockefeller Foundation from 1917 to 1929, and was a close personal associate of Rockefeller Jr. Although Roger Greene at an early stage had favored close ties between the CMB and the Rockefeller Foundation, this attitude had changed by the early 1930s. At the time of the young Rockefeller's appointment to the CMB, Greene registered his surprise, terming it a "step backward to closer relationships" with the Foundation.[37]

John D. Rockefeller III, only twenty-four years old at this time, was asked to undertake an in-house review of the CMB. His youthful and naive enthusiasm—which greatly irritated Greene—is revealed in a letter to Vincent: "Never having made an investigation of this nature before I am not quite sure how to go at it but it is really lots of fun."[38] Nevertheless, Rockefeller's survey produced genuine insight into the complicated overlapping of interests. Five years after the RF had been supposedly freed from responsibility for PUMC, Rockefeller III wrote:

> The Foundation and the College are closely related both due to the fact that the directors of the CMB are, to a large extent, either on the Foundation board or closely related with it and since all of the supplies of the College which are bought in this country are procured through the Foundation. In other words, we have an interlocking directorate and the Foundation acts as agents for the PUMC in this country.[39]

Given this skewed locus of authority, it is not surprising that misunderstanding prevailed between the RF/CMB/PUMC complex and Roger Greene, especially in financial matters. Each year from 1929 through 1933, PUMC attempted to remain within the budgetary limitations imposed by the five-year decreasing grants from the RF to

35. "Report on Reorganization of Rockefeller Boards," 1928, p. 3.
36. Ferguson, *CMB and PUMC*, p. 68.
37. Greene to Eggleston, April 21, 1930, *RGP*.
38. Rockefeller III to Vincent, September 18, 1931, *RFA*.
39. Rockefeller III to Vincent, June 18, 1932, *RFA*.

CMB Inc. This effort was facilitated by a fluctuating exchange rate which increased the buying power of U.S. dollars in China. Chinese silver dollars, per American dollar, increased from the previous rate of 2:1 to over 4:1 by 1930. Thus, PUMC was able to provide for the requirements of increases in the salary schedules and a slight expansion of the College while remaining within the U.S. gold provisions.

This modest growth greatly alarmed RF President Max Mason. In 1933 he wrote apprehensively to Vincent: "A rough estimate of the situation at the present time would indicate that the policy of the P.U.M.C. during the past five years has been one rather of expansion and not one of the production of economies."[40]

The resounding stock market crash of 1929 and the ensuing Great Depression did not greatly affect CMB Inc. and RF securities until about 1933, at precisely the time when a review of the Foundation's supplemental grants to the PUMC was expected. Alan Gregg wrote Greene that "just at the end of a period of very great financial uncertainty in this country" the RF Trustees would be inclined against future commitments to PUMC.[41]

Meanwhile, in New York the notion persisted that PUMC ought to be able to obtain some local Chinese funding. The difficulties of securing this aid were more evident to Greene than to those in New York, but he did conceive of a plan to increase the income from the CMB endowment: investment in Chinese securities. As income dwindled in the American depression, Greene assessed the financial strength of the Chinese market in 1933 and suggested that a portion of the endowment be invested in Shanghai. This would give the PUMC Trustees in China genuine fiscal responsibility, for management of the investments would be in their hands.[42] CMB Inc. appeared to take this recommendation quite seriously, consulting with Wall Street financiers and the State Department as to the wisdom of such a decision. However, the final report, submitted by Rockefeller III, spoke of "conflicting advice" and advised a policy of "watchful waiting."[43]

40. Mason to Vincent, May 19, 1933, *PUMC Papers.*

41. Gregg to Greene, April 10, 1933, *RGP.*

42. Greene, "Memorandum from the Director of the China Medical Board, Inc., on the *proposal for a silver endowment,*" c. 1933, *RFA;* Greene to Rockefeller III, November 23, 1933; January 2, 1934, *RFA.*

43. L. M. Dashiell [Treasurer of CMB] to Members of the Finance Committee, CMB, September 28, 1933; Fosdick, "Confidential Memorandum on Interview with Stanley Hornbeck, Chief of the Division of Far Eastern Affairs of the State Department," January 3, 1934; Rockefeller III, "Report to the China Medical Board by its Special Committee of One"; all in *RFA.*

The American attitude of retrenchment was especially difficult to accept in Peking during the early thirties. For those continuously associated with PUMC, these years witnessed the fulfillment of their dream: to provide the medical leaders of modern China. As the Nationalist government sought to strengthen medical institutions and services, PUMC graduates and faculty were in increasing demand. It was not a time to cut back on the services of the institution, but rather to expand them. Roger Greene now became the ardent advocate of this view. Conceding that American institutions might also be in financial straits, he went on to argue: "I think it is a fact that no institution in the United States . . . carries such a heavy responsibility for the future as this College, which almost alone is endeavoring to maintain a high standard of medical education and investigation in China."[44]

Greene's arguments began to sound especially hollow and repetitive when in early 1934 the Rockefeller Foundation Trustees were exposed to an entirely new concept of aiding China, an approach which directly and indirectly questioned PUMC's usefulness. Selskar M. Gunn, Vice President of the RF in Europe, who had made several trips to China, submitted a proposal for an interdisciplinary approach to China's social problems. Included in his report was a penetrating criticism of PUMC, emphasizing its excessive financial largess. It is clear in correspondence between Gunn and Greene that each felt he was in competition for Foundation funds.[45] It must have been a severe blow to Roger Greene when in December 1934 the trustees approved Gunn's request for a three-year grant of one million dollars for what became known as the China Program.[46]

Greene worked diligently to reduce the PUMC budgets, but his nagging for favorable financial treatment grated on those in the home offices responsible for budgeting the resources of the Foundation. During the years 1933 and 1934 the correspondence between Greene and Margery Eggleston, Secretary of the CMB in New York, noticeably lost warmth. In later years both Raymond Fosdick and John D. Rockefeller III remembered their frustration in responding to Greene's unyielding advocacy.[47] The tensions between Greene

44. Greene to Eggleston, April, 1935, quoted in Ferguson, "The PUMC," Chapter 14, p. 47.

45. Gunn–Greene correspondence, January–March, 1934, *RGP*.

46. Selskar M. Gunn, "China and the Rockefeller Foundation," January 23, 1934, Hoover Library, Stanford, Calif.; James C. Thomson, *While China Faced West: American Reformers in Nationalist China, 1928–1937* (Cambridge, Mass.: Harvard University Press, 1969), includes a chapter on The China Program, pp. 122–150.

47. Interviews with Raymond Fosdick, July 27, 1970; and John D. Rockefeller, III, June 13, 1973.

and Rockefeller III, primarily over financial issues, were particularly acute. Complicated and fluctuating exchange rates made even routine transactions a hassle. During this same period, John D. Rockefeller, Jr., became increasingly concerned about Greene's unwillingness to press for a strong department of religious and social work. This was to prove the straw that broke the camel's back.

Rockefeller's surveillance of the religious life of PUMC stemmed from several personal commitments made to the previous missionary owners of the College. In 1915 he wrote an open letter to all missionary groups in China pledging "to select only persons of sound sense and high character, who were sympathetic with the missionary spirit and motive."[48] At the property sale with the London Missionary Society, Wallace Buttrick had given "the strongest assurance that if the transfer was carried out the work of the College would be continued on its present line as a Christian Mission College."[49] In 1928, at the time of the reorganization of the PUMC Trustees, Rockefeller personally wrote the former missionary members: "I need not assure you that I shall be no less alert in the future than in the past to do what lies within my power to preserve and perpetuate the fine Christian spirit upon which this enterprise was built."[50] These were not legal commitments, but for Rockefeller they were binding moral ones.

Roger Greene had repeatedly registered his firm opposition to restricting the autonomy of the PUMC Trustees. Upon reading the 1928 letter of Rockefeller Jr. which especially mentioned the department of religious and social work, Greene countered that the trustees should be "quite free to maintain or discontinue this department as they see fit."[51] When the religious director Y. Y. Tsu had threatened in 1930 to resign because of faculty indifference, and this situation had been brought to the attention of Rockefeller Jr., Greene was quite specific: "I am myself much disturbed by the way in which the supposed autonomy of the College is apparently to be limited in respect to this matter. If pressure is brought to bear on the College by the Advisory Committee [former American PUMC Trustees] with some of its members in such influential posi-

48. Rockefeller Jr. to missionary societies, April, 1915, RFA.

49. Quoted from the London Missionary Society, Director's Minute Book in Bowers, "The Founding of PUMC," p. 321. See also "Memorandum of Agreement between the Trustees of the London Missionary Society and the Rockefeller Foundation," June 2, 1915, RFA.

50. Quoted in Ferguson, "The PUMC," Chapter 16, p. 29. See also Margery Eggleston, "Religious Work in the Peking Union Medical College—Agreements and Commitments," April, 1930, RFA.

51. Greene to Vincent, July 18, 1929, in Ferguson, ibid., p. 32.

tions, it would be something to which I can hardly be reconciled."[52]

As PUMC had developed, faculty were not limited to those who were Christians, and religious instruction was never a part of the curriculum. The Department of Religious and Social Work, which conducted voluntary religious services, would probably not have become controversial had it not been for the continuing need to make cuts in the College budget. In 1929–1930, a committee comprised of PUMC professors, C. E. Lim (Lim Chong-eang) and Wu Hsien, searching for unnecessary expenditures, commended the work of the department but did not feel it was a "legitimate charge to the College budget."[53] Although they and other professors, including Greene, were in favor of at least cutting the activities of the department, no action was taken until the resignation two years later of its director, Y. Y. Tsu.

In 1933, Greene recommended that the replacement for Tsu be appointed on a half-time basis. This precipitated a letter from Rockefeller III to his father: "It would be well for you to write Mr. Greene a general letter about the religious work of the College. A word directly from you would, I feel, make him realize more fully the religious aspects of the responsibility which the College assumed when it took over much of the work of the missionary societies some years ago."[54] This brought a letter from Rockefeller Jr. to Greene which reaffirmed his personal commitment to the continued Christian character of PUMC:

> I realize that radical changes in thought along religious lines have taken place since the founding of the P.U.M.C. and that there is growing up a new school of thought as to how the fundamental and eternal principles underlying Christianity can best be promoted in the world and Christian character developed. On the other hand, so long as the P.U.M.C. stands, there can never be a question as to the duty of all those currently responsible for conducting the institutions to carry out with sincerity and wholeheartedness the full spirit of the understanding with the missionary societies upon which it was founded.[55]

The PUMC Trustees were more cautious than Greene when considering reducing the religious budget. Well aware of the hand that buttered the bread, they were reluctant to challenge the known wishes of Rockefeller Jr. Mary Ferguson, then secretary of the PUMC Trustees, records: "A majority of the Chinese Trustees were

52. Quoted in Ferguson, *CMB and PUMC*, p. 97.
53. *Ibid.*, p. 94.
54. Rockefeller III to Rockefeller Jr., June 9, 1933, *RFA*.
55. Rockefeller Jr. to Greene, August 16, 1933, *RFA*.

in favor of maintaining the department on a full-time basis—both for the value of its service to the College, and also because it seemed discourteous to oppose something so much desired by Mr. Rockefeller and his associates."[56]

The appointment of a full-time replacement for Y. Y. Tsu in 1933 seemed to settle the issue, and even resulted in a personal letter of appreciation from Rockefeller Jr. to Greene.[57] But Dr. Thomas Cochrane, formerly a director of the Union Medical College as well as London Missionary Society trustee representative, visited Peking in the spring of 1934 and wrote to Rockefeller of his dissatisfaction with the religious atmosphere of the College. Cochrane was particularly upset at the lack of religious fervor among the scientific staff: "The Staff is not being selected with due care in relation to the idealistic aims of the College. The Religious Director and the Religious Department do not enjoy a *status*, nor are they given a *scope*. . . . I say it solemnly and advisedly, the Institution is on the down-grade in things which are most essential."[58]

Cochrane came to New York, and in an interview with Rockefeller III he further blamed Greene for the situation: "In Dr. Cochrane's opinion, Mr. Greene was too pro-Chinese; that is he was trying to put the P.U.M.C. in a position to be turned over to the Chinese too fast, which was detrimental to the best interests of the college."[59] Compounding this religious disenchantment, Tsu's replacement, the former YMCA worker Egbert M. Hayes, was in the habit of writing personal letters to Rockefeller Jr. describing the successes and the failures of his undertaking. A most pessimistic account, titled "Impressions after six months in P.U.M.C.," was sent to Rockefeller Jr. in April 1934, shortly after Dr. Cochrane had registered his complaints.[60]

Both George Vincent and Raymond Fosdick well understood the difficulties of perpetuating Rockefeller's personal commitment to the missionary societies. Vincent wrote at the time of Cochrane's visit: "It is a difficult problem to combine an efficient training in modern medicine with evangelical piety."[61] Fosdick, years later,

---

56. Ferguson, *CMB and PUMC*, p. 98. Earlier, in 1930, Vincent visited China and reported to Rockefeller Jr. on the affirmative attitude of the trustees with regard to the religious department, Vincent to Rockefeller Jr., October 2, 1930, *RFA*.

57. Rockefeller Jr. to Greene, November 17, 1933, *RFA*.

58. Thomas Cochrane to Rockefeller Jr., March 16, 1934, *RFA*.

59. Rockefeller III, "Memorandum: Dr. Thomas Cochrane," April 2, 1934, *RFA*.

60. Egbert M. Hayes, "Impressions after six months in P.U.M.C.," April, 1934; Hayes to Rockefeller Jr., April 11, 1934, *RFA*.

61. Vincent to Rockefeller III, April 21, 1934, *RFA*.

remarked that it had been a "bad commitment."[62] Nonetheless, neither tried to dissuade Rockefeller from his continuing advocacy of the department of religious and social welfare.

By the spring of 1934 an impasse was reached between Roger Greene in Peking and the Rockefeller circle in New York. Greene's personal characteristics, earlier described by Alan Gregg as a "reserved bearing, an intensity of feeling, a sense of personal responsibility for the PUMC, and conspicuous singleness of purpose," had done nothing to ameliorate his personal relations with the Rockefellers.[63] While the religious issue was only a personal anxiety to Rockefeller Jr., the financial debates caused justifiable concern within the Foundation. One might have anticipated the outcome of these controversies, but the *manner* in which they were resolved elevated the issue to a major institutional crisis.

In April 1934, Alan Gregg advised Greene to resign from his position as Resident Director of the CMB Inc., suggesting that the duality of Greene's roles contributed to trans-Pacific misunderstandings: "Your services are known and respected but your advocacy of PUMC is feared because you are still in the Jury—i.e. the CMB."[64] Greene complied, thereby hoping to strengthen his major position—that of Vice-Director of PUMC, directly responsible only to the PUMC Trustees.

In July 1934, Greene returned to New York, fortified with a considerably pared down budget, ready to begin extensive financial discussions with the CMB and RF officials. Much to his surprise, George Vincent, newly reinvested with the chairmanship of the CMB, requested Greene's resignation from his PUMC post. Pressed by Greene to explain this totally unforeseen development, Vincent stated that it was because Greene had come into conflict with Raymond Fosdick, Vincent himself, and John D. Rockefeller, Jr.[65]

Several days before Greene had arrived in New York, Gregg had received a hurried, unexpected letter from Rockefeller III which detailed the role of his father in Greene's firing: "As a result of conversations with Father, it has been decided to ask Mr. Greene to resign as director of the PUMC in the near future and to send Dr. Houghton out in his place."[66] Rockefeller Jr. denied later that the religious question had been the cause of firing Greene, writing

62. Interview with Fosdick, July 27, 1970.
63. Gregg to Greene, March 20, 1933, *RGP*.
64. Gregg to Greene, March 20, 1934, *RGP*.
65. Ferguson, *CMB and PUMC*, p. 87.
66. Rockefeller III to Gregg, June 26, 1934, *RFA*.

instead that he had become "increasingly difficult to work with," and stating: "The religious work has not been a factor in the situation." [67] It seems irrefutable, however, that the religious question had been one element in the crumbling relationship between Greene and the inner Rockefeller circle. [68] There is a certain irony in this, for Greene himself was a religious person; his opposition was not to religious activities *per se* but to outside intervention in internal policies of the institution.

Roger Greene, Vice-Director of the PUMC, was immediately responsible to the PUMC Trustees. The irregular channels utilized to request his resignation defied the authority delegated to the Chinese trustees. Moreover, not only had the trustees not been consulted, not a single meeting of CMB Inc. took place from the spring of 1934 until that December. [69] The decision to fire Greene, made by the inner coterie of Fosdick, Vincent, Rockefeller Jr., and Rockefeller III, was a severe blow to the years of gradual transfer of power to China. This intervention clearly indicated that the RF and CMB Inc. had no intention of relinquishing authority—even to an American administrator. Whatever the policy justification, the cavalier dismissal of Greene indicated the degree to which the New York clique, in their own minds as well as in actuality, still managed PUMC. Professed intentions to the contrary, the PUMC Trustees remained a symbolic body.

Upon hearing of the enforced resignation of Greene, the PUMC Trustees rebuked New York and voted unanimously to retain Greene. They accurately perceived that the issue was much more than the career of just one man: the legitimation of their own authority was in doubt. In a circular note passed among the trustees in Peking titled, "For Private Information of the Trustees," the following statement came to the crux of the issue:

> There is obscurity as to the degree of independence both of the P.U.M.C. and the C.M.B. If the C.M.B. is entirely independent of the R.F., how is the intervention of the Chairman of the R.F. [Rockefeller Jr.] to be explained? [70]

In a personal letter to Greene, Ting Wen-chiang, recently elected as a trustee, urged him not to worry if the trustees' action in voting

67. Rockefeller Jr. to Francis Hawkins, December 7, 1934, *RFA*.
68. Ferguson cites Gregg to Greene, August 2, 1934 in which Gregg states that Greene's irregular dismissal was based on the religious question, "The PUMC," Chapter 16, p. 57.
69. Conversation with Mary Ferguson, July 20, 1972, Washington, D.C.
70. "For Private Information of the Trustees," n.d., *RGP*.

to retain Greene should antagonize New York. If that occurred, Ting stated that the Trustees were a nominal body anyway and ought to resign.[71] None did, perhaps because the debate continued for nearly a year. And Y. T. Tsur, the Chairman of the PUMC Trustees, took a more cautious approach. In a telegram to Vincent he remonstrated: "In long association with Greene we have found him conscientious progressive tactful openminded impartial efficient administrator." However, in a letter written two weeks later, while reiterating his support of Greene, Tsur also pledged "our sense of obligation to the China Medical Board, Inc. for the support without which the College could not exist."[72]

Greene undoubtedly reflected his own bitterness in a personal letter several months later, but his observation of the trustees' dilemma is astute. Referring specifically to the attitude of Y. T. Tsur, Ting Wen-chiang, and Wong Wen-hao, who at that time were among the most active of the trustees, he stated:

> They are coming to believe that the Rockefeller inner group is untrustworthy as well as unwise and unfair. The expression of such feelings is to some extent restrained by the absolute dependence of the PUMC on the CMB and RF, and by the hope of future financial favors for China from the RF.[73]

The ten months following Greene's forced resignation were complicated. Henry Houghton was appointed as the new CMB Inc. representative in China, and it was New York's intent that ultimately he would be named Greene's successor as Vice-Director of PUMC. But the PUMC Trustees made repeated requests for Greene's continuance. And when he returned to China in the fall to preside over a transition, Greene was asked formally by the PUMC Trustees to withdraw his resignation. Confronted with strong support for Greene in Peking, the CMB Inc. backed down temporarily and allowed Greene to remain as Vice-Director for several months. Fosdick even made a conciliatory visit to China, staying in Greene's home in Peking and meeting personally with the PUMC faculty and trustees. At times during this period Greene seemed to believe that a compromise solution would be reached. But the China Medical Board and the Rockefellers did not change their minds.[74] After months of fruitless negotiations, the Trustees recognized that for

71. V. K. Ting [Ting Wen-chiang] to Greene, October 29, 1934, *RFA*.

72. Tsur to Vincent, October 25, 1934; November 13, 1934, *RFA*.

73. Greene to Jerome Greene, May 6, 1935, *RGP*.

74. Ferguson, *CMB and PUMC*, pp. 105–110; also, Tsur to Vincent, November 22, 1934, *RFA*.

the good of the college—or, more frankly, to assure continued financial support of PUMC—they had to accept Greene's ouster. In April 1935 he resigned.

The blow to the authority of the PUMC Trustees, however, was nearly crippling. Four years later Greene's successor, Henry Houghton, described the continuing attitude of the Trustees:

> The Trustees, especially the Chinese members, are still somewhat dubious about the functions and relationships of the China Medical Board. In part this is probably a result of the exercise by the Board in 1934 of its charter powers of ownership. The wounds of that episode were very deep and the scars will not dissolve, I think, for a long time.[75]

Houghton's observations were made two years after an attempt had been made to clarify the relationship between the CMB and PUMC Trustees. The PUMC Trustees had ratified a document which clearly stated that they had the sole right to choose the director of the College. But elsewhere it elaborated upon the overseeing rights of CMB Inc.:

> The Chinese Medical Board, Inc. is obligated by its charter to keep itself currently familiar with the policies, programs, and accomplishments of the College, and to review these from time to time in order to evaluate the general trends and quality of performance as related to the objectives of the Founders as stated above.[76]

Without a single Chinese member, CMB Inc. remained a vague and amorphous body to those in Peking. Empowered with final judgment over the institution as well as being the funnel for funds, it is no wonder that the PUMC trustees saw the CMB as a "mysterious and hostile body."[77]

Henry Houghton replaced Roger Greene as Peking middleman in 1935, first as CMB Resident Director, and then at the time of the Japanese occupation in 1937 as Acting Director of PUMC. He held this latter position until early 1942 when both he and the institution were captured by the Japanese. Houghton's return to Peking was at the direct request of John D. Rockefeller, Jr., with whom Houghton, over the years, had established warm family ties. Rockefeller apparently had confidence that Houghton would be responsive to New York's concerns.[78] Houghton did make some headway in solv-

---

75. Quoted in Ferguson, "The PUMC," Chapter 19, p. 45.
76. Ferguson, *CMB and PUMC*, p. 254.
77. Quoted in *ibid.*, p. 111. The statement is by Houghton.
78. Information supplied by Mary Ferguson.

ing the financial conflicts between New York and Peking by a plan to slash the PUMC budget drastically from US$727,258 to $473,047.[79] But, like Greene and in spite of his personal ties, Houghton also crossed swords with New York and the Rockefellers, first on the issue of receiving money from the Chinese government, and second on the role of the PUMC Trustees. By this time, it was John D. Rockefeller, Jr., however belatedly, who was arguing for the transfer of some authority to the PUMC Trustees.

Although it had always been the goal to solicit Chinese financial support for PUMC, there is no indication that the directors or trustees of PUMC ever actively sought Chinese funds. Realistically, they knew that in China PUMC appeared to be supported by the boundless munificence of the Rockefellers. Other Sino-Western institutions, much less well provided for, had little success in raising Chinese funds. In early 1937, however, the Ministry of Education offered to contribute Mex.$50,000 to PUMC's operating budget. Houghton rejected this offer on the basis that it would compromise the political independence of the institution:

> I do not propose to sell out the freedom of this institution and the maintenance of its scientific and educational standards for a contribution amounting to less than two percent of our annual upkeep. When the Government becomes a financial partner it immediately begins to mould institutional policies and practices to its own particular pattern.[80]

When Rockefeller III learned of this he expressed alarm at the willingness of PUMC's administration to forego possible Chinese financial support.[81] The Marco Polo Bridge Incident shortly put Peking in the hands of the Japanese, and any support from the exiled Nationalist government became an academic question.

More disturbing to those in New York were reports of Henry Houghton's disinclination to cooperate with the PUMC Trustees: "They [the Trustees] were themselves not recognized as having important responsibilities of being in the Board for any purpose than to authorize periodic financial appeals to the CMB for funds."[82] Sohtsu G. King, Chairman of the Trustees, further stated: "Dr. Houghton was asked three years ago to train a Chinese for the position

79. "Survey Commission of PUMC Report," Docket, Board of Trustees, PUMC, September 23, 1936, *RGP*.

80. Ferguson, *CMB and PUMC*, p. 135.

81. *Ibid.*, p. 134.

82. "Extracts from the report of Mr. Lobenstine [Chairman CMB, 1936–1945] to the China Medical Board, Inc. on his return from China," November, 1939, p. 1, *RFA*.

of Vice-Director. He has not 'bothered about it.' The Trustees know little of what is going on." [83]

These accounts caused considerable consternation among RF trustees and in the CMB. Rockefeller III's recourse was a familiar one. He asked his father to write Houghton a letter re-emphasizing the ultimate aims of the College:

> He should constantly be building up the Chinese staff for the day when they will take over the institution. . . . It is essential that he work closely with the Trustees and that there be a feeling of mutual confidence for in the last analysis we are *depending on the Trustees for the eventual* operating of the College. [84]

Rockefeller Jr.'s subsequent six-page letter to Henry Houghton in October 1940 is a revelation of his poignant perception of the historical dilemma of Peking Union Medical College. Nineteen years after the founding of PUMC, Rockefeller finally sensed the need to lodge responsibility in the hands of the Chinese trustees, and his comments on this subject deserve to be quoted at some length:

> They [the Trustees] should be made not only to feel but to *assume* the responsibility which is rightly theirs for forming its policies and for making decisions both as regards its present operation and the more important questions relating to its future. I would make it clear to them that you, as the chief administrative officer, were there to aid them in forming and carrying out their plans and policies and not they there to simply approve your program. There are an unusual number of men of outstanding ability on the Board. Men of that type will be interested to give generously of their time, thought and effort only as they feel that the responsibility rests squarely on their shoulders. [85]

Rockefeller went on to suggest that the Board of Trustees be brought in on a number of key decisions: the possible relocation of the school; the reorganization of the departments; and exploring "in what ways the College can tie in with the medical education program of China."

Rockefeller's letter is personally revealing, but it came far too late to be significant in PUMC's history. By 1940 a degree of surrealism persisted about the institution which was just barely operating in a city controlled by the Japanese. World War II brought to a close this chapter in Rockefeller Foundation–PUMC relations. In a very real sense there was no dramatic denouement in administrative

---

83. *Ibid.*, p. 2; see also Ferguson to Lobenstine, February 10, 1940, *RFA*.
84. Rockefeller III to Rockefeller Jr., September 9, 1940, emphasis in original; also, Rockefeller III to Rockefeller Jr., September 13, 1940, *RFA*.
85. Rockefeller Jr. to Houghton, October 2, 1940, *RFA*, emphasis in original.

relations. But before closing so inconclusively, it is important to reflect for a moment on the Rockefeller Foundation and its Peking middlemen.

It has perhaps been unfair to concentrate primarily on the conflicts between New York and Peking. Certainly there was great strength in the continuity and quality of persons on both sides of the Pacific during this quarter century. If it were possible to compare the RF's progress in devolving authority to China with mission boards or other Sino-Western institutions, it might well emerge as one of the more progressive institutions. At present few such monographic studies of other institutions, which would make such a comparison possible, exist.

On the other hand, the conflicts themselves illustrate what a straightforward chronological account might not: the wide gap between the goals and actions of the Foundation. Professed intentions to the contrary, one is left convinced that the Foundation's investment in PUMC was too great to be turned over to the Chinese, and that even in different times CMB Inc. would have remained a perpetual American "endowment-holding body" with all of its commensurate prerogatives.

The conflicts also illustrate the personal role of the Rockefeller family in Foundation affairs. Again, broader studies are necessary before one can come to the conclusion that John D. Rockefeller, Jr., dominated overall Foundation policy. This study indicates, however, that on at least two issues Rockefeller's personal convictions carried decisive weight: China and religion. The involvement of the Foundation in China was an extension of the personal philanthropies of the Rockefeller family, and it was an area in which they continued to make private donations.[86] A sense of identification with PUMC, strengthened by his personal role in the earliest negotiations and commitments, remained with Rockefeller throughout his life. Religion was an especially personal concern, and in China at least, it prompted his continuing extra-institutional role. Occasionally beneficial to the institution, Rockefeller's intervention in religious and other matters nonetheless greatly obscured channels of authority and undermined confidence in autonomy.

The weight of Rockefeller's influence on Foundation officials is also indicated by the manner in which some of the trans-Pacific

---

86. Rockefeller Jr. personally contributed $100,000 to Jimmy Yen's Mass Education Movement in 1928. See Thomas B. Appleget to Rockefeller Jr., December 17, 1928, *RFA*. According to Dr. Joseph Ernst, Archivist of the *RFA*, the Rockefeller family personally contributed over one and a half million dollars to China between 1913 and 1950.

conflicts were resolved. After 1929 he had no legal role in PUMC's affairs, being neither a member of the CMB or the PUMC Trustees. Problems involving PUMC and China were, however, routinely passed onto him by his son. Rockefeller Jr.'s penciled notations on some of these documents indicates his continuing interest in these affairs.[87] When Rockefeller III, who remained active on the CMB, felt that an issue needed addressing, he would summarize the arguments and then ask his father personally to write the individual involved. Several letters by John D., Jr., to Greene, and numerous letters to Houghton, are indicative of this process. During this period at least, Rockefeller III seems to have relied on his father's influence rather than his own. The unique authority of the father may not have been passed on to the son.

The Rockefeller family was at the disbursing end of the Foundation's funds and authority. At the other, in this case, were the PUMC Trustees. These included eminent Chinese such as J. Heng Liu, Y. T. Tsur, Sohtsu King, and Hu Shih. Men of political moderation, their personal experiences in America and involvement in other Sino-Western institutions left little doubt that during the twenties and thirties financial control of these institutions would probably remain in the hands of the American donors. As they saw it, their primary task was not to jeopardize the flow of funds to China. They did hope to assert some independence in the utilization of these funds and independence in the actual administration of Sino-American institutions. Well-acquainted with the prevailing American apprehension over Chinese "management," they sought with tact and perseverance to demonstrate their responsibility.

That they sometimes backed down in asserting their rightful authority reflects the psychological result of unilateral financial aid more than it does the timidity of the individuals. For all its good intent, Rockefeller's 1940 letter to Houghton did not mention transferring PUMC's endowment to China or decreasing the authority of CMB Inc. And yet King's own response to Rockefeller was first to continue pleading for funds for a "first-rate institution," and only second to welcome Rockefeller's belated confidence in the trustees. Almost as an afterthought he raised the hope that "in due course that responsibility . . . for finances can be arranged."[88] Problems of power, and especially the transfer of authority, become exceedingly complicated when a treasure house dazzles and recipients must be "grateful" to the donors.

87. Dr. Joseph Ernst, Rockefeller Family Archives, identified these markings for me.
88. King to Rockefeller Jr., December 12, 1940, RFA.

In the middle, between the Family and the Trustees, were the Foundation's Peking middlemen. This position, be it CMB Resident Director or Acting PUMC Director, was at the crux of a devolution process which never took place. Here the discrepancies between Foundation goals and actions became operative. And here the American reluctance to delegate authority to Chinese became most obvious.

In spite of his contradictions and pitfalls, in spite of his obvious paternalism, there is a poignancy about Roger Greene's China career which evokes sympathy. In part, this is because he tried to "howl down the puppets of Great Wealth."[89] When leaving his post as American Consul-General in Hankow to become a member of the RF First Medical Commission in 1914, he wrote to his brother Jerome: "As regards the consular service, however, I begin to wonder whether I want to stay in it. I am getting a little tired of American red tape."[90] During the next twenty years Greene confronted a personalized kind of American red tape, and he was never able to cut through it. He could never accept the transcendent authority of the Rockefeller family in the Rockefeller Foundation. Only belatedly did Greene begin to realize a portion of what had gone wrong. In a letter to his friend Nelson Johnson, the American Minister in China, Greene reflected on his forced resignation:

> I suspect that it is mainly due to friction between me and John the third, who though a very young man assumed a dictatorial manner towards me from the beginning. I will admit that I was not very tactful in my reaction to that treatment, never dreaming that the older men would take the youngster so seriously as they have done.[91]

It is hard to tell whether Greene also realized what else had gone wrong—that in his unyielding personal identification with PUMC he lost the necessary flexibility to be a successful broker between New York and Peking.

89. Alan Gregg used this phrase in another context, Penfield, *The Epic of Alan Gregg*, p. 206.
90. Greene to Jerome Greene, March 1, 1914, quoted in Ferguson, "The PUMC," p. 23.
91. Greene to Johnson, October 10, 1934, *RGP*.

FOUR The Oil Prince's Palace

*. . . a certain preciousness which has reduced the usefulness
of PUMC.*

Alan Gregg,
"Memorandum for the China Medical Board," 1941

VIVID CHINESE COLORS—jade-green roofs, vermillion pillars, and red-, blue-, green-, and gold-carved eaves—contrasted sharply with sterile antiseptic laboratories, stark rows of hospital beds, white-coated doctors, and starchly capped nurses in the seventy acres and fifty-or-so buildings which comprised the Peking Union Medical College. As scientific white glared and yet also merged with Chinese hues, so too the College, the hospital, and their policies, programs, and personnel present a unique mosaic of a Sino-American institution in the Republican period.

Employment at PUMC for Westerners and Chinese alike brought the good life of the "years that were fat." For foreigners and a few Chinese an ample, if not luxurious, home was provided in the North or South Compound, with housekeeping helped by *amahs*, "boys," and cooks. Summer homes at Peitaiho or Tsingtao cooled the warm months, and the cocktail, dinner, and dance circuit of Peking's Legation Quarter brought amusement and entertainment to the harsh winters. The private homes and public reception rooms at PUMC in turn provided teas, dinners, scientific forums, and cultural "happenings" for the international intellectual community of Peking. As one professor later reflected, "Academically and socially, life could not be more delightful than Peking." [1]

1. "Grant Reminiscences," p. 296.

One should not conclude, however, that the faculty of PUMC was isolated from the Chinese. Peking, after all, was not Shanghai, where apartheid policies hampered frequent social intercourse. A mecca for the intellectuals of China, Peking during the twenties and thirties became a cosmopolitan city, stimulatingly open and culturally alive. For some foreigners at PUMC the high culture of the past was appreciated and studied; many became amateur collectors of Chinese art. Others mingled freely with the educated Chinese of the city, forming eating clubs which sought out the finest in Mandarin cuisine, or became active members of the *Wen-yen hui* (the Friends of Literature Society), or the Chinese Social and Political Science Association.

Esthete is not an accurate characterization because the political and economic problems of China were also subjects of prolonged discussion and speculation. During the twenties in particular various warlords struggled for control of the former imperial city, and the relative quiet of the Nanking era was a superficial one. But, for most at PUMC, the context was one of comfort, and the discourses were those of reason. These were scientific spectators who viewed with detached intensity the revolutions of modern China.

The Chinese faculty were more than mere spectators; they epitomized the transformation of the Confucian literati into an international, modern elite. Although in the beginning they appeared as second-class citizens of PUMC, and throughout the period were paid on a different salary scale than their Western colleagues, these men were nonetheless first-class citizens of Peking. A Chinese assistant professor might be paid less than a glassblower imported from Europe to make the scientifically precise test tubes required in the laboratories,[2] but one Chinese professor lived in a converted hideaway of the Dowager Empress Tz'u-hsi, complete with swimming pool, tennis courts, and riding stables.[3]

Salaries, on the whole, were higher than any paid by missionary or Chinese institutions; and fringe benefits, such as sabbatical years in America or Europe, insured that these men became scientific citizens of the world. Listing in the *International Who's Who of Medicine*, not to mention *Who's Who in China*, personal recognition by European governments such as the Soviet Union, publication in international medical journals—all of this and more accrued to the best of the Chinese professors at PUMC.

2. Henry Houghton, "Memorandum on the Organization and Program of the Peiping Union Medical College," 1935, *RGP*. The glass blower was paid Mex.$12,600; the Chinese assistant professor, Mex.$9,102.

3. This was Wu Hsien. See Daisy Yen Wu, *Wu Hsien, 1893–1959* (Boston: privately printed, 1960), pp. 5, 72.

There was privilege in the PUMC community, but for Occidental and Oriental alike there were diligence and brilliance as well. Each appointment was a matter of careful consideration by leaders of medical science in the United States, and their selections ultimately proved to be outstanding. Nearly one-half of the Western professors eventually returned to the United States to become either full professors or deans of medical colleges.[4] Liberal research time allotments of 50 percent of one's academic load, together with the small student body, allowed many hours for scientific study.

The results seem to justify this exceptional freedom: from 1919 to 1925 alone over 300 articles were published in Chinese, American, and European journals.[5] Few of their discoveries were as dramatic as Davidson Black's uncovering of Peking Man in the caves of Choukoutien, but by mid-century the patient and persistent research on kala-azar, malaria, schistosomiasis, trachoma, nutrition, and the Chinese pharmacopoeia, had provided scientific tools with which to treat China's disease-ridden population. While to the historian much of the research appears procedural, two decades of painstaking, meticulous experiments and uncounted hours of basic research contributed to the impregnation of the scientific method on Chinese soil.

Research frequently produced genuine scientific collaboration between Chinese and Westerners, and friendship between equals occasionally resulted. Davidson Black and noted geologist Ting Wen-chiang were good friends, each in his own way recognizing, but attempting to minimize, the self-assumed superiority of the Westerner and the defensive sensitivity of the Chinese. Black appears to have noticed the outrageousness of the 18th Biennial Meeting of the China Medical Association where all officers were Western but some major scientific papers had Chinese authors. When Black died several years later, Ting would urge that concepts of nation and race were trivial when compared with the quest for scientific truth.[6]

J. Heng Liu accepted advice from John Grant in the organization of the National Health Administration, and also joined him in a raucous three-day celebration of New Year's Eve in the bars of

4. "Grant Reminiscences" includes an appended list of 29 PUMC faculty who became deans or professors, pp. 117, 117A. Bowers, *Medicine in a Chinese Palace*, includes details on the careers of most of the prominent Westerners.

5. *Bibliography of the Publications from the Laboratories and Clinics of the Peking Union Medical College and Hospital, 1915–1925* (Peking: PUMC Press, 1926).

6. Furth, *Ting Wen-chiang*, pp. 53, 60; Dora Hood, *Davidson Black: A Biography* (Toronto: University of Toronto Press, 1964), p. 67.

Shanghai. Their friendship was one of intimacy, and endured for more than forty years.[7]

These relationships were made possible by comparable educational backgrounds, yet even in the PUMC community such camaraderie was unusual. This closeness was, however, more characteristic of the scientific community than of the missionaries who worked with the underprivileged, the merchants who sought a financial profit, or the diplomats preoccupied with the nuances of extraterritoriality.

Peking's main Hatamen Avenue brought a varied patient clientele to the Rockefeller Hospital. Sun Yat-sen's final operation and autopsy were performed under the watchful gaze of his son, Sun Fo, and an entourage of military generals. Generalissimo and Madame Chiang Kai-shek came for periodic checkups. Bertrand Russell was treated for pneumonia. The Peking police transferred psychopathic cases from the prisons. Rickshaw teams gathered indigents from the streets. And nearby coolie laborers arrived for free treatment. At the dedication of the College in 1921, a local paper reported that the plant was supplied with pure distilled ice drinking water, its own private telephone exchange, 500 electric fans, a complete laundry, and, in statistics inspired by a reporter's imagination, it was calculated that there were 530,654 square feet of tiled walls, linoleum surfaces, and wooden floors to be cleaned![8]

In 1930, this luxurious hospital contained 346 beds, treated 5,071 in-patients and 134,312 out-patients. Four special clinics were held for out-patients by the Department of Medicine—heart, tuberculosis, kala-azar, and an all-inclusive one for employees. An elaborate system assigned each patient to a resident who filled out a complete medical history and reported the case to the chief resident. Ultimately the visiting staff, consisting of the clinical faculty of the College, toured the wards.[9]

It was the punctilious *efficiency* of the hospital which so impressed Chinese and foreigners alike. An American army intelligence report found the PUMC:

> ... an example of Western organization and efficiency which may well fill the foreign heart with pride. ... In passing through its wards and out-patient departments few foreign faces are seen. The mechanism of

7. "Grant Reminiscences," pp. 312–313. Denise (Mrs. John B.) Grant, "Around the World in 81 Days; September 8 to November 28, 1957," pp. 47–49, unpublished 102-page manuscript in her private possession, Washington, D.C.

8. *Peking Leader*, 20 September 1921, p. 2:1.

9. Peking Union Medical College Hospital, *Report of the Superintendent, 1930* (Peking: PUMC Press, 1931), pp. 19–23.

the hospital runs smoothly and quietly to the casual eye. . . . Chinese doctors and nurses are in constant and capable attendance. A splendid system splendidly administered is evident.[10]

A teaching hospital provides the vital transfer from knowledge learned in the laboratory to knowledge applied to the patient. Furthermore, as a social institution it reflects in microcosm the health conditions of the area. Although the PUMC hospital thus insured that medical research was permeated with the human realities of China, the doctors saw the Chinese patients divorced from their environment—scrubbed, bathed, and placed *individually* in immaculate white beds. Curative medicine necessitates a one-to-one relationship between a doctor and a patient, and the treatment of individual illness was absolutely essential. But there was always the possibility that this would dim awareness of China's teeming masses.

There was also the difficulty of transferring Western organization and efficiency to situations *outside* the walls of PUMC. This is particularly well demonstrated in the frequent missions of PUMC surgical teams to the civil wars and natural disasters of the Republican period. A few examples should suffice. In 1923 Dr. George Char was appointed Honorary Medical Advisor to Feng Yü-hsiang and spent several months organizing a military hospital near Peking. In 1925, again coming to the aid of the so-called "Christian" general as he marched from Peking to Tientsin, the entire surgery department was enlisted in maintaining the base hospital at Nanyuan for several months. In 1931, during the floods of the Yangtze, the area of Wuchang was placed under the medical supervision of 20 PUMC doctors and 40 nurses. Also in 1931, the Nationalist government appealed to the College's moralistic obligation to provide medical aid to the anti-Communist front in Kiangsi.[11]

In summarizing these and many other charitable ventures, the head of the surgery department, Dr. Harold Loucks, repeatedly stressed the problems encountered on those missions. In Kiangsi, "the local army organization was under the old type of medical officer who resented the appearance of outside personnel." In Honan, "the local hospital officials (graduates of the Army Medical College) were jealous of their positions and reputations and re-

10. Lt. W. G. Wyman, "Comments on Difficulties Encountered by Foreign Medical Workers in China," Report No. 8127, October 27, 1931, p. 1, Record Group 165, 2273/I-3, National Archives, Washington, D.C. Hereinafter referred to as *NA*.

11. Harold Loucks, "Military Surgery," pp. 1–4, included in Wyman, "Comments on Difficulties."

sented any suggestions from others." Loucks lamented that the only medical accomplishment during one six-week absence from PUMC by six senior medical men was the performance of 25 operations. Everywhere, PUMC relief teams were unable "to conduct *efficient* hospital service."[12]

Undoubtedly, these medical forays produced some positive results. Feng Yü-hsiang was so grateful for the medical assistance that PUMC provided in conjunction with a China Inland Mission hospital in Kaifeng that he asked L. Carrington Goodrich, assistant director of the CMB, what he could donate to that hospital. Goodrich suggested that the hospital needed X-ray equipment. Several months later a bag of Mex.$4,000 was delivered from Feng to Goodrich to buy an X-ray machine for the Kaifeng hospital.[13] This outreach was crucial, but for the most part these missions only brought frustration to the administration and faculty of PUMC. Writing near the end of 1931, Loucks concluded: "The returns to the College, whether considered in terms of field experience, political status or humanitarian accomplishments have been—except in one or two instances—wholly insignificant."[14]

This collage of impressions of PUMC presents the recurring ambiguity of the institution. As in a kaleidoscope, the views constantly merge and then diverge from selflessness to sanctimoniousness, from participation to insulation, from altruism to paternalism, and much depends on the eye of the beholder. There is a constancy to this ambivalence, and yet there is change as well. PUMC was not a static institution during two decades of existence prior to its closure during World War II. The most dramatic alteration was in the composition of the faculty, especially in the steady growth of the Chinese component. There were other modifications as well —though they were more tenuous—in the content of the curriculum and in the gradual identification of the College with the pressing medical needs of China. Since these latter were connected in part to the medical and educational program of the Nationalist government, their evolution was a truncated one.

The faculty must be considered first. In 1920 there were 22 Westerners and nine Chinese in the faculty, including the lower levels of assistants and associates. By 1940 there were only ten Westerners and 109 Chinese. The Rockefeller Foundation was deservedly proud of this record. The total numbers and percentages are impres-

---

12. *Ibid.*, p. 3. Emphasis added.
13. Interview with L. Carrington Goodrich, October 15, 1971.
14. Loucks, "Military Surgery," p. 5.

sive, but they represent in part the growth of the College as well as the more rapid addition of Chinese at the bottom of the scale. In order to explore the Sinification of a Western institution, the process of elevating Chinese faculty must be explored. Additionally, it must be admitted that in reality two separate pay scales existed: one for Westerners, one for Chinese.

At the beginning of its work in China, the Rockefeller Foundation was anxious to provide adequate compensation to its Western faculty in order to attract and hold high calibre men. It was inevitable that some of the earliest professors would be discouraged by slow growth and relative isolation from scientific colleagues. Reid Hunt, visiting professor of pharmacology from Harvard University in 1923, wrote of his disappointment in the quality of students. He seemed surprised that they were not of the stature of Harvard or Johns Hopkins, conjecturing: "I think that the difficulty arises in part from a slowness on the part of the students to grasp technical English, and partly from early environment."[15] Henry Houghton despaired of pathology professor Carl Ten Broeck's adjustment problems:

> Ten Broeck complains that he is not much interested in staying on here because there are so few men to work with him and under him, and he doesn't get on very sympathetically with the Chinese. By that I do not mean that he has not proved to be a good teacher—quite the contrary; but he takes such a pessimistic attitude toward our making much of any progress with them that it colors all of his views.[16]

Not all of the new professors were so discouraged. Dr. Adelbert Fuchs, an internationally renowned ophthalmologist from Vienna, a visiting professor during 1923–1924, wrote in glowing terms of the students he had guided in studies of the eye, one of China's most pressing health needs.[17]

But it was in anticipation of the difficulty of securing truly well-qualified medical scientists that the Rockefeller Foundation had made liberal salary provisions. Heads of the departments were paid Mex.$10,000 (US$5,000) in 1921, and associate professors Mex. $7,000 (US$3,500). Simon Flexner's notations on the budget statistics indicate that he felt this was excessive since the salaries were higher than in the United States where the cost of living was much more: "Price down to values in this country. All relatively high. For

15. Reid Hunt to George Vincent, November 3, 1923, *SFP*.
16. Houghton to Greene, January 7, 1923, *RGP*.
17. A. Fuchs, "Report on the Year's Work, 1923–24," *SFP*.

example all $7000 salaries to $5000 at most are $5000 to $3500." [18]

Franklin McLean, the first director, justified the salary range in a 20-page memorandum to the Rockefeller trustees. He reminded the trustees of their obligation to provide living quarters for all Western staff, retirement allowances, and a furlough every four years. He cited the standard missionary salaries, using the Methodist Episcopal Board as an example. Their average salary for a man with three dependents was $1,750 gold, or Mex.$3,500. McLean argued for higher compensation for PUMC faculty: "It is neither necessary nor desirable for the families of all the members of the staff of the PUMC to economize to the same extent as is practiced by the families of missionaries." In concluding his appeal to retain this relatively luxurious salary scale, McLean frankly stated: "It has always been assumed that some additional inducement as to financial arrangements or living conditions must be offered in order to attract individuals from the U.S. to China." [19] High salaries continued.

The first few Chinese appointees to the PUMC faculty were paid on the same scale as Westerners. [20] In 1922, however, as the trustees looked forward to the steady increase of Chinese faculty, the question of separate salary scales was raised. The arguments in favor of equal pay for Chinese professors were perceptive. If discrimination was evident, Chinese faculty would become discouraged. If Westerners received higher salaries, they would feel superior. Also, Chinese professors were not allowed to compensate earnings with a lucrative private practice. And finally, Chinese with foreign training had family and social obligations equal to Westerners.

The arguments opposed to equal salaries represent for the most part the preferred status of foreigners in China. High salaries induced Westerners to live abroad. Living costs for Westerners were higher than for Chinese. It had been customary for foreigners to receive higher salaries, even in Chinese or Japanese schools. One argument, however, raised a genuine dilemma:

> It is felt that a disservice will be done to the cause of medical education
> if men trained in the Peking Union Medical College become accustomed

18. "Peiping Union Medical College—Budget, 1920–1921," p. 5. Flexner's penciled notation.

19. Franklin McLean, "Memorandum Concerning Obligations of Trustees to the Staff of the Union Medical College," January 16, 1920, p. 11, *SFP.*

20. For example, F. E. Dilley, Associate in Surgery, and J. Heng Liu, Associate in Surgery, were both paid Mex.$5,000 in 1920–21. See "Budget 1920–1921," p. 6.

to higher salaries than they can hope to get outside ... for they will be deterred from going away from the Peking Union Medical College to play the part they should in other schools.[21]

The salary quandary which faced the PUMC administration was characteristic of any biracial institution established by an affluent society in an underdeveloped country. Separate salary scales perpetuated the relative affluence of the foreigner, with unavoidable psychological discrimination. On the other hand, equitable salaries created a native elite dependent on a false economy.

Throughout most of this period, PUMC dealt with this dichotomy by adroitly ducking the issue. Roughly equitable salary schedules were designed, but a *sub rosa* commutation payment to Western faculty substantially raised their earnings. The PUMC annual budget contained only the published salaries. The China Medical Board yearly added a commutation, or bonus, which was paid to Western faculty in U.S. dollars rather than Chinese currency.[22] In most other benefits there was parity. Until the mid-thirties, when financial stringency had become the watchword, Chinese and Western professors received equal sabbatical opportunities.

Sources are too few to determine what effect the *de facto* separate salary scale had on relationships between Chinese and Western faculty members.[23] Occasionally, correspondence between Peking and New York reflects controversy on this topic within the College. In 1925 Roger Greene sent a special memorandum to New York entitled "Salary Schedules," in which he reaffirmed the general conviction that, although it was undesirable to maintain unequal salaries, differences in living standards made this a necessity.[24] A year later Henry Houghton commented on the other side of the coin by noting the wide discrepancy between PUMC's Chinese salaries and those of government institutions.[25] Many years later Dr.

21. "Exhibit A—Policy in Regard to Salary Scale and Furloughs of Chinese Staff of Peking Union Medical College, 1921," p. 4, *SFP*.

22. A file labelled "Commutation," in the *PUMC Papers* reveals the details of the commutation payments after 1929. See "Exhibit E-a: Estimate of Cost of Excess Salaries for Foreign Staff of Peking Union Medical College During the Year 1929–1930, Sums to be Requested from the Rockefeller Foundation." In some cases the commutation payment was considerable: Francis Dieuaide, Department of Medicine, received US$2,250 in addition to his regular salary of US$5,750.

23. Two former Chinese faculty members interviewed seemed to accept the necessity for paying higher salaries to their Western colleagues, but their attitudes cannot be taken as representative. Interview, Dr. Bacon Chow, October 1, 1971, Baltimore, Maryland; Interview, Dr. I. C. Yuan, October 12, 1971, New York City.

24. Greene, "Salary Schedules, December 5, 1925," *RGP*.

25. Houghton to Greene, January 4, 1926, *RGP*.

Reinhard Hoeppli, the Swiss head of the Department of Parasitology, who was as close to his Chinese colleagues as anyone, wrote that relations between Chinese and foreign staff were not as harmonious as they might have been: "One of the main reasons was a certain envy of the Chinese staff, as the foreign staff received higher salaries."[26]

The American record only mentions one serious altercation. In order to minimize the effect of an unstable exchange rate, the Trustees in 1930 approved salary payments in gold instead of Chinese currency to Western faculty. But the Chinese professors continued to receive their salaries in local currency. Since these arrangements practically doubled the buying power of the foreigners, the Chinese on the faculty were outraged. Greene admitted the inequity of this policy:

> Our Chinese staff is much upset over the action in regard to gold salaries of foreign staff, and I may be in for a bad time, though I hope I can pacify them with the help of our Chinese trustees. It is a fact that the cost of living is rising also for the Chinese staff, and particularly for those who have chosen a rather foreign way of living.[27]

But the protests were disregarded, and this procedure continued.

Discrimination and what one Yenching professor termed *yi-lai hsin-li* (a psychology of reliance)[28] were perpetuated by PUMC's salary policies. Even with separate schedules, the salaries of most PUMC Chinese professors remained considerably higher than those paid by locally comparable Chinese institutions. For example, by 1935 the salary range for a Chinese assistant professor at PUMC was Mex.$5,200–6,000, whereas the *goal* for a similar position at the four national medical colleges was Mex.$3,600–4,800.[29] Furthermore, it was well known that actual salaries of Chinese institutions were considerably below the government's target.

There was perhaps a rational basis for PUMC's system, and it was undeniably more equitable than at most other Sino-American institutions. Few can deny that higher salaries for both Westerners and Chinese was one method of maintaining standards of excellence. Nonetheless, differential salaries solved none of the problems inherent in binational schools. Undeclared commutation payments to Western faculty appeared racially discriminatory, whereas high

26. Hoeppli to Loucks, July 7, 1968, *PUMC Papers*.

27. Greene to Margery Eggleston, March 6, 1930, *RGP*.

28. West, "Yenching University," p. 324.

29. F. C. Yen, "Economics of Medical Schools and Hospitals in China," *CMJ* 49 (1935): 888.

salaries for Chinese faculty, compared with those outside PUMC, were inappropriate.

A more nagging issue than salaries, for all were essentially well-remunerated, was the question of the promotion of Chinese staff. Although the increase in higher level positions for Chinese is quite evident, it was not accomplished with ease. At the outset, it was assumed that the majority of the faculty would be Westerners. Additionally, the top slots would be held by foreigners, even if Chinese of equal educational qualifications emerged. Dr. Houghton summarized this attitude in 1924:

> With regard to the appointment of foreigners to posts *higher than those we give to Chinese of equal training* . . . it seemed to us in the case of obviously temporary appointments of this nature—to be held by men who are taken away from their own country and are in some important respects deprived of opportunities for advancement in what is to be their permanent lifework—that it was fair to pay a premium, and that it would be recognized by our Chinese as on the whole being a just procedure.[30]

It was ostensibly the goal of these first Western professors to train their replacements, but this is a considerable expectation of the human psyche. There were inevitable variations in individual approaches to reducing the foreign contingent. Seventy-one foreigners were appointed to faculty rank in the years 1918–1942 and their average tenure was seven years. While this indicates some turnover, foreign control at the policy level was pervasive: of the sixteen foreigners who stayed for ten years or longer, eleven were heads of departments. By 1937 there were five Chinese departmental heads, but seven Western chairmen remained.

After the initial adjustment, many aliens came to see themselves as permanent fixtures at PUMC, and they were tardy, to say the least, in training their successors. In a 1926 letter of uncommon irritation, Richard Pearce wrote to Greene about Dr. Bernard Read, chairman of the Department of Pharmacology: "Has he stupidly . . . prevented the development of good Chinese who have worked under him?"[31] Physiologist Robert Lim (Lim K'o-sheng), one of the few Chinese who achieved the rank of professor during the twenties, was upset in 1928 that Francis Dieuaide, chairman of the Department of Medicine, had not trained any Chinese for teaching responsibilities in this most crucial department.[32]

For the Westerner in China during the twenties and thirties it

30. Houghton to Greene, August 5, 1924, *RGP*. Emphasis added.
31. Pearce to Greene, June 29, 1926, *RGP*.
32. Greene to Pearce, April 27, 1928, *RGP*.

was difficult to view with genuine enthusiasm the transfer of responsibilities to the Chinese. Houghton relayed the personal trauma: "We have all been having heart-searchings of late, in the light of these good young Chinese that are coming along, and trying to realize as impersonally as we can the fact that our turn [to leave] may come next."[33]

Although the Rockefeller Foundation *Annual Report* continually stressed the rapid growth of the Chinese faculty, significant increases did not occur until after 1928. Chinese were regularly employed as assistants or associates in departments. This accounts for the rise in their percentage of the whole (see Table 1). But in 1925–1926, for example, there were only four Chinese, as compared with 22 Westerners, of assistant professor rank or above. After this, as indicated in Table 2, the increase was more noticeable. By 1930–1931, there were 13 Chinese in major faculty positions including four of full professorial rank. It should be noted that although the total number of Westerners decreased from 45 to 22 in the years between 1925 and 1935, this decrease occurred *only* at the levels below assistant professor. In contrast with Houghton's earlier assumption that Westerners would be replaced by Chinese, Westerners of faculty rank—that is, assistant professor or higher— actually remained relatively constant during that period.[34] Promotion of Chinese thus had *not* taken place at the expense of Westerners.

That the initial increase in Chinese faculty occurred most dramatically during the period 1925–1930 was the result of two interrelated factors. The first was the increasing number of PUMC "returned" graduates. After several years of training abroad, as well as PUMC internships, these men were beginning to mature to the faculty level. Also, Chinese graduate students at PUMC, matriculating from other medical institutions, had occupied lower level positions for some time. The availability of these qualified men within the immediate orbit of PUMC slowly but continually necessitated their advancement.

The second reason was the heightened sense of Chinese nationalism which challenged Western educational control during and after the establishment of the Nanking government in 1927. PUMC's American administration tended to minimize internal pressures for Chinese advancement, but the changing national climate inevitably

33. Houghton to Greene, March 1, 1925, *RGP*.
34. There was more fluctuation in faculty representation than is indicated by these five-year intervals. The peak of Western faculty was in 1932–33, when there were 26 of faculty rank.

TABLE I

Western and Chinese Faculty at
Peking Union Medical College

	Western	Chinese
1920–1921	22	9
1925–1926	45	44
1930–1931	28	88
1935–1936	22	102
1940–1941	10	109

NOTE: Data derived from the *PUMC Annual Announcement*, 1920–1941. In this case, "faculty" refers to professors, associate professors, assistant professors, instructors, and associates.

TABLE 2

Comparison of Faculty Positions Held by Westerners and Chinese

	1920 – 1921		1925 – 1926		1930 – 1931		1935 – 1936		1940 – 1941	
	Western	Chinese	Western	Chinese	Western	Chinese	Western	Chinese	Western	Chinese
Professor	8	0	9	0	11	4	8	5	7	7
Associate Professor	3	0	8	4	9	0	7	4	3	10
Assistant Professor	0	0	5	0	1	9	4	11	0	27
Subtotal	11	0	22	4	21	13	19	20	10	44
Lower Ranks	11	9	23	40	7	75	3	82	0	65
Total	22	9	45	44	28	88	22	102	10	109

NOTE: Data derived from the *PUMC Annual Announcement*, 1920–1941.

affected promotion policies. Roger Greene, in a 1928 letter to Assistant Secretary of State Nelson Johnson, described the situation:

> We do, of course, encounter some ebullitions of national feeling and a tendency to be rather critical of proposed foreign appointments as against promotion of Chinese, but this has not been serious. A sufficient number of the Chinese staff are so interested in their work and in the welfare of the College that they are not disposed to press their nationalism too far.[35]

Greene's policy to appoint Chinese when they "could be found as good, all things considered, as any foreigners that we are likely to be able to secure"[36] resulted in the dual policy of continued recruitment of Western scientists and gradual appointment of Chinese. From 1926 to 1935, new appointments were fairly evenly divided between Chinese and Westerners.

Several of the smaller departments had Chinese professors as chairmen by the late twenties, notably biochemistry, physiology, and radiology.[37] The two major departments, medicine and surgery, which provided training during the last years of a student's program and were the core of clinical practice, remained predominantly Western during this period. In his 1926 survey of the PUMC faculty, David Edsall, Dean of Harvard Medical College, noted that there were several promising Chinese in clinical medicine:

> ... but the most promising are young and would not be fitted for very responsible work in the most difficult of all departments for four or five years. It will be even longer before any Chinese will be fitted for the professorship of medicine. It requires prolonged study, clinical experience, and training in research to a degree that no other department does.[38]

Edsall did believe that the Department of Medicine had too many foreigners, but that at least four well-qualified ones, each in separate specialities, should continue for some years to come. The Western faculty of the Department of Medicine fluctuated between five and eight during the next ten years.

The Department of Surgery, which Edsall had thought might move more rapidly toward Chinese leadership, also continued to employ a high percentage of Westerners throughout this period. In fact, there were *no* Chinese appointments to the level of assistant professor or above from 1924 until 1937, although Chinese filled

---

35. Greene to Nelson Johnson, May 17, 1928, *NJP*.
36. Greene to Pearce, November 5, 1927, *RGP*.
37. Wu Hsien, Robert Lim, and J. Hua Liu, respectively.
38. Edsall, "Memorandum on PUMC," p. 5.

the lower positions of residents, assistants, and associates. At first glance this seems to reflect an obvious reluctance on the part of the chairman, Harold Loucks, to turn authority and responsibility over to Chinese. This may have been true; but on closer examination, other employment problems are evident. In many ways an unchallenged system, rather than personal prejudice, was the determinant of faculty appointments.

From 1923 until 1929 only three students (out of 56) at PUMC specialized in surgery. Other medical schools within China graduated increasing numbers of medical students, but many of the best came to PUMC for their years of internship and residency. PUMC increasingly turned to its own graduates, graduate students, or lower level research assistants for new faculty positions in all fields. This meant that of the Chinese faculty appointed, most had worked their way up slowly from the bottom. For example, of the 12 Chinese who were assistant professors in 1932, a number had degrees from American medical schools, but most had then come immediately to PUMC to serve as residents or lower level associates. Several of the group had degrees from other institutions within China, but they had also come immediately to PUMC for further training. Only one of the twelve was an actual graduate of PUMC. But by 1937, of the sixteen Chinese assistant professors, eleven were PUMC graduates, and most of the others had worked their way up from the bottom.[39]

Several conclusions can be drawn from this recruitment system. Prolonged residency, apparently necessary for medical maturity, coupled with the restricted enrollment of PUMC, suggests it was probably remarkable that the PUMC Sinified its various teaching departments as rapidly as it did. The reluctance to recruit Chinese professors of more advanced rank from the staff of other institutions, thus insuring educational diversity as well as some equality of status between colleagues, is more difficult to evaluate.

In the first several years of its existence, PUMC was able to secure exceptionally well-qualified Chinese trained abroad for its faculty positions.[40] By the late twenties, the better medical students within China were undoubtedly enrolled at PUMC, and the better graduates of many other institutions came for advanced study. However, Chi-

39. Complete biographical information on Chinese professors at PUMC is not available; the above has been deduced from the known PUMC graduates along with some information on the other professors in the *Chinese Medical Directory, 1936* (Shanghai).

40. For example, J. Heng Liu, Wu Hsien, C. E. Lim, J. Hua Liu, and T. M. Li, all of whom trained abroad and came immediately to PUMC.

nese students continued to obtain advanced medical degrees abroad in great numbers. Additionally, there were over twenty other medical colleges within China at the time. While medical publications of the period indicate that the standards of the schools might have been low, a number of reputable medical scientists did teach in these institutions. But after 1925 there were *no* Chinese from outside PUMC appointed directly to the position of assistant professor or above. All were groomed in lower positions. Whatever the rationale for this in-house recruitment, the result was definitely an inbred faculty at PUMC.

A system which depended upon students rising to positions of relative equality with their former professors created inevitable discrimination even without the additional factor of nationality. It is not surprising that the Western faculty felt their students were not ready, and that their Chinese students wondered "whether [foreigners] recognized the potential of the people under them."[41] No substantial changes occurred in the policy of the appointment of Chinese faculty until the mid-thirties, when educational currents in China necessitated a reappraisal of PUMC's policies and programs. Before considering these factors, the varying changes in curriculum content should be explored.

The "modification of American educational curriculum to the needs of China" was a rhetorical phrase liberally scattered through PUMC's history. Ernest Burton stressed that Western educational practices had no claim to perfection, and that "no mere importation of American or European courses as such" should occur.[42] The speeches at the 1921 dedication, including those by William Welch, John D. Rockefeller, Jr., and Edward Hume, had urged the adaptation of PUMC's curriculum to the exigencies of China. In 1924 the Rockefeller Foundation *Annual Report* stressed the marked development of Chinese national consciousness: "It is certainly desirable, if not essential that Western methods should be carefully adapted to Chinese conditions."[43] But no one indicated *how* this was to be accomplished.

The first curriculum was patterned as closely as possible after that of The Johns Hopkins Medical School. Major strengths of that program were laboratory training and clinical demonstration in hospital wards. In 1924, on the premise that "Chinese students need

41. Interview with Bacon Chow, October 1, 1971. Chow felt that some of the Chinese in lower ranks during the thirties were better qualified than their Western superiors.
42. Ernest Burton, "Report," p. 425.
43. Rockefeller Foundation, *Annual Report, 1924*, p. 251.

supervision,"[44] there was experimentation with a new unit system of teaching. This primarily involved a great increase in classroom hours and daily recitations. Both Western and Chinese faculty became dissatisfied with this change. Edsall, who was a visiting professor in 1926, observed that PUMC's students needed more independence, not more supervision.[45] Robert Lim wrote that "the attitude 'that Chinese students are not practical'" was harmful and "due in part to the fact that the student is over-instructed."[46]

Under Dr. Francis Dieuaide, head of the Department of Medicine from 1926 to 1935 and concurrently chairman of the Curriculum Committee, the rigid structure of hours and excessive requirements was modified. Recitation practices were abandoned, and the schedules altered to include larger percentages of time in the laboratories and hospital wards. Class attendance was abolished and the grading system was changed from frequent testing to an annual evaluation of a student's progress by the professors with whom he had worked. According to Dieuaide, this progressive course, which increased flexibility, also promoted a more mature student body.[47]

These curriculum changes reflected some consideration of how to teach Chinese medical students, but Edsall went further and indicated the need for increased adaptation of Western pedagogical methods: "In a large proportion of the departments, both pre-clinical and clinical, the general methods and the details of training the students are essentially a direct transplanting of Western methods to China."[48] Edsall also attested to the need to re-examine the content of medical education. Although this eminent American educator believed that there was a body of medical knowledge which was universal, he felt that specific Chinese medical problems should also be covered: "such matters as the particular habits of life of the Chinese as to occupation, diet, housing, etc., the striking differences as to the kinds of diseases seen . . . demand that different slants be given to the teaching . . . in order to make the effect increasingly indigenous rather than something exotic."[49]

The only major curricular attempt "to make the effect increasingly indigenous rather than something exotic" occurred in the field of public health. Interestingly, this modification was later to be

44. "History of the CMB, 1931," RGP, p. 73.
45. Edsall, "Memorandum on PUMC," p. 10.
46. Lim to Greene, November 6, 1924, PUMC Papers.
47. Francis R. Dieuaide, "Medical Education and the Curriculum at the Peiping Union Medical College," CMJ 48 (1934): 1017–1045. Also interview with Dr. Dieuaide, March 30, 1972.
48. Edsall, "Memorandum on PUMC," p. 15.
49. Ibid., p. 16.

extended from PUMC to major medical schools in the United States. The Professor of Public Health at PUMC from 1921 until 1934 was John Grant, the son of Canadian missionaries to Ningpo. In 1925 Grant enlisted the cooperation of the municipal police in establishing a public health station which provided medical services for Peking's first ward, an area of approximately 100,000 people in which PUMC was located. More importantly, it served as the training ground for Chinese public health specialists. Although Grant initially met opposition within the PUMC faculty, *all* students from 1926 on were required to spend a four-week clerkship in the public health station, a period of time equal to that of clerkships in medicine, obstetrics, and surgery. This represented a major innovation in Western medical education, was recognized as such by American medical educators and was duplicated in the thirties to a certain extent at Vanderbilt, Johns Hopkins, and Harvard.[50] By the mid-thirties other medical schools in China were beginning to focus attention on public health training; but PUMC consistently required more hours in this field than any other school.[51]

For the most part, however, the curriculum at PUMC followed the course of American medical schools. Dieuaide, as head of the Curriculum Committee, kept a close watch over the yearly developments in American curricula at major U.S. medical colleges—recording them on a large chart. Slight adjustments in hours, or in sequence of courses, were followed faithfully at PUMC.[52]

With the exception of comments by Edsall, and some pressure from within PUMC, especially by John Grant, there was no real stimulus prior to 1930 to alter radically PUMC's teaching program. From the time of its entry into China, by virtue of its financial endowment and close affiliation with the prestigious international medical education programs of the Rockefeller Foundation, PUMC dominated China's medical education. But when the Nationalist government sought to prescribe standards of education for the entire country in the late twenties and early thirties, new influences challenged what Alan Gregg later so aptly termed the "preciousness" of PUMC.

50. Public health at PUMC will be examined more extensively in Chapter 6. For the impact of Grant on American medical education, see W. S. Leathers, "The Integration of the Teaching of Preventive and Clinical Medicine," *Journal of the Association of American Medical Colleges* 14 (1939): 23.

51. Lee T'ao, "Some Statistics on Medical Schools in China for 1932–1933," *CMJ* 47 (1933): 1034.

52. Interview with Dieuaide, March 30, 1972. Interview with Mary Ferguson, November 22, 1971, Sandy Spring, Maryland. Miss Ferguson described the large chart and constant tabulation of hours.

Some of the new voices were to come from students and professors at PUMC itself; others were European members of the League of Nations' Health Organization. A unifying element in their varying approaches was concern for medical *services* as well as medical standards. They felt China should adopt a centralized program of national health care and medical education. Furthermore, the overriding problem to be solved was the distribution of medical services to the rural *hsien* in addition to the urban areas. The national issue became whether or not China should adopt a "two-track" system of medical education: medical colleges to train high-level physicians and special medical schools to train medical practitioners. During this debate, Peking Union Medical College, as a unique institution and as a "model," increasingly came under attack. The first major volley in the argument was the 1931 publication of Knud Faber's *Medical Schools in China*.

Faber, Professor of Medicine at Copenhagen University, was asked by the League of Nations' Health Organization on behalf of the Chinese government, to evaluate China's medical education. He was specifically asked to comment on the Ministry of Education's tentative "two-track" policy. His resulting report, based on a three-month survey in the fall of 1930, was the first major reassessment of medical education in China since the Rockefeller Foundation's First Medical Commission in 1914.[53] Although Faber did deprecate the meagre laboratory facilities and absence of clinical teaching at many government and private medical colleges, standards of scientific excellence were not his watchwords. The Scandinavian educator introduced his study by citing the fact that there was roughly one modern-trained physician per 80,000–100,000 people in China. In the United States there was one per 800; in Sweden, one per 2,860. If China set as a goal one per 8,000, there was a need for 50,000 medical doctors!

Faber approved the proposed dual-track system for China, and included in his report a model curriculum for the novel special medical schools. He candidly described the existing inadequacies of many of the government schools, and he also suggested which ones should form the nucleus of the higher level medical colleges. Not unexpectedly, Faber recognized the superior nature of PUMC:

> With a hospital of 250 beds and extraordinarily well equipped with all the necessary facilities for pre-clinical and clinical teaching and re-

53. Knud Faber, *Report on Medical Schools in China* (Geneva: League of Nations Health Organization, 1931). It should be noted that Faber evaluated and supported, but did not himself originate, the proposal for medical special schools. Crozier, *Traditional Medicine*, p. 54, is misleading on this point.

search, this is an excellent medical school and its influence on the development of modern medicine in China cannot be over-estimated.[54]

But he recommended that the enrollment be expanded, and that it become more closely integrated into a national system of medical education:

> The present facilities of the Peiping Union Medical College are relatively extensive, certainly for China, but they provide only for the instruction of classes of twenty-five students. General considerations and the small additional facilities necessary to train 50 students in a class make it appear logical to provide for this number.[55]

Faber observed that most of PUMC's graduates had become teachers in other medical schools or directors of projects within the National Health Administration. He suggested that the normal school function be crystallized, and that PUMC concentrate on graduate rather than undergraduate training.

Faber was a guest in Roger Greene's home in Peking, and he seems to have spent several days visiting and lecturing at PUMC. His recommendations for Chinese medical education, however, were rejected by many of PUMC's professors. Francis Dieuaide himself led the counterattack. Several months after Faber's visit, Dieuaide addressed the PUMC community on the question of standards of medical education. Although he never mentioned the League of Nations by name, Dieuaide implicitly rejected Faber's proposals.

Dieuaide discussed the major revolution taking place in Russian medical education under the Soviet government, and specifically compared the PUMC curriculum with that of the Bolshevik model. The Russians had devised a several track system to prepare specialists in specific fields of medical services to the community. In Dieuaide's opinion, this was teaching techniques, not science. He himself rejected lower level technical schools of medicine: "The question then arises, 'Is it ever desirable to erect technical schools of medicine?' The answer is, they will exist in any case, even as they now exist in every country in the world, but it does not seem desirable to set about bringing such institutions into existence."[56]

The PUMC professor of medicine conceded that the Soviet model was of interest to China in that similar social conditions existed: both countries had large populations and few modern students.

54. *Ibid.*, p. 14. Faber's estimate of a 250-bed hospital is wrong, for the hospital report for the previous year listed 346 beds.

55. *Ibid.*, p. 31.

56. F. R. Dieuaide, "Medical Education and Some Recent Experiments," *National Medical Journal of China (NMJC)* 17 (1930): 298.

But he appealed to medical educators in China to reject the Russian approach:

> On any terms the task of educating the number of physicians theoretically needed is stupendous and must take the better part of a century. But the graduation of large numbers of poorly qualified physicians would slow the progress of modern medicine. . . . Medicine needs the best possible protagonists for its cause and will not find them among technicians.[57]

Several years after Faber's trip to China, the Yugoslav Andrija Stampar became the "expert" on health in China for the League. He also advised the government on educational matters, and further stressed the need for PUMC to modify its program:

> But for some time it has been felt that the institution has not yet been made to yield its maximum utility, and the opinion expressed that from an institution of such impressive character, the populations as a whole should receive greater benefits. With these suggestions in mind, the authorities have recently given much thought to the future of the college and the role which it is most fitted to play in the medical services of China.[58]

These and other exhortations for the transformation of PUMC's program were based partially on the tremendous discrepancy which existed between that favored institution and all other medical schools in China. A comparison of some of the annual budgets in 1934 will illustrate this: the PUMC budget was Mex.$3,167,700; the next closest at Mex.$289,949 was that of Cheeloo Medical College in Tsinan. The largest budget for a Chinese-operated medical school was Mex.$230,016 for the College of Medicine of the National Peiping University. The best of these Chinese facilities, the National Shanghai Medical School, had a budget of only Mex.$173,803. Newly-established provincial schools, which were to act as special medical colleges with lower entrance requirements and a shortened curriculum, were nominally funded. The Chekiang Provincial Medical School received only Mex.$8,806 and the Yunnan Medical School only Mex.$14,400.[59]

These statistical comparisons are not fair to PUMC, for its budget included a nursing school, large hospital, and the complete mainte-

57. Ibid., p. 299.

58. Stampar, "Health and Social Conditions in China," in M. D. Grmek, ed., Serving the Cause of Public Health: Selected Papers of Adrija Stampar (Zagreb: Andrija Stampar School of Public Health, 1966), p. 145.

59. Lee T'ao, "Some Statistics on Medical Schools in China for the Year 1933–1934," CMJ 49 (1935): 898–899. It should be noted that PUMC's figures were reported accurately, for Lee was on the PUMC staff.

nance of its extensive plant, while most of the other figures included the expenses of the medical school only. Nevertheless, three
million dollars to $300,000, or a *ten-fold* differential, is simply over-
whelming. While a crisis in Chinese medical services prevailed,
it is no wonder that a public determination existed to ensure that
PUMC's largess would be utilized more effectively and economically.

From 1934 until 1937 the Chinese government annually inspect-
ed Peking Union Medical College. After the first review the Ministry of Education advised that PUMC:

1. Increase the number of enrollments for new students;
2. Correct the "over-emphasis" of using English as the teaching
medium;
3. Adopt Chinese as the main language of administration;
4. Readjust the luxurious state of living among the students.[60]

A year later the College was reinspected to ascertain whether
these reforms had been implemented. This 1935 commentary on
PUMC from the Ministry of Education's Commission on Medical
Education is a fascinating document. It probably reveals fairly widespread Chinese opinions of PUMC. And it might well have been
written by Chu Chang-keng, a 1929 PUMC graduate. Chu was the
General-Secretary of this Commission, and a leading proponent of
drastically modifying China's medical education. Other members
of this group were well acquainted with PUMC, and at least one of
them, P. Z. King, had been associated with PUMC for many years.
As a further ironic twist, the Rockefeller Foundation's China Program contributed approximately one-half of the annual budget of
this commission.[61]

The 1935 evaluation concluded that *none* of the 1934 proposals
had been put into effect. The student body had not been expanded.
According to Roger Greene, this was because there were too few
qualified applicants and facilities would be inadequate. The Chinese officials rejected this reasoning. Their survey of the student
body indicated that 100 percent had come from private universities,
primarily missionary institutions. They concluded that the use of
English for the entrance exam discouraged applicants from Chi-

60. "Recommendations for the P.U.M.C.—April, 1935." Confidential translation
of the document received from the Ministry of Education, p. 1, *RFA*. This document
describes both the 1934 and 1935 inspection of PUMC by the Chinese government.

61. Marshall Balfour, "Memorandum on Rockefeller Foundation Activities in China, 1935–1944," p. 3. This report was in the private possession of the author who
was head of the China Program from 1938–1943. Interview, February 15–16, 1972.
C. K. Chu, "The Revised Medical Curricula," *CMJ* 49 (1935): 837–846, discusses
some of the functions of the Commission.

nese universities. Furthermore, their own interviews with PUMC professors Robert Lim and Wu Hsien indicated that the prestigious college's laboratories and classrooms could easily accommodate 32–42 students instead of 25, and with only slight readjustment, 50 students.

The Ministry of Education acknowledged that Western faculty members could not teach in Chinese, but it saw no reason for *Chinese* professors not to teach in Chinese: "the Chinese teaching staff is growing in size and there is no reason why the Chinese teachers cannot start to use their mother tongue as the medium of teaching." [62] Since medical terms were increasingly being translated into Chinese, it was felt that PUMC professors and students were vital in spreading the vernacular terminology. In addition, the administrative language had not been changed to Chinese. Greene indicated to the inspectors that this would have been financially prohibitive and nonessential: "It is hard to understand what Mr. Greene means by 'not essential.' Financially it costs very little by using Chinese language in comparison with the annual expenditures of the College." [63]

The government inspectors also noted that no change had taken place in the "luxurious life of the students"; therefore, the atmosphere of the entire campus needed diversifying. Faculty life-styles as well as student privileges should be adjusted to "the social and financial status of the country." The PUMC community should familiarize itself with "the life of the majority of the population, the poor class, in order to bring about a sympathy with that section of society." [64] PUMC students also needed to cooperate more fully with students of other governmental schools.

In summarizing these negative conclusions, the Ministry of Education rhetorically invoked the sanctions of John D. Rockefeller, Sr., the American founder:

> Unfortunately, the Founder's object has not been adequately interpreted in the steps taken by the Administration to secure realization. The Chinese government has also greatly desired that the establishment of the P.U.M.C. should play a more significant role in the development of medical education in China. . . . In order to fulfill the Founder's work, it is the duty of the Chinese government to supervise the administration of the College more closely. [65]

Increased supervision appeared in three new guidelines for the College. First, science should be taught by focusing on Chinese prob-

62. "Recommendations for the P.U.M.C.," p. 2.   63. *Ibid.*, p. 3.   64. *Ibid.*
65. *Ibid.*

lems. Teaching emphasis, accordingly, should be on public health, parasitology, and bacteriology. Second, the Chinese department should be enlarged to an equal standing with the scientific departments, and should specifically teach Chinese medical terminology. Students should learn how to translate medical papers and theories into the Chinese language. Third, all Chinese staff should produce their articles in both English and Chinese, and the papers of Westerners should also be translated into Chinese. Heretofore, *none* of the scientific papers from PUMC had been published in Chinese. Concluding these new requirements, the government observed in one of its most telling indictments: "It is too much of a regret that the contributions of the College cannot be referred to by most of the Chinese medical schools, as well as the medical profession throughout the Country, on account of the language difficulty."[66]

From 1934 to 1937, these and other governmental regulations were to annoy greatly some administrators at PUMC. Dieuaide, himself chairman of the Curriculum Committee for nearly a decade, wrote in October 1934:

> The medical profession and medical schools have always been charged with traditionalism and over-conservatism. No doubt in various times and places the charges have been and are justified. Medical practice, however, is not an activity into which it is to the public advantage to have suddenly and frequently introduced radical innovations. A wise conservatism, which does not shut out new departures, and yet demands careful consideration and experimentation, is entirely proper to medical education.[67]

The response from New York was more favorable. After reading the 1935 governmental directives, Alan Gregg wrote to Selskar Gunn that although it is "doubtful whether it is within the province of the Ministry to concern itself with the number of students enrolled," other of the regulations were understandable.[68] Later, John D. Rockefeller III was almost enthusiastic: "I find myself rather generally in sympathy with the recommendations. . . . At least it is something to have them take a real interest in the school since it is our thought to eventually turn the institution over to the Chinese." Wondering if a few of the requirements were impractical, he wrote: "At the same time I do think that the ultimate objective indicated in most of the recommendations is reasonable and to be

66. *Ibid.*, p. 4.
67. Dieuaide, "Medical Education and the Curriculum," p. 1018.
68. Gregg to Gunn, July 31, 1935, *RFA*.

worked for."[69] The appeal to the aims of the Founder had brought a response from the grandson.

Some members of the Chinese faculty were also arguing for adaptation of PUMC's program. Both Wu Hsien and Robert Lim (Lim K'o-sheng) had recognized the critical issues facing China's medical profession. Lim, in his Presidential Address at the 1930 meeting of the National Medical Association, had drawn attention to rural health needs: "The question which must be faced is how to render effective health service to the mass of our population which is almost entirely rural." Charting a new course for medical education, he presented some specific ideas for curriculum change:

> I should like to suggest that while we must aim at attaining a standard not inferior to the best in the Occident, it is not essential to copy the methods of the West in all details. . . . There are possibilities of modification of the medical curriculum and departments and yet maintain satisfactory scientific standards. For example, we may very well teach the "normal biology of man," in place of the three or four separate subjects of anatomy, physiology, biochemistry, and pharmacology.[70]

In 1932 Wu Hsien, writing under a pseudonym in the *Independent Critic*, had described the paramedical teams being organized by the Public Health Division of the Mass Education Movement in Ting Hsien, and the problems yet to be solved in the adequate delivery of medical care to the rural countryside.[71] Four years later he wrote a long and thoughtful article on the difficult problems facing the medical profession. These included: conflict between traditional and modern medicine, regulation of medical practitioners, and varying approaches to the teaching of medicine. For Wu Hsien, noting the variation in standards, the inadequate distribution of doctors to rural areas, and a dearth of financial resources, it was the pedagogical problem which was most critical. Using statistics reminiscent of Faber, Wu Hsien noted that China needed approximately 40,000 doctors in order to provide one doctor per 1,000 people. At the present matriculation rate of 500 students from the 27 medical schools, it would be *80 years* before China would have barely sufficient medical service.[72]

69. John D. Rockefeller, III to Alan Gregg, August 20, 1935, *RFA*.

70. Robert Lim, "Presidential Address," *NMJC* 16 (1930): 118, 119.

71. Wu Hsien, under pseud. T'ao Ming, "Ting Hsien chien-wen tsa-lu," [Notes on Miscellaneous Experiences at Ting Hsien] in *Tu-li p'ing-lun* No. 4 (1932), p. 16.

72. Wu Hsien, under pseud. T'ao Ming. "Yü yu-jen lun i-wu shu," [A Discourse with Friends on Medical Affairs] in *Tu-li p'ing-lun* No. 201 (1936), pp. 39–42.

Recognizing the crisis in China's medical modernization, Robert Lim, the ardent, nationalistic activist, and Wu Hsien, the quiet, serious scholar, nonetheless concurred in the belief that China still needed a school like PUMC. With its standards of excellence, PUMC should stand at the apex of a national system which also included *chuan-k'o* (special schools) of varying technical grade. But they also argued that PUMC itself needed a thorough-going revision. Their aim was not to dilute the standards of excellence, but to ensure that PUMC's services were more consistently available for a national system of medical education.

Crisis, standards, national integration—these were the criteria which brought PUMC to a mid-decade reappraisal of its policies and programs. Heretofore, procedures had evolved primarily out of the context of the Flexnerian reforms in American medical education, not in tandem with the Chinese environment. The philosophical reassessments of the mid-thirties are difficult to evaluate because they were obscured, and perhaps nullified, by the Japanese occupation of Peking in 1937. They are significant, however, because they chart a new direction for the privileged PUMC.

Administrative change was first heralded by a report titled "Memorandum on the Organization and Program of PUMC" issued in November 1935 by Henry Houghton, a year after he had returned to China. It will be recalled that Houghton returned to China in the fall of 1934 as CMB representative during the crisis brought on by Greene's resignation. During the years in which Houghton and Greene had jointly been involved with PUMC, 1920–1927, there appeared little difference in their views of PUMC's program. But when Houghton returned after seven years of absence, attitudes in New York and pressure from Chinese nationalistic movements, and perhaps his own inclinations, had greatly altered his thinking. Houghton was assisted in this evaluation of PUMC by four persons: J. Heng Liu, Robert Lim, G. Canby Robinson, and Charles Leach. The two Americans were visiting professors in medicine and public health, respectively. Having only been at PUMC a short time, their contributions reflected none of the vested interests of long-term PUMC faculty.

In his path-breaking report Houghton declared that during the coming years five major issues needed to be resolved: the scope of PUMC; the nature of graduate instruction and its relation with the government; religion; making the institution more Chinese; and improving relations with the CMB. He candidly admitted: "In some respects there is a luxury of provisions in professional and auxiliary staff which runs beyond that of most of the better medical schools in the U.S."[73]

He then outlined the sociological conditions *within* China which influenced medical education. First, at long last, came the recognition of the continuing importance of traditional Chinese medicine. Second, the international factions in medical education which were strongly influenced by the foreign country of their medical training—Japan, Germany, France, Great Britain, and the United States. Third, Houghton noted the "conservative" nature of rural China, emphasizing that most Chinese people lived an agrarian life. Therefore, "its permeation with medical service and notions of healthful living should be the principal objective of medical education."[74] Finally, he described the problems of a society in flux.

Houghton then summarized the Nationalist government's health policies, indicating that these plans would decisively influence PUMC's programs. If the country was to adopt socialized medicine, then education and training must necessarily be adapted to this fact of life. He suggested that PUMC could perhaps serve as a curriculum laboratory, as he also recognized the need for a variety of standards of medical education.

PUMC graduates were already represented in the National Health Administration (*Weishengshu*). But to "be represented in such a movement, however, only by occasional graduates who may be available and interested, and by the rarified atmosphere of high standards, is not enough. Thought must be given to ways in which immediate, practical, and concrete assistance can be given."[75] Emphasizing teacher education as PUMC's most relevant contribution (as Knud Faber also had done), he noted that the institution had not been sufficiently utilized within China for graduate teaching.

Deploring the "holier than thou" posture of the institution, Houghton made a number of specific suggestions aimed at identifying the College "more fully with its environment." Permanent Chinese leadership of all departments, as well as increased representation at the other faculty levels, was urgently needed. Foreign teachers were a necessity in order to keep abreast of international medical science, but these individuals should not be in administrative positions. Nor should they occupy the junior positions for which plenty of Chinese were available. Houghton also acknowledged that the

73. Houghton, "Memorandum on the Organization and Program of PUMC," p. 6.
74. *Ibid.*, p. 9.
75. *Ibid.*, p. 19.

commutation system of secret payments to foreigners brought justified irritation and criticism—although he did not propose a specific
solution.

More than twenty years after Welch and Flexner had advocated
teaching in English, Houghton declared: "A breaking down of the
barriers that now exist because of the language problems is one of
the most important tasks that faces the college." He urged a "gradual extension of the use of the national language in teaching, especially in laboratory courses in demonstrations." [76] Additionally, every
department should be made bilingual.

It is puzzling that Mary Ferguson later wrote that "Dr. Houghton
voiced no harsh criticism of existing practices nor did he recom-
mend radical changes in program or direction." [77] His references
to bilingual teaching were a departure from previous policies, and
if the criticisms were not harsh, the tone and thrust of the document
was quite different from the previous administration. Roger Greene
certainly disagreed with Houghton: his written rebuttal was nearly
as long as Houghton's original evaluation. [78]

As a result of Houghton's report, a Survey Commission was
appointed by the PUMC Trustees in 1936 "to formulate a statement
of the policies and objectives of the College, to make an impartial
and intensive survey and study of the institution and its financial
requirements in the light of these policies and objectives." [79] This
group met through the spring and fall of 1936. A principal topic
was the reduction of expenses commensurate with expected income from the CMB Inc., but educational policies were also debated.

The final recommendations of the Commission's Subcommittee
on Educational Policy, written by Robert Lim, are especially significant. A wider treatment of preventive medicine within the curriculum was urged, as well as closer cooperation with the North China
Council for Rural Reconstruction. This Council was funded under
the China Program of the Rockefeller Foundation, and aimed at
coordinating university personnel in an attack on the rural problems
of China. An effective bilingual system of education was also to
be instituted at PUMC. Recognizing the historical significance of
using Chinese in addition to English as the medium of instruction,

76. *Ibid.*, p. 39.
77. Ferguson, *CMB and PUMC*, p. 113.
78. "R. S. Greene's Comments on Dr. Houghton's Report," 37 pages, *RGP*. Greene
received a copy of Houghton's report, as well as other PUMC documents, because
he remained a PUMC trustee until 1938.
79. Ferguson, "The PUMC," Chapter 18, p. 1.

Lim noted: "the importance of this decision is obvious, and its consequences will be increasingly significant as time goes on."[80] Furthermore, the educational subcommittee approved a plan to admit 36 to 40 students into each class, and graduate courses were to be restructured as teacher-training programs.

The need to reduce the number of Western faculty, in part because of the financial straits of the institution, was also addressed by this Survey Commission. In late 1936 the PUMC Trustees approved the Commission's controversial recommendation that all indeterminate appointments (a status similar to tenure) be cancelled. New appointments were to be tendered, but they did not guarantee headship of a division or department as in the past. To further implement this new policy of reducing the Western faculty, a committee of senior Chinese professors was appointed to review all academic departments and assess instances where Western personnel could be replaced by Chinese already on the staff. As a result of these changes, aimed directly at increasing the Chinese staff in leadership positions, a number of Western professors left for the United States, including Francis Dieuaide.[81] Foreigners of full professorial rank continued to outnumber Chinese until 1940 when they became equal (see Table 2), and only a few departments actually passed into Chinese hands. But a clear pattern for Sinification had been established.

Strengthening the teacher training graduate programs had frequently been mentioned among the plans to integrate the curriculum of PUMC more closely with that of the general needs of medical education in China. In June of 1937, the College finally approved a memorandum accepting the Ministry of Education's invitation to constitute and register a Graduate School of Medicine. As recounted earlier, Houghton had firmly rejected financial assistance from the Chinese government, and the memorandum concluded on a wary note: "In submitting this application for registration, we wish to record our conviction, in which we are sure the Ministry will concur, that true graduate work in medicine requires the greatest possible degree of freedom and elasticity."[82] The next month—before anything could be accomplished—this tentative experiment in cooperation with national education was aborted: the Marco Polo Bridge incident was soon followed by the Japanese occupation of Peking.

80. Robert Lim, "Report of the Sub-Committee on Education," in Docket, Board of Trustees, September 23, 1936, p. 2, RGP.
81. Ferguson, CMB and PUMC, pp. 130–131.
82. Ibid., p. 128.

The 1937–1938 PUMC *Annual Announcement* formally proclaimed that instruction was to be given in Chinese and English, but that is about the extent of the implementation of the educational reforms proposed by the Survey Commission. War-time conditions decreased student enrollment, and effective cooperation with other universities in seeking solutions to China's rural problems was at an end. Some of the professors and students fled to southwest China. For those who remained, a new set of problems faced the isolated institution. The reforms proposed during the years 1935–1937 can hardly be called revolutionary, yet they were serious attempts to modify the program of PUMC to the exigencies of China itself. Like many of the gradualist plans during the Republican period, they came too late and were too few, and were finally cut short by World War II.

FIVE

"To Serve Our Dear Old China"

We, who had the inestimable privilege of being at the PUMC,
are so enchanted about the glorious institution that any-
thing we say or write is totally biased, and with reasons,
our reasons!

Loo Chih-teh, PUMC '29, 1972

CHINA'S STUDENT POPULATION of the 1920s
and 1930s has repeatedly been analyzed in terms of its shifting
nationalistic allegiance from the Kuomintang to the burgeoning
Chinese Communist Party.[1] The professional education and maturation of this elite group has been largely obscured by more fer-
vent political questions. Yet, their professional significance cannot
be over-emphasized: the first of these classes became young adults
in the optimistic 1930s, were in their productive forties during the
war-torn 1940s, and would surely have become natural administrative and educational leaders by the 1950s. The graduates of the
waning days of the Nanking era are even today only in their sixties. It was from these college graduates, less than one-hundredth
of one percent of the population during the Kuomintang period,
that leadership for technological advances and educational modernization—to a degree in Republican China and to a greater degree on Taiwan and in the People's Republic of China—have come.

The 313 graduates of PUMC were an elite group in the medical
sciences, hand-picked and individually trained as the future medical leaders of China. They were not the first generation of modern

1. John Israel, *Student Nationalism in China, 1927–1937* (Stanford: Stanford
University Press, 1966); Jessie Lutz, *China and the Christian Colleges, 1850–1950*
(Ithaca, N.Y.: Cornell University Press, 1971).

medical scientists and physicians in China. That designation had already been earned by "returned students," whose education had begun with the Confucian classics and ended with a degree from Oxford, Johns Hopkins, or Tokyo University. Their professor of biochemistry at PUMC, Wu Hsien, was such a man, having taken the civil service examinations at the age of 11 before attending a modern high school. He was awarded a Boxer Indemnity Scholarship to study in America, and he spent ten years in Massachusetts, earning his B.S. from the Massachusetts Institute of Technology and his Ph.D. from Harvard. Wu was best known for his work in the denaturation of proteins. But during a self-imposed exile in the United States following World War II, he also wrote a *Guide to Scientific Living* which combined Confucian humanism with Western scientism.[2]

PUMC students, members of the second generation of medical scientists, had no need to synthesize a Confucian background with their modern education. Although vestiges of tradition remained in their homes, their education was *in toto* modern; furthermore, it took place for the most part in China, and not abroad. This is not to say that they were not "Westernized." In fact, they were perhaps more Westernized, or at least modernized, than their intellectual predecessors. But their acculturation had evolved more naturally than that of an earlier generation. Wu Hsien, for example, had married a stranger, arranged by his parents, shortly before going to school in the United States. When he returned, finding no compatibility with the uneducated girl, he made the difficult decision to divorce his first wife. Wu's second marriage was to a graduate assistant in PUMC's biochemistry department, who had an American educational background similar to his own.[3] For his PUMC students, family control over marital arrangements appears to have lessened decidedly: at least eight men married fellow classmates, and in most cases both went on to promising careers.[4]

Chinese educational patterns persisted underneath the Americanisms of PUMC, but for the most part they were subtle. *T'unghsueh* (school and classmate) bonds continued their kinship-like

2. Wu Hsien, *Guide to Scientific Living* (Taipei: Academia Sinica, 1963).

3. His second wife wrote a biography of Wu, see Daisy Yen Wu, *Wu Hsien, 1893–1959.*

4. Unless otherwise indicated, general information on PUMC students has been gathered from PUMC's *Annual Announcement*, for the years 1920–1941. Copies are located at the China Medical Board office in New York and in the Library of Congress. This yearly report included native provinces and premedical institutions for all students attending PUMC, and until 1937 included brief summaries of the occupations and location of its graduates.

tenacity, and some students were to follow a favored professor through wars and across a continent. But it was the Westernized atmosphere of PUMC which was most noticeable.

It has often been observed that Protestant missionary educators transferred the small college, community campus, and *in loco parentis* atmosphere of American denominational colleges to their educational institutions in China. Nonetheless, it is a surprise to come upon the words of PUMC's school anthem. The chorus recalls vaguely a Yale fight song, considerably at variance with the restrained sentiments of the traditional Confucian elite:

> PUMC forever,
> The College of Our Choice,
> Let us not now, aye, never, aye, never,
> Forget our mother's voice.

The first stanza is not much different:

> Hurrah for PUMC
> The College of Our Choice
> Tis here we learn such precepts
> As makes our hearts rejoice.
> We've learned the truths of science,
> We've learned to study men.
> We've learned to know each other;
> We part to meet again.

Other lines glorify the medical skills learned:

> She's taught us ills to lessen,
> And how disease to cure,
> By killing all bacilli
> We heal the rich or poor.

And the personal commitment to the Hippocratic oath:

> Its ours to help the wretched
> To guard the public health,
> To serve our dear old China
> Without a thought of wealth.[5]

The maudlin message is reminiscent of any school song; but the phraseology, particularly, "To serve our dear old China," was clearly written by a foreigner. That it would be practically impossible to translate such a phrase into Chinese did not matter: all communication within the College, including the school song, was in English.

5. *The Unison, 1924* (Peking: PUMC Press, 1924), p. 144. The words were written by a Lorin Webster, a visitor to PUMC.

Three times prior to World War II the students at PUMC published a yearbook, *The Unison*. Its pictures of drama groups, clubs, class outings, scientific forums, and class officers reveal a campus community apparently knit together by the same organizations as the cloistered Ivy League schools of the American East Coast. The 1924 and 1928 dedications, years that spanned intensive anti-imperialist movements, went to John D. Rockefeller, Senior, and John D. Rockefeller, Junior, respectively. The 1934 dedication was perhaps more understandable: it went to Roger Greene.[6] The school song, and the yearbook, published in English with a few Chinese translations, were but an imitative veneer for a student body whose essence lies somewhere else. That they were tolerated at all reveals much about these student generations at PUMC.

Who were these PUMC students, and where were they from? Heinrich Necheles, Associate Professor of Physiology from 1924 to 1932, made the following observation based on a survey of his students:

> Their provenance is, in the greatest part, from relatively wealthy families, many of which have Westernized ideas. Nearly all of the students have been brought up under modern influences in modern Chinese or Western, some Mission schools: only a small fraction of them have ever been in foreign countries.[7]

John Grant, Professor of Public Health for nearly fifteen years, recalled that "PUMC recruits from the upper class."[8]

A few biographies substantiate the elite and Westernized nature of the PUMC student backgrounds. The descendants of two of China's most prominent statesmen, Tseng Kuo-fan and Liang Ch'i-ch'ao, were enrolled: Tseng Hsien-chiu, '40, was the great-granddaughter of Tseng; and Liang Pao-p'ing, '24, was the son of Liang. Winston W. Yung, '31, was the great-grandson of Yung Wing, an 1854 Yale graduate.[9] Yung Wing, the first "returned student," was responsible for the Educational Mission of 1874, a short-lived experiment in American education for Chinese youths. I. C. Yuan (Yuan I-chin), '27, one of the few PUMC students from interior Hupeh, grew up in Hankow where his father was a Chief Justice in the State Court following the 1911 Revolution. A student of law in Japan for seven years, Yuan's father taught Western legal his-

6. *The Unison*, 1924, 1928, and 1934, all published by the PUMC Press.

7. Heinrich Necheles, "Psychology of Chinese Students in the Light of Medical Education," *CMJ* 42 (1928): 748.

8. "Grant Reminiscences," p. 300.

9. Interview with Mary Ferguson, November 22, 1971.

tory in Hankow and was active in the reform of prisons and other judicial procedures.[10] Chow Hua-k'ang, class of 1940, was the son of Y. T. Tsur (Chou I-ch'un), a Harvard graduate and long-time PUMC trustee.[11]

More biographies would undoubtedly include more children of Chinese "returned students." Another avenue to wealth and the West was the military. Fang I-chi, '27, from Kiangsu, was perhaps only one of many sons of military fathers. There were exceptions to this list of upper-class students: Yao Hsun-yuan, '25, a native of Chihli, came from a peasant family and himself had been employed as a carpet-maker. Missionary assistance enabled him to continue his education, first in mission schools, later at PUMC. Yao's background was apparently unusual. More than forty years later a classmate recalled, with the amazement of scholar-gentry gentility, the rough, calloused hands of this Chinese physician.[12]

The modern orientation of many of these families came from their residence in urbanized areas of the coastal provinces. Table 3 illustrates the predominance of four treaty-port provinces: Kiangsu, Hopeh, Kwangtung, and Fukien. That these provinces furnished students with a more Westernized orientation than other parts of China is specifically corroborated in Y. C. Wang's study of the origins of Chinese students who studied abroad from 1909–1949.[13] Despite this Westernized background of most PUMC students, it would be erroneous to conclude that this new acculturation totally eclipsed the traditional heritage. Professor Necheles noted that the *toys* of Western technology were not among the possessions of Westernized Chinese families. According to Necheles, it was familiarity with the toys of modern science which conveyed an instinctive technological sense to many Western children. He also observed that the modern Chinese family continued to be influenced much more strongly by literature than their American counterparts:

> The student believes too much, therefore, in textbooks (the printed word) and known authorities; his mind is not opened sufficiently to criticism. Technically, he lacks most of the experience of the western

10. Interview with I. C. Yuan, October 12, 1971.

11. Howard Boorman, ed., *Biographical Dictionary of Republican China*, 1: 402–403.

12. I. C. Yuan described to me the backgrounds of Fang I-chi and Yao Hsun-yuan, March 31, 1972.

13. Y. C. Wang, *Chinese Intellectuals and the West* (Chapel Hill: University of North Carolina Press, 1966), pp. 156–159. The only significant deviation is in the greater representation from Hopeh at PUMC: Hopeh ranks second for PUMC, sixth in Wang's study. PUMC's location in Hopeh, coupled with the isolation of the institution from 1937–1943, are sufficient explanations.

TABLE 3
Native Provinces of PUMC Graduates (1924–1943)

Kiangsu	59
Hopeh	50
Kwangtung	45
Fukien	43
Chekiang	27
Hupeh	20
Shantung	11
Hunan	9
Honan	8
Kiangsi	7
Anhwei	5
Manchuria	5
Szechwan	3
Shansi	3
Formosa	1
Hong Kong	1
Abroad	6
No record	10
TOTAL	313

NOTE: Data derived from the *PUMC Annual Announcement*, 1924–1941. It should be noted that 1943 degrees were granted following completion of studies after the end of World War II.

child, and although he has often good manual abilities, applied science is further away from his instinctive grasp than in the case of his western brother.[14]

Even more revealing than their home provinces is the kind of educational institutions attended prior to admission to PUMC. It should be recalled that PUMC maintained its own three-year premedical school from 1918 to 1925. Almost all of the 64 students graduating between 1924 and 1930 attended this school. Their earlier educational experience was quite diverse: it ranged from middle school graduation alone to a full college degree. Thirty-three different institutions were attended by these 64 students: 19 designated as colleges, and 14 middle schools. Most of the institutions were missionary-sponsored, but a number were Chinese-managed. These included Peking University, Szechwan Teachers College, Shansi 1st and 5th Middle Schools, and Tientsin Government Middle School. Admission to PUMC's premedical school was highly selective. In 1923, 136 students took the entrance examinations, and only 28 were admitted. For the students enrolled, divergent academic backgrounds were evened out with a heavily concentrat-

14. Necheles, "Psychology of Chinese Students," p. 749.

ed course of English, biology, chemistry, and physics. Of the total number of 205 individuals admitted to the premedical college, 100 ultimately went on to the PUMC, and of these 84 received the M.D. degree.[15]

The PUMC premedical school program was suspended by the China Medical Board in 1925. It had been originally intended by Drs. Flexner and Welch as a stop-gap measure. In the intervening years, a number of missionary and Chinese colleges had raised their levels of scientific training. The China Medical Board's contributions to laboratory equipment, buildings, and salaries for a number of these colleges had brought about greatly accelerated programs in chemistry, biology, and physics.[16] The colleges supported included eight missionary schools and three Chinese institutions: St. John's University, Fukien Christian University, Canton Christian College, Ginling College, Yale-in-China, Yenching, University of Nanking, Soochow University, Southeastern University, Tsinghua University, and Nankai University.[17]

By far the largest donations had gone to Yenching, and in 1926 the premedical instruction at PUMC was fully turned over to Yenching. The Rockefeller Foundation agreed to grant Yenching Mex. $138,765 over five years to maintain and further strengthen its science departments. When this did not prove sufficient, the RF in 1929 agreed to add US$250,000 in endowment funds to bolster Yenching's premedical facilities.[18] Prior to 1920, Yenching's science instruction had been in Chinese, but the impact of PUMC's language policy had also affected Yenching, as one professor remembered:

> The decision that the teaching in the Peking Union Medical College would be in English, under the new management, instead of Chinese as before, affected Yenching profoundly. Hitherto the colleges which united to form Yenching had done their science teaching almost entirely in Chinese. . . . Now a sudden shift to teaching science in English was made, a change which was welcomed by most of the students, for though they would have to work harder, they would be better prepared for study abroad, an ambition cherished by almost everyone.[19]

15. Ferguson, CMB and PUMC, p. 39.
16. Lutz, China and the Christian Colleges, pp. 177–178.
17. Ferguson, CMB and PUMC, p. 39.
18. Rockefeller Foundation, Annual Report, 1925, p. 353; West, "Yenching University," pp. 272–294, discusses the confused negotiations and matching grant problems surrounding this assistance.
19. Dwight Edwards, Yenching University (New York: United Board for Christian Higher Education, 1959), p. 161.

TABLE 4
Premedical Institutions of PUMC Graduates (1931–1943)

Yenching University	137
Soochow University	19
Shanghai University	17
Fukien Christian University	12
Ginling College	11
University of Nanking	10
St. John's University	5
Lingnan University	3
18 Other Institutions enrolling 2 or less students	21
Abroad	6
No record	8
TOTAL	249

NOTE: Most students graduating prior to 1931 attended PUMC's own premedical college. Data is derived from the *PUMC Annual Announcement*, 1931–1941.

Fifty-five percent of PUMC's graduates from 1931 until 1943 attended Yenching University, most of them receiving their B.S. degrees from that institution (Table 4). Even more startling than this domination by Yenching as a feeder institution to PUMC is the fact that only *five* students during this entire period came directly from specifically Chinese institutions: two were transfers from the National Central Medical College and the Peking Government Medical College, one each from the Universities of Amoy, Tsinghua, and Nankai. *All* the rest were from missionary-sponsored colleges!

Because the entrance examinations and all instruction at PUMC were in English, graduates of missionary institutions, which emphasized this foreign language, had an obvious advantage. Statistics are unavailable for students who took the entrance examinations but failed to qualify. Perhaps this would reveal a number of students from Chinese institutions. Another possibly restrictive factor was expense: PUMC tuition fees were Mex.$100 a year as compared with Mex.$20 at the National Central Medical College in Shanghai and the Medical College at Peita.[20] Furthermore, the Westernized flavor of PUMC may have been unattractive to some of the new youth of modern China.

It is well to pause for a moment and reflect upon the significance of the missionary education backgrounds of nearly all PUMC students. Four years in a Westernized collegiate campus followed by at least five years at PUMC meant nearly a decade of adaptation

20. Lee T'ao, "Some Statistics, 1933–1934," p. 896.

to the Sino-Western synthesis offered by these institutions. Some members of their generation, and of later generations, would term this a *denationalizing* experience, a most perjorative description in an era of intense nationalism. The degree of alienation between the student minority attending missionary institutions and the majority attending Chinese institutions has been little explored. Perhaps the most decided difference was an economic one: many Chinese universities were practically tuition-free, whereas all missionary colleges charged fees.

Attendance at a missionary college did not necessarily mean that a student embraced Christianity, but he was more likely to do so than at a purely Chinese college. There was, however, a steady decline in the percentage of students claiming to be Christians at the Christian colleges during the Republican period. At Yenching, for example, 88 percent of the student body was reportedly Christian in 1924, but by 1935 supposedly only 32 percent.[21]

Although the religious activities at PUMC remained of great interest to John D. Rockefeller, Jr., his concern seems in fact to have had minimal impact on the campus community. In 1927 an unsigned letter from a member of the PUMC staff appeared in the Bulletin of the China Christian Educational Association describing the atmosphere:

> Our college is in a very peculiar situation as far as religious work is concerned, because as it is at present, the Faculty are concerned with the development of the institution as a scientific school and not as a religious project. Teachers are invited to the school not for their religious interests but for their professional proficiency. Whatever religious work that is done is purely voluntary as far as student requirements are concerned. As in all professional and especially medical institutions, we are up against the unconscious but pervasive materialistic view of life which negates the religious or spiritual conception. But there is a small number of teachers who are deeply interested in religious work and a small group of students who form the working nucleus among their fellow students.[22]

Nearly ten years later, in 1936, at the time of the Survey Commission, a PUMC student analyzed for the faculty committee the history of student religious affiliation. He characterized the first few years at PUMC as a time when it was acceptable to be religious, and the period during and after the Northern Expedition as a time of intense anti-religious sentiment. By the mid-thirties, religious

21. West, "Yenching University," p. 411.
22. "Religious Life in Christian Universities and Colleges of China, 1927–1928," China Christian Education Association, Bulletin No. 24 (1928), pp. 42–43.

concerns were seen by most students as being too trivial to be of importance at all. Fifty percent were entirely indifferent to Christianity, 20 percent showed occasional interest, 25 percent were strongly interested, and 5 percent actively anti-religious.[23]

The *hsüeh-ch'ao* (student storms) which swept Chinese universities during the twenties and thirties were also active on missionary campuses. Students at missionary institutions were sympathetic participants in the nationwide strikes which erupted following the May 30, 1925, shooting of 11 Chinese students by British-led police in Shanghai. Some were leaders in the Restore Educational Rights movements of 1924–1926 which sought to eradicate Western control of missionary schools. According to Jessie Lutz, constant exposure to Western authority perhaps only intensified anti-imperialist sentiments:

> Though Christian college students were benefiting from the educational work of Christian missions, their public declarations revealed that they often harbored deep resentment over the dominance of foreigners in the schools, the religious requirements, and the isolation of the institutions from Chinese cultural and national life.[24]

By the mid-thirties, Yenching University students were among the leaders in this anti-foreign movement.

It appears certain that whatever their individual roles in college might have been, PUMC students could not have escaped exposure to the xenophobic, anti-Japanese, anti-imperialist expressions which fanned the student demonstrations during the 1920s and 1930s. But one should be cautioned against assuming that the majority of students in China were activists. John Israel, in his *Student Nationalism in China, 1927–1937*, writes:

> We have observed that slightly more than half a million college and middle school students formed an educated elite among nearly half a billion Chinese. But the course of student political activities was plotted by a mere handful of leaders. Although an extraordinary national crisis or an imperialist affront could rally youths by the thousands to demonstrate in the streets and public squares, young scholars usually remained at their desks.[25]

Furthermore, in considering the participation or nonparticipation of PUMC students in various nationalistic outbursts, it should always

---

23. "Report of the Sub-Committee on the Department of Religious and Social Work," Docket, Board of Trustees Meeting, September 23, 1936, p. 2, *RGP*.

24. Lutz, *China and the Christian Colleges*, p. 246.

25. Israel, *Student Nationalism in China*, p. 7.

be kept in mind that these were scientific *graduate* students, intent upon the individualistic pursuit of a clearly defined goal.

The only student demonstration which appears to have affected PUMC seriously was the national upheaval caused by the May 30 incident in Shanghai in 1925. The killing of Chinese students by concession police under British command occasioned widespread reaction against British imperialism by merchants and laborers as well as students. Robert Lim, Professor of Physiology and himself British-trained, led the PUMC students in street protests. Roger Greene attempted to minimize these disturbances in a letter to George Vincent:

> Our students held out against considerable pressure from outside and completed all their class work, but at last lost their nerve and voted two to one to ask the faculty to postpone the examinations till September. . . . Our own students said very clearly that they would not strike, not because they were less patriotic than the other students, but because they differed with the others as to the means by which they should express their patriotism. They felt that as students in a professional course their best means of serving their country was through completing their studies.[26]

Whether these were truly the sentiments of PUMC students, or Greene's expostulation of them, is difficult to determine. Loo Chih-teh, PUMC '29, later prominent on Taiwan, has recalled: "The majority wanted to get on with their studies, finished [sic] the course and obtained [sic] their diplomas within the prescribed period, instead of wasting their time in politics of which they had no idea of what the difference of opinion was about."[27] There was perhaps some desire to identify with the nationwide strike, for as Loo also remembered, PUMC was closed prior to examinations, which were rescheduled for the following year.

PUMC students do not appear to have been prominent in any of the other major student movements. In 1935, when Peking became the focus for anti-Japanese agitation, the student body of PUMC was not represented. The 1935 report of the three-man directorship, Wu Hsien, Preston Maxwell, and Robert Lim, casually noted: "PUMC students took no part in the demonstrations of 1935."[28] One must tentatively conclude that, as graduate students intent on an exacting career, PUMC students were little influenced by the

26. Roger Greene to George Vincent, June 15, 1925, *RGP*.

27. Loo Chih-teh to the author, November 20, 1972. Dr. Loo is Director of the National Defense Medical Center, Taipei, Taiwan.

28. "Report of the Administration Committee on the Work of PUMC, July 1, 1935 to February 29, 1936," in Docket, Board of Trustees, March 11, 1936, p. 2, *RGP*.

Peking Union Medical College class in anatomy, 1924.

ebb and tide of Chinese nationalism. Themselves the beneficiaries of Rockefeller oil money, expressions of anti-imperialism were muted in the well-equipped laboratories of PUMC.

The intensity of PUMC did not reside in political awareness, but rather in scientific scholarship. While it is usual, and revealing, to discuss a Sino-American institution in terms of degrees of Chinese nationalism, and the self-assumed authority of the Westerner, the essence of PUMC must also be sought in a more traditional academic setting. The only way to understand PUMC completely is to explore it on its own terms: it was a medical college, *par excellence*. It was not just that the Department of Anatomy was housed in a three-story building complete with museum, cold-storage room, animal room, and histological laboratory;[29] or that the library included 50,000 German dissertations;[30] or that the faculty had Ph.D. degrees from such illustrious schools as Johns Hopkins or Harvard—there was an ineffable spirit of scientific inquiry which permeated the institution.

At a time when specialization was quite new in American medical

29. Black, "PUMC Department of Anatomy," pp. 27–29.
30. "Report of Mr. James F. Ballard, purchasing agent for the PUMC College Library, from Leipzig, Germany," May 2, 1920, *RFA*.

education, PUMC students were taught even the most fundamental subjects by experts in those fields. For example, a first-year student learned his anatomy from Davidson Black, his biochemistry from Wu Hsien, and his physiology from Robert Lim. Not only were these men internationally acclaimed medical scientists, they continued their own pioneering research in paleontology, nutrition, and nervous diseases within the laboratories of PUMC. Visiting professors further stimulated the investigative atmosphere, for each brought the latest knowledge in international medical discoveries to China.

It was this exposure to specialized information and research of high quality which set PUMC students apart from both their peers in China and many in the United States. Furthermore, there is no doubt that most of these students responded with alacrity to this intense academic environment. Year after year, the bibliography of scholarly work produced by PUMC added to its list of authors the names of its Chinese graduates.[31]

This gradual transfer of research leadership from the Western faculty to their Chinese students can be illustrated by tracing one of the most challenging of the research projects undertaken at PUMC, a search for the cause of kala-azar. The elusive nature of kala-azar makes this an especially exciting story, and provides a hint, at least, of the absorbing research at PUMC.

Kala-azar had first been identified as a distinct disease in 1903 when an Englishman, William B. Leishman, had isolated identifiable parasites in the bloodstream of an infected person from India. The causative agent, named after him and another British scientist, Charles Donovan, as *Leishmania donovani*, occurs as Leishman-Donovan bodies in the organ tissue of diseased persons of the Mediterranean, India, and China. Persons infected were characterized by severe anemia, distended bellies, enlarged spleens or livers, and if left untreated, the disease was usually fatal.[32]

The first modern statistical survey of its incidence in China was undertaken in 1911 by Samuel Cochrane, who utilized reports of missionary hospitals to diagram an endemic area primarily north of the Yangtze River. After his investigations, descriptions of the

31. A complete bibliography exists for the scientific writings from PUMC, in three volumes, titled, *Bibliography of the Publications from the Laboratories of PUMC College and Hospital, 1915–1925, 1925–1935, and 1935–1941*, printed by the PUMC Press in Peking.

32. For a general discussion of kala-azar, see Philip Manson-Bahr, *Manson's Tropical Diseases*, 16th edition (London: Balliere, Tindall and Cassell, Ltd., 1966), pp. 107–143.

disease, various methods of diagnosis, and experimental techniques were frequently reported in issues of *The China Medical Journal*, while British doctors in India, and others in the Mediterranean, attempted to discover the life-cycle of the *L. donovani*.[33]

In 1923, Charles W. Young, of PUMC's department of medicine, submitted a proposal for field studies on kala-azar to the China Medical Board. Young requested special financial support for equipment and trained personnel. He hoped to discover improved methods of diagnosis and cure—and eradication—by "discovering how it is transmitted to human beings."[34] Funds were approved by the CMB, and for a number of years PUMC conducted a special kala-azar field study.

Young had already by this time considerably advanced the knowledge of the geographical distribution of kala-azar victims. A series of maps published in October 1923 of Chihli (Hopeh), Kiangsu, Shantung, Anhwei, and Shantung provinces indicated the *hsien* which regularly reported cases to the widely scattered mission hospitals and clinics. These maps suggested an endemic area which roughly corresponded to territory encompassed by the Huai River to the south, the Shansi hills to the west, and the Great Wall to the north. Within this region the most seriously affected zone was the alluvial plain of the Yellow River.[35]

In January 1924 the PUMC field studies unit, consisting of Young, Marshall Hertig, and Liu Pao-yung, along with a number of Chinese technicians, moved into Hsuchowfu in northern Kiangsu, a locality of especially high incidence. It had been estimated that nearly 10 percent of the people in this area suffered from kala-azar. Cooperating with Presbyterian missionaries, they established contacts in a number of surrounding villages. Victims were treated and their environmental conditions studied.[36]

The team's experiments attempted to verify several hypotheses which had been postulated for the way in which kala-azar was transmitted to man. One theory was that man was the reservoir host of the parasite, but that it was transmitted from person to person by an intermediate host, probably an insect of some kind. Local village assistants helped to gather a number of insects from

33. A good summary of early work in China is in Charles W. Young, "Kala-azar in China," *CMJ* 37 (1923): 797–799.

34. "Proposal for Field Studies by the Staff of PUMC—Kala Azar, May, 1923," *SFP*.

35. Young, "Kala-azar in China," pp. 800–802.

36. Detailed discussion of their field studies is in Charles W. Young, *et al.*, "The Kala-azar Transmission Problem: Field and Laboratory Studies in China, I: Epidemiology," *American Journal of Hygiene* 9 (1929): 228–233.

afflicted homes, including flies, bedbugs, and fleas. These were then exposed to hamsters which had been infected with a laboratory case of kala-azar. After biting the kala-azar hamster, the insects were examined for *L. donovani*, and several proved susceptible.[37]

A second hypothesis was that the reservoir host was not man, but possibly a rodent, and that an intermediary host, such as an ectoparasite of the rodent, conveyed the disease to man. In this connection, rats, mice, and hamsters caught in Chinese villages were examined, but none proved to be natural carriers of Leishman-Donovan bodies.[38]

Earlier investigations in the Mediterranean had suggested the possible role of the sandfly as a transmitter of kala-azar. Young, Hertig, and Liu surmised that in China also there was a possibility that the sandfly was involved: its natural habitat corresponded to the endemic area of northern China. However, sandflies only proliferated and were abundant during the summer months. If they were indeed the intermediary hosts, the occurrence of the disease should show seasonal variation. But in the limited number of case studies available at that time, no periodic cycles were indicated.[39]

The Northern Expedition of 1926–1927 disrupted these Kiangsu kala-azar studies, and Young's untimely death in 1928 terminated his own research. But his years of effort defined the areas of future investigation. During the late 1920s and through the 1930s, research on kala-azar proceeded in many parts of China: at mission hospitals, Chinese medical colleges, and PUMC. At PUMC, professors and students of several different departments were actively engaged.

The avenue of transmission continued to be explored in a variety of ways. In 1927 James Cash, Professor of Pathology, collaborated with Hu Cheng-hsiang (C. H. Hu), a Harvard '21 M.D. serving as an assistant in the department, in the critical discovery that the skin of affected persons contained a high concentration of Leishman-Donovan bodies, speculating that bodily contact was a means of transmission.[40] Hu and Lee Chung-en (C. U. Lee), who was

37. *Ibid.*, pp. 240–242.
38. *Ibid.*, pp. 242–246; Young, *et al.*, "The Kala-azar Transmission Problem: Field and Laboratory Studies in China, II: Susceptibility of Various Rodents to Infection with *Leishmania donovani*," *American Journal of Hygiene* 10 (1929): 183–200.
39. Young, *et al.*, "Studies in China, I," pp. 234–235.
40. J. R. Cash and C. H. Hu, "Kala-azar: Demonstration of *Leishmania donovani* in the skin and subcutaneous tissue of patients; Possible Relation to the Transmission of the Disease," *Journal of the American Medical Association* 89 (November 5, 1927): 1576–1577. Cash also described his work on kala-azar in a letter to Henry Houghton, January 9, 1928, *SFP*.

an assistant in the Department of Medicine and an M.D. from Leeds University in England, invented a new apparatus for feeding sand-flies in a project which continued to explore the possibility of their involvement in the *Leishmania* life-cycle.[41]

Hu, Lee and Dorothy Huei, a graduate student, came up with the novel suggestion that transmission might take place when a person slapped a sandfly, thus discharging parasites onto the skin. They devised technical ways in which to investigate this possibility.[42] Chung Huei-lan (H. L. Chung), PUMC '29, and Timothy J. Kurotchin, Assistant Professor of Bacteriology, experimented with the susceptibility of the squirrel to kala-azar in the hopes of discovering a more useful laboratory animal, but they achieved only modest results.[43]

Other research was devoted to more effective means of diagnosis and treatment. Chester S. Keefer, Associate Professor of Medicine, Oo-kek Khaw (O. K. Khaw), assistant in parasitology, and C. S. Yang, a graduate student, conducted experiments on the best treatment for the anemia which was typical of kala-azar patients. The effectiveness of blood transfusions, iron supplements, and nutritional supervision were evaluated.[44] Chung Huei-lan noticed a certain uniformity in the sedimentation rate of the blood of kala-azar patients, suggesting a more efficient means of diagnosis than had heretofore been utilized.[45] Hu Cheng-hsiang then explored other pathological expressions of kala-azar which also aided in the recognition of the disease.[46] C. U. Lee and Chung Huei-lan summarized many of these clinical findings in an article in 1935 setting forth a description of the early manifestation of Chinese kala-azar.[47]

In the meantime, research in Europe and India continued to mention the possibility of the sandfly as insect carrier, and a new reservoir host was proposed—the dog. In the Mediterranean area,

41. C. H. Hu and C. U. Lee, "New Technique for Feeding Sandflies (Phlebotomus) for Experimental Transmission of Kala-azar," *Proceedings of the Society for Experimental Biology and Medicine* 26 (1929): 277–278.

42. C. H. Hu, Dorothy Huei, and C. Y. Lee, "Slapping as a Factor in Transmission of Kala-azar by Sandflies (Phlebotomus)," *Ibid.* pp. 280–284.

43. Chung Huei-lan and T. J. Kurotchin, "The Susceptibility of the Squirrel to Kala-azar," *NMJC* 16 (1930): 616–624.

44. Chester S. Keefer, O. K. Khaw, and C. S. Yang, "The Anemia of Kala-azar with Special Reference to Treatment," *NMJC* 15 (1929): 731–742.

45. Chung Huei-lan, "The Sedimentation Rate of the Blood of Patients with Kala-azar," *CMJ* 48 (1934): 1101–1112.

46. C. H. Hu, "The Pathological Anatomy of Human Kala-azar with Special Reference to Certain Hitherto Less Well Recognized Changes," *CMJ* 50 Special Supplement (1936): 1–12.

47. C. U. Lee and H. L. Chung, "A Clinical Study of the Early Manifestations of Chinese Kala-azar," *CMJ* 49 (1935): 1281–1300.

dogs were found to suffer from their own variety of kala-azar, but there was no proof that the canine and human varieties were the same. Complicating these findings were studies in India which seemed to rule out both the sandfly and the dog as host animals.

Drawing on European studies, Feng Lan-chou (a Yale-in-China graduate who had come to PUMC for advanced medical work), Chung Huei-lan, and Reinhard Hoeppli, Professor of Parasitology, decided to examine dogs in Peking for the natural manifestation of kala-azar. Heretofore, dogs utilized in PUMC laboratories had been considered free from kala-azar. Feng, Chung, and Hoeppli's investigations revealed 12 cases of canine leishmaniasis.[48] Further examinations of 587 normal dogs in Peking by Chung, Lee, C. W. Wang and W. T. Liu (the latter two both graduate students), revealed that eight dogs, or 1.4 percent, were natural carriers of *L. donovani*. The number was small, but it indicated the possibility of the dog as a reservoir host.[49]

In connection with their canine studies, Chung Huei-lan and Feng Lan-chou examined sandflies caught in the vicinity of a kala-azar infected dog. The species *Phlebotomus chinensis* revealed a significant percentage which carried the *Leishmania* flagellates. Since these were naturally infected sandflies caught in the household of a kala-azar dog, the conclusion that they had contracted the disease from biting the dog seemed certain.[50]

These studies seemed to verify the applicability of the European thesis: the dog was the reservoir host, and the sandfly the vector of kala-azar. It still remained to be proven that canine and human kala-azar were one and the same thing, and that the disease was transmitted to man by the sandfly. It will be recalled that Young and his colleagues had postulated a decade earlier that if the sandfly was indeed the transmitter, then a seasonal difference in the incidence of kala-azar should be observed. I. C. Yuan and Chu Fu-t'ang (both PUMC '27 graduates) and C. U. Lee compiled a statistical record of all the kala-azar cases treated at PUMC of children under one year of age. These cases would have only been

48. Feng Lan-chou, Chung Huei-lan, and Reinhard Hoeppli, "Canine Leishmaniasis with Skin Lesions Observed in Peiping," *CMJ* 55 (1939): 371–382.

49. Chung Huei-lan, C. W. Wang, C. U. Lee, and W. T. Liu, "A Report on the Examination of 587 Normal Dogs in Peiping for *Leishmania* Infection," *CMJ* 56 (1939): 354–359.

50. Chung Huei-lan and Feng Lan-chou, "Natural Infection of *Phlebotomus chinensis* in Peiping with *Leishmania* Flagellates," *CMJ* 56 (1939): 47–51; Chung and Feng, "The Development of *Leishmania* in Chinese Sandflies Fed on Dogs with Canine Leishmaniasis," *Ibid.* pp. 35–46.

exposed to kala-azar for one season. From studying the case histories, and in some cases interviewing the parents, it was extrapolated that all had contracted kala-azar from May to September, the months when sandflies were abundant.[51] A year later Chung Huei-lan published an article on the relationships between canine and human kala-azar which offered nearly conclusive scientific proof that the disease of the dog was identical to that of humans.[52] Thus, by 1940 the chain of transmission of *L. donovani* in China could be drawn with a degree of surety: dog to sandfly to human. The eradication of the disease was only dependent upon the extermination of the kala-azar dog and the *Phlebotomus* sandfly.

PUMC's kala-azar research shows a close collaboration between Westerner and Chinese, and between professor and student. It perhaps illustrates Sino-American cooperation at its finest. By the late 1930s, the primary investigators were Chinese, many of them PUMC graduates, and most of whom had become full-fledged faculty members. These men became quite prominent in their respective fields. Hu Cheng-hsiang and I. C. Yuan became heads of PUMC's departments of pathology and public health, respectively. In 1947, C. U. Lee became Director of PUMC. Chung Huei-lan in medicine, Chu Fu-t'ang in pediatrics, and Feng Lan-chou in malariology all became outstanding medical scientists in the People's Republic of China.

Not all research at PUMC probed so deeply into the public health conditions of modern China as the studies on kala-azar, but certainly much of it did. Thus, while a profile of the PUMC student includes the fact that he spoke in English, wrote his scientific treatises in English, and was constantly exposed to the Americanisms of the institution, it also includes his participation in the search for answers to the major medical problems of China.

The goal of PUMC from the outset had been to train the medical leaders of modern China. The standards and curriculum were designed to produce more than competent physicians: to train professors, scientists, and public health administrators. An analysis of the careers of the first ten graduating classes (1924–1933) demonstrates the impact of PUMC students upon Republican China. Com-

51. I. C. Yuan, F. T. Chu, and C. U. Lee, "The Seasonal Incidence of Kala-azar in Infants and Its Significance in Relation to the Transmission Problem of the Disease," *CMJ* 56 (1939): 241–261.

52. Chung Huei-lan, "On the Relationship between Canine and Human Kala-azar in Peiping, and the Identity of *Leishmania canis* and *Leishmania donovani*," *CMJ* 57 (1940): 501–518. See also Hoeppli's summarizing article, "The Epidemiology of Kala-azar in China," *CMJ* 57 (1940): 364–372.

plete occupational data for these graduates from the time of their matriculation up to 1937 appears in Appendix A. Obviously those graduating in 1924 and 1925 had had more than ten years in which to establish themselves, whereas the class of 1933 had had only four. Nonetheless, the direction of their careers can also be delineated.

The medical specialities of these alumni exhibits a predictable diversity, and are illustrated in Table 5. The appeal of the public health department is noted by its being second largest in the number of graduates. It is perhaps surprising that surgery, then the most glamorous of all fields in the United States, rates only fourth—behind medicine, public health, and obstetrics.

Of more interest, perhaps, than the medical specialties of these men and women, is the fact that 55 percent studied abroad before 1937 following their graduation from PUMC (see Table 6). The ratio is higher, 71 percent for the graduates prior to 1930, indicating that a longer time span under peacetime conditions would probably have raised the entire percentage. For the most part, these graduates studied in the United States at Johns Hopkins, Harvard, and the Rockefeller Institute on grants from the China Medical Board. Most of these students received advanced degrees from American institutions. The China Medical Board followed strict regulations as to

TABLE 5
Medical Specialties of PUMC Graduates (1924–1933)

Medicine	21
Public Health	16
Obstetrics & Gynecology	12
Surgery	11
General Practice	10
Pediatrics	8
Maternity & Child Welfare	7
Ophthalmology	6
Radiology	4
Pharmacology	3
Tuberculosis	3
Bacteriology	3
Dermatology & Syphilology	3
Otolaryngology	2
Pathology	2
Anatomy	1
Physiology	1
Neurology & Psychiatry	1
Urology	1
Medical Administration	1
TOTAL	116

NOTE: Derived from the *PUMC Annual Announcement*, 1924–1933.

TABLE 6
PUMC Graduates (1924–1933)
Studying Abroad Before 1937

Class	Students Graduating	Students Studying Abroad
1924	3	3
1925	5	4
1926	8	5
1927	10	6
1928	14	11
1929	16	11
1930	8	4
1931	14	8
1932	21	8
1933	17	4
TOTAL	116	64

NOTE: Data derived from the *PUMC Annual Announcement*, 1937–1938.

the tenure of these fellowship grants, designed as one professor in China remembered, to "Hold Him Here."[53] Grants were not issued until the applicant indicated precisely where he would be employed upon *returning* to China. Only rarely were they renewed for a longer stay in the United States. As a result of these precautions, as well as the demand for these graduates within China, *every* graduate from 1924 to 1933 had returned to China by 1937, or shortly thereafter. Not only did they have specific aims in China, these students were usually in their late twenties or early thirties when they first went abroad. These conditions seem to fit Y. C. Wang's conclusion regarding students who studied abroad in general:

> If the Chinese experience is of any general significance, it would seem that foreign study has a maximum chance of success only if the students are mature in age, have definite objectives in mind, and limit their sojourn to fairly short periods.[54]

Nonetheless, the extensive and prolonged education of PUMC graduates might have resulted in an over-trained, over-specialized elite without a function in the society to which they returned. These medical scientists were fortunate in that they matriculated during the golden age of the Republican period: medical colleges in China were rapidly expanding; a Central Field Health Station, the coordinating body for all medical education and research, was established

53. Interview with Dr. Snapper, October 14, 1971.
54. Wang, *Chinese Intellectuals and the West*, p. xiii.

in Nanking; and provincial health administrations were being founded throughout China. That the national interest in public health was due in large part to two PUMC professors, John Grant and J. Heng Liu, will be explored subsequently. Suffice it to note here that this general situation facilitated ready employment for PUMC graduates.

The first six graduating classes, 1924–1929, demonstrate especially well the pattern of leadership which accrued to the doctors from PUMC. An examination of their positions in 1937 (see Appendix A) supports the Rockefeller Foundation contention that it trained medical leaders for China. Three different categories have been selected to illustrate elite positions within the field of medicine.

1. *Superintendents or directors of hospitals, directors of provincial health administrations, and commissioners of municipal health administrations.* Ten of the 56 graduates fall into this category of medical administrators, and they represent a variety of institutions. For example, superintendents of hospitals included Huang K'e-kang, '28, Superintendent of Kiangsi Provincial Hospital in Nanchang, and Chia K'uei, '26, Superintendent of Hopeh's Provincial Medical College Hospital in Paoting, an experimental college started during the thirties. Fang I-chi, '27, was Commissioner of Health for Kiangsi Province, and Yao Hsun-yuan, '25, was Yunnan's Provincial Health Director. Li T'ing-an, '26, was Commissioner of Public Health for Greater Shanghai, and Ch'en Chih-ch'ien, '29, was Director of Public Health for the Mass Education Movement at Ting Hsien.

2. *Departmental heads at hospitals, colleges, or national health administration agencies.* Eleven graduates fall into this category, and a few examples will indicate the nature of their positions. Three were directly associated with the Central Field Health Station at Nanking: Lee Shih-wei, '26, was head of the Department of Obstetrics and Gynecology; Ch'en Heng-i, '28, head of the Department of Surgery; and Jung Tu-shan, '29, Chief Roentgenologist. Hsiang-Ya Medical College in Changsha had two PUMC graduates as departmental chairmen: Yang Chi-shih, '26, was head of the Department of Medicine, and his wife, Li Jui-lin, '29, head of the Department of Obstetrics and Gynecology. Another woman graduate, Shen Chi-ying, '27 (wife of Wu Ch'ao-jen, '28), was Chairman of Peking's Committee on Maternal Health and Director of the City Birth Control Clinic.

3. *Professors at medical colleges.* This third category contains the largest number of these graduates—21. Significantly, 14 remained

at PUMC in positions ranging from assistant to associate professor. The other institutions represented were Hsiang-Ya Medical College; Kwong Wah Medical School, Canton; Lingnan University; Army Medical College, Nanking; National Medical College of Shanghai; Henry Lester Institute of Medical Research, Shanghai; Central University Medical School, Nanking.

Thus, by 1937, 42 of the 56 early graduates were in leadership positions in China. Of the remaining 14, seven were in private practice, two on the staffs of hospitals, four on the staffs of public health organizations, and one not practicing.

Predictably enough, the 60 graduates of the years 1930–1933 had gained less prominence by 1937. But there were two hospital superintendents and three heads of departments at medical colleges. However, that is about the extent of visible administrative leadership. It is perhaps more meaningful to divide these later graduates into types of institutions which employed them: hospitals, public health departments, and colleges. Eleven graduates served on the staffs of various hospitals, ten were employed in the national public health administration, and 37 were associated with medical colleges. Only one was engaged in private practice, and one was not practicing at all.

The China Medical Board was proud of PUMC's public record, especially the high percentage occupied in the teaching profession and in the public health field. It is interesting to compare the occupations of PUMC's graduates with those of another medical school in China, Cheeloo School of Medicine of the Shantung Christian University in Tsinan (see Table 7). A union missionary medical college, teaching in Chinese, Cheeloo was perhaps the best of the missionary medical colleges. Graduating 313 students between

TABLE 7

Graduates of Cheeloo and PUMC: Comparative Occupations

	Private Practice	Hospitals	Public Health	Teaching	Miscellaneous
*Cheeloo**	38%	37%	11%	9%	5%
*PUMC***	6%	21%	20%	51%	2%

*Cheeloo Medical College graduated 313 students between 1915–1934. This analysis is based on their occupations in 1935. Randolph T. Shields, "Distribution of Cheeloo Medical Graduates, January, 1935," p. 1, Archives of the Presbyterian Church in the U.S., Montreat, North Carolina.
**PUMC graduated 116 students between 1924–1933. This analysis is based on their occupations in 1937. *PUMC Annual Announcement*, 1937.

1915 and 1934, the positions of these physicians in 1935 forms a definite contrast with that of the richer, better equipped, and more selective PUMC.

The most striking difference in this comparison between PUMC and Cheeloo alumni is in the field of teaching. Only 9 percent of Cheeloo's graduates became teachers, as compared with 51 percent of PUMC's graduates. This is perhaps the clearest indication of the degree to which PUMC students became the acknowledged leaders in the medical field. Additionally, only 6 percent of PUMC's graduates were in private practice, as compared with 38 percent of Cheeloo's. In other words, PUMC staffed the medical institutions—hospitals, colleges, and public health administration, while others had to provide the day-to-day dispensing of medical service.

Although the careers of PUMC students are markedly different from those of Cheeloo, and probably from most of the other medical schools in China, their geographical distribution is quite similar. In 1935, two professors at the National Medical College in Shanghai analyzed the locations of 5,390 physicians, 87 percent of whom were Chinese, 13 percent Western. Even for a country in which coastal, urban areas had provided the primary contact with Western ideas, the results were surprising. Nearly 50 percent of all modern physicians were located in two provinces: 37.3 percent in Kiangsu and 11.2 percent in Kwangtung. In more graphic human terms, Kiangsu provided one physician for every 16,000 people; for the rest of China there was only one modern physician per 81,000 people. Nor was the maldistribution confined to two eastern provinces, since four cities—Shanghai, Nanking, Peking, and Mukden—contained a highly disproportionate share of the medical doctors.[55]

The north China location of PUMC shifted the largest congregation of PUMC graduates to the province of Hopeh (see Map 1), which ranked third in the Shanghai professors' tabulation. Thirty-seven percent of the 116 alumni from 1924–1933 were in this single province, and 34 percent of the total (39 doctors) were in Peking itself. But the second largest concentration of PUMC graduates predictably was in Kiangsu, with 31 percent, and most of these were in Nanking and Shanghai. In fact, 73 of the 116 (63 percent) were located in these three cities—Peking, Nanking, and Shanghai.

The exceptionally dense concentration in Peking requires some discussion because all but three of these 39 alumni were still at PUMC. Time had dispersed many of the 1924–1929 graduates away

55. Chu Hsi-ju and Daniel G. Lai, "Distribution of Modern Trained Physicians in China," *CMJ* 49 (1935): 542–552.

MAP I. *Location of PUMC Graduates (1924–1933) in 1937*

China and Manchuria	100
South East Asia	2
Abroad	14
Total	116

SOURCE: *PUMC Annual Announcement,* 1937–1938

from the medical college. By 1937, only 12, or approximately 21 percent, remained at their alma mater. More than one third of the 1930–1933 graduates, however, were still in residence at PUMC by 1937. Even though from four to seven years had elapsed since their graduation, 23 students remained at their mother institution in capacities ranging from resident to instructor—none had achieved actual faculty rank during those years. Since nine of the students abroad in 1937 were on leave from PUMC, inclusion of them in this list of PUMC locations would further raise the number. It was this phenomenon of the umbilical ties of PUMC which led to frequent charges that its graduates were incapable of adaptation to Chinese institutions of lower grades.

Western-oriented, highly specialized, very influential, and residing primarily in Peking, Nanking, or Shanghai—this is the overall profile of the PUMC graduates of 1924–1933 during the Nanking era. It has often been observed that those who were the intellectual leaders between the decline of Confucianism and the advent of Communism were an apolitical elite, embracing modernity, but contributing little to national integration. The urban and institutional orientation of scholarly PUMC graduates does indeed suggest a wide gulf between themselves and the common people.

This general characterization of PUMC's graduates leads us back to the question of whether or not Peking Union Medical College, a hybrid Sino-American institution, really ever took root in China. One must answer both yes and no. Administratively the College remained firmly under the control of the China Medical Board *and* the Rockefeller Foundation. Until administrative authority was transferred from New York to Peking, or until New York and Peking at the very least shared equally in policy making, the growth of Chinese leadership was stunted. But the increasing Sinification of the faculty, some curriculum modifications, and the leadership positions assumed by PUMC graduates *in China* do indicate that in other ways the institution was beginning to send shoots into Chinese soil. Judging by the urban location of most PUMC graduates, however, many of these roots appear to have remained quite shallow.

Still, this generalized profile of PUMC alumni does not tell the whole story. The positions held in 1937 are revealing, but indicate little of the specific nature of their contributions to modern medicine in China. Most were clearly engaged in preserving the PUMC tradition of research and teaching, in providing leadership in urban medical colleges and public health institutions. Except in the Epilogue, the remaining chapters in this study do not further describe this majority group. Now the focus narrows to a small group of

PUMC activists who were directly involved in adapting Western medicine to China. The remaining chapters trace some of their careers, some of their programs. The primary focus is on PUMC graduates and associates who sought *"how* to adapt to the soil and the water." It should begin with John B. Grant, perhaps their most remarkable professor.

SIX John Grant, Medical Bolshevik

*It is far more important to support Chinese efforts that are
60% efficient than western ones that are 100%.*

John Grant, "Diary of Shansi Trip," 1922

J OHN GRANT differed in many ways from his colleagues among the Peking-bound PUMC entourage aboard the *Empress of Asia* in 1921. For one thing, Grant was returning to the
land of his birth, China. For another, his temperament and view-
points were soon to earn him the appellative "medical bolshevik,"
hardly a typical nickname for one of the staff of the prudent Rockefeller Foundation.[1] More importantly, he had the unusual intellectual flexibility necessary for adapting medical practice and peda-
gogy to the overwhelming needs of China.

Grant's adult sojourn in China was to last for seventeen years,
1921–1938, fourteen of which he spent as Professor of Public Health
at PUMC and three as Co-director of the Rockefeller Foundation's
progressive rural China program. A leading Chinese economist
years later attributed any accomplishments in social medicine during the Republican period to the leadership of this same John Grant,
concluding that he was the "spirit of public health" for modern
China.[2]

1. "Grant Reminiscences," p. 231. Dr. Saul Benison conducted this Columbia University Oral History Project. His interviews were completed shortly before Grant's
death in 1962.
2. Interview with Franklin Ho, formerly Director of the Nankai Institute of Economics, July 22, 1970, New York City.

Grant was born in 1890 to Canadian missionaries in the treaty port of Ningpo. The small hospital which his father directed provided childhood memories of the problems of modern medicine in traditional China. The missionary son recalled years later that in those days of the early twentieth century poorer classes more frequently turned to the Western charity hospital than their gentry neighbors. He also long remembered the hauteur of Western racism which prevailed in some missionary circles. For example, contacts with Chinese were banned at the union missionary school he attended: "Well, in Cheefoo, if we were found talking to an outside Chinese, we were caned."[3] As an adult, and with little affectation, Grant sought to destroy this concept of separateness. Scarcely six months after his PUMC appointment, he wrote of his desire to establish an international club: "One of the chief drawbacks to general comity with the Chinese is the lack of a common meeting place."[4] Grant personally solved this problem by frequenting Peking restaurants or bars with his ever-expanding circle of Chinese friends.

Grant returned to Canada to attend Acadia College in Nova Scotia, but he travelled back to Ningpo for a year upon graduation. There he occupied himself by writing articles on the history of Ningpo for a foreign weekly newspaper. Then Grant proceeded to medical school at the University of Michigan from which he received his M.D. in 1917. When he joined the International Health Board (IHB) of the Rockefeller Foundation that same year, Grant fully expected to be sent immediately to China. Instead he found himself assisting in the RF county health program in Pitt County, North Carolina for nine months. Grant's philosophy of social medicine, his demand for the integration of preventive and curative services, and his emphasis upon the local community as the vehicle for medical care, all derived in important part from this brief North Carolina interlude.

The public health and preventive medicine movement had arrived late on the scene in the development of modern medical organizations in America.[5] This was in part due to the fact that

3. "Grant Reminiscences," p. 13.
4. Grant to Victor Heiser, January 7, 1922, *CMBC*, Box 78. All subsequent material cited in this chapter also comes from Box 78.
5. For background on public health, see: George Rosen, "The Evolution of Social Medicine," in Howard E. Freeman, *et al.*, ed., *Handbook of Medical Sociology* (Englewood Cliffs, N.J.: Prentice-Hall, 1963), pp. 17–61. George Rosen, "Public Health," *International Encyclopedia of the Social Sciences*, 13 : 164–170; René Sand, *The Advance to Social Medicine* (London: Staples Press, 1952); and Richard Shryock, *The Development of Modern Medicine* (New York: Alfred A. Knopf, 1947).

until the late nineteenth century, the science of preventive medicine hardly existed. The belief that disease could be prevented and communicable disease contained had always been latent, and in many cultures social and culinary taboos for millenia had aimed at keeping the individual well. But widespread and effective scientific means of preventing and controlling epidemics were not fully possible until the late nineteenth century. Not until scientists such as Louis Pasteur and Robert Koch identified the microorganisms responsible for specific diseases did control of contagious diseases become possible. As the related sciences of bacteriology and immunology developed in the late nineteenth century, so too did international public health programs.

By the twentieth century, public health organizations in many European countries were able to cooperate closely with physicians and hospitals engaged in traditional individual curative medicine. But in the United States, where individual enterprise remained the ideal, public health organizations were considered as potential threats to the private practice of American physicians. Encountering an adamant lobby in the American Medical Association from an early date, the scope of public health organizations was narrowly drawn. State, county, and municipal public health personnel could only be concerned with preventive measures; they were not allowed to encroach on the practice of private physicians. For example, if public health workers, while conducting eye examinations of school children, discovered bad eyesight or trachoma, there were no complementary public health physicians to treat these disorders. The cure or treatment was dependent on the child visiting a private physician. In impoverished areas this crucial follow-up often did not occur.

As a member of the Rockefeller Foundation's county health project in North Carolina, Grant was involved in progressive attempts to involve the state government in supporting community health agencies.[6] But in the rural South these efforts seemed especially thwarted by the separation of preventive and curative medicine. Grant came away determined to avoid this unnecessarily fragmented medical system.

While Grant had been in medical school and later in North Carolina, the International Health Board had been debating sponsoring public health activities in China. The IHB was the major component of the Rockefeller Foundation during its early years, and under the leadership of Wickliffe Rose it had successfully con-

6. "Grant Reminiscences," pp. 45–49.

ducted the famed hookworm campaign in the American South. At this time it was also undertaking malaria and yellow fever control projects, and extending its public health surveys to Europe and Latin America. Underlying these efforts was the desire to launch long-term indigenous public health agencies which would be financially sustained and professionally staffed by local government agencies. Given Wickliffe Rose's premise that public health activities were useless unless native political forces were able to provide continuing leadership, the prognosis for China in the early twentieth century was pessimistic.

But in 1916 the International Health Board did appoint Dr. Victor Heiser, a former U.S. public health officer in the Philippines, as their representative in the Far East. Heiser travelled throughout southeast Asia, the Philippines, Japan, and China, surveying existing sanitation facilities and recommending various improvements. In the fall of 1916 he visited China, journeying through the coastal cities of Canton and Shanghai, as well as to the hinterland population centers of Hankow and Changsha. Heiser was particularly worried about the lack of city sanitation. But since the Rockefeller Foundation was concurrently undertaking its international study of hookworm, his first proposal was to control and treat hookworm in the P'inghsiang mines of Hunan.[7]

Accordingly, in late 1917 Grant was named associate director of the hookworm survey in China. Preliminary surveys had indicated that 85 percent of the miners working in wet underground conditions at the P'inghsiang mines were infected by hookworm. The IHB program was a pilot demonstration, designed to illustrate to the mining authorities effective sanitary means of controlling hookworm. It was during this time that Grant first met T. V. Soong, then general secretary of the Han-yeh-p'ing industrial complex which included the Hunan mines, and later to become a brother-in-law of Chiang Kai-shek.[8]

The project appears to have lasted just over a year. Its somewhat abortive conclusion led Grant to an analysis of the unusual frustrations of public health work in China. Asserting that the P'inghsiang effort had accomplished little, his report stated that the customary policy of the International Health Board was too narrow and would be ineffective in China. It had been impossible to work with a Chi-

7. Victor Heiser, "Notes of 1916 Trip," vol. 2, September 2–October 26, 1916, pp. 624–788. For Heiser's autobiography see his *An American Doctor's Odyssey* (New York: Norton, 1936).

8. Rockefeller Foundation, *Annual Report, 1917*, pp. 36, 154–156; *Annual Report, 1918*, pp. 77, 175; "Grant Reminiscences," p. 62.

nese business firm in planning public health measures. Hence there must be a new attack: intensive public health education throughout China, training of business executives in the fundamental importance of public health awareness, establishing a model sanitation center, and endeavoring to press for national public health legislation.[9] Grant had just written his return ticket to China.

After these two years of field work in North Carolina and China, Grant enrolled in 1920 at the newly-established Johns Hopkins School of Public Health to study under Drs. William Welch and Sir Arthur Newsholme. The latter had been instrumental in the public health movement which had just had a great success in the creation of Great Britain's Ministry of Health in 1919. His emphasis on state responsibility for medical care was to influence Grant profoundly.[10]

While Grant was at Johns Hopkins, the China Medical Board decided to appoint a professor of public health at PUMC who would also be a member of the IHB. It was undoubtedly his China background as well as his fluency in Chinese which prompted an inquiry from George Vincent to Welch requesting an evaluation of John Grant. Dr. Welch's reply is illuminating: "He has ability, enthusiasm, industry, and an interesting and attractive personality and character. . . . I am inclined to believe that he will be stronger on the administrative side than on the investigative." Welch also revealed that Grant's revered professor, Sir Arthur Newsholme, observed that he was "a little too cock-sure in his judgments of some sanitary problems."[11]

In 1921 then, this brash young man received the appointment in public health at PUMC. He became concurrently the International Health Board's representative to China. Less than a year after he had arrived in Peking, Grant's letters and activities revealed the bold strokes with which he was to seek to raise a country's public health consciousness. By the end of 1922, the main themes of his China career had appeared in embryonic form: educating Chinese political leaders, training Chinese public health specialists, designing an urban demonstration health center, and always relying on Chinese instead of Western leadership.

During his first year in China, Grant held numerous discussions with authorities in Peking, Nanking, Shanghai, and Shansi province about the problems of health and sanitation. In Shansi, he was

9. "The Most Efficient Manner in Which the International Health Board May Accomplish Its Fundamental Purpose in China," (n.d.), WWP.

10. "Grant Reminiscences," p. 100.

11. Welch to George Vincent, December 22, 1920, WWP.

entertained by the progressive war-lord Yen Hsi-shan. In Peking, his meetings included several sessions with the Minister of Education, T'ang Erh-ho.[12] Grant came away from these sessions convinced of the importance of convincing political leaders about the state's public health responsibilities. One way he attempted this was to encourage W. W. Yen, the Minister of Foreign Affairs, and Alfred Sao-ke Sze, the Chinese Minister to Washington (both future PUMC Trustees), to visit Johns Hopkins School of Public Health. Grant had become convinced that the Ministry of Foreign Affairs, and its representatives, was a vital link to national public health awareness.[13]

The Foreign Affairs Ministry might appear to be a circuitous route indeed to achieving a national focus on public health, but Grant had perceptively detected an important link between China's concern for national sovereignty and effective public health controls. The issue of extraterritoriality dominated the horizon of Chinese political consciousness. Grant seized upon the notion that Chinese control over quarantine, at that time being administered by the treaty-port powers, would be a first step in convincing the imperialist nations that Chinese were qualified to administer not only port health facilities, but internal legal jurisprudence as well. Western fear of tropical diseases and unsanitary conditions in Asia had been an important psychological reason for retaining control over exports and imports from China. Grant recognized that if the Chinese government and medical profession decided to train qualified quarantine inspectors and public health officials for its ports, one justification for the perpetuation of extraterritoriality would have been removed.[14]

Chinese leaders did begin to lobby for control of quarantine regulations, and Grant continued to expand his contacts with Chinese officialdom. He also focused on the need for well-trained Chinese public health experts. In his dealings with the few Chinese working in public health, Grant had been repeatedly struck by their lack of training and perspective. Describing their limited horizons

12. Grant, "November 10, 1922," *CMBC*.

13. Grant to Welch, March 14, 1922, *WWP*.

14. *Ibid.* An interesting footnote to Chinese-American relations during the Republican period is that the U.S. *discouraged* and actively *opposed* Chinese management of quarantine service. With the assistance of the League of Nations, a Quarantine Service was established in 1928, and by 1930, most European nations had accepted the Chinese authority. As late as 1935, United States vessels refused to accept the authority of the Chinese quarantine officers. For example, see M. M. Hamilton to Stanley Hornbeck, "Memorandum," March 10, 1930, File 893.12/2 League Survey, Record Group 29, *NA*; Nelson Johnson to Secretary of State, Cordell Hull, Dispatch #237, June 8, 1934, File 893.12/85, Record Group 59, *NA*.

by a Chinese proverb, "Sitting in a well and attempting to see the whole heavens," Grant encouraged the most active to study abroad for a year or two.[15] He also labored on their behalf for fellowship funds from the Rockefeller Foundation. This ultimately led to the Foundation providing over 75 U.S. fellowships in public health for Chinese students between 1922 and 1949.[16]

Grant was well enough aware of the compelling medical needs of China to see overseas training as only a temporary and transitional measure. In February of 1922, he completed a health survey of Peking in which he concluded that public health measures were "almost completely absent." Grant listed three causes of death as most easily preventable: infant mortality, smallpox, and gastrointestinal diseases.[17] Two months earlier, in a letter to S. H. Chuan, Director of the Army Medical Program, Grant had outlined an urban demonstration unit which would provide training for the local police and board of health in communicable disease control, food inspection, pre- and postnatal care, sewage disposal, and so on.[18] Several years later this design would come to fruition as Peking's First Urban Health Demonstration Station.

In these early proposals and letters, Grant repeatedly endeavored to pass the initiative to a Chinese colleague. For example, in a late 1921 letter to S. M. Wu (Hu Hsuan-ming), he wrote: "Do you know the new Minister of Education? . . . I have been wondering of the feasibility of putting a public health plank in his platform. I had already set about doing this personally but it seems to me that such an initiative would be one that could very well be handled through you and your organization."[19] The outlines of his own philosophy as a "Western advisor" were becoming clear: "The foreigner in China is everlastingly thinking in terms of the foreigners as being the only worth-while thing in China and the foreigner in China has done practically nothing in being able to get the Chinese to adopt his methods." Grant concluded that it was far more

15. Grant to C. T. Wang, November 9, 1922, *CMBC*.
16. "The Rockefeller Foundation Fellowship History File: Fellows from People's Republic of China." This record was provided to me courtesy of Dr. Virgil Scott of The Rockefeller Foundation.
17. John Grant, "Report of a General Health Survey of Peking, China," February, 1922, Rockefeller Foundation Archives, China Series 601, IHB Stacks, Box 55. Hereinafter citations from the Foundation Archives China Series will read *FA* (601/IHB/55). The middle category is the program designation; if it is omitted, the material comes from the general 601 series.
18. Grant to S. H. Chuan, December 9, 1921, *CMBC*.
19. Grant to S. M. Woo (Wu), December 27, 1921, *CMBC*.

important to support Chinese efforts that are "60% efficient than Western ones that are 100%."[20]

Grant may have been cautious about undertaking a project when he could find Chinese to do it instead, but he was quite bold in committing the Foundation to schemes that had not been approved. After his trip to Shansi, for example, he wrote to the war-lord Yen Hsi-shan: "I feel sure that our New York office would be very glad to enter into some kind of agreement with your government."[21] It should be kept in mind that Yen's was only one of many war-lord regimes of the period. This kind of activity alarmed New York. George Vincent wrote Welch: "We are a little disturbed at the eagerness with which Doctor Grant is undertaking his duties . . . and is going ahead more rapidly than we are prepared to follow."[22] This concern prompted a letter from Wickliffe Rose to Grant which urged a more evolutionary approach: "Nothing urgent in this field but hope you may come to be recognized authority. We have not considered it probable that China will be prepared to undertake public health activity at this time. Development may be pretty slow."[23]

The evolution of public health programs in twentieth century China had indeed been slow. But, given the slowly emerging modern consciousness, the very existence of a few programs is notable. Yuan Shih-k'ai, as Viceroy of Chihli (Hopeh Province), had set up a sanitary division in the police department of the city of Tientsin, and some other municipalities followed suit. This resulted in the establishment of a Sanitary Administration under the Ch'ing administration in 1905. The functions given to this office included inoculations, quarantine, and supervision and control of physicians, but for the most part it was inactive. The lack of government commitment and higher priorities assigned to other problems were two reasons, but the absence of qualified individuals was another.[24]

20. Grant, "Diary of Shansi Trip," February 16–22, 1922, *FA* (601/IHB/55), pp. 18–19.

21. Grant to Yen Hsi-shan, February 19, in *Ibid.*, p. 27.

22. Vincent to Welch, April 28, 1922, *WWP*.

23. Rose to Grant, May 22, 1922. Notes from this letter are contained in "Notes from JBG's Personal File, China, Work While at PUMC," prepared from the files of the Rockefeller Foundation for Saul Benison. This document contains summaries, and apparently a number of direct quotations from 58 letters to, from, or concerning Grant from 1922 to 1935. When letters from this document are cited, *JBG's File* will be noted. The document is in the possession of Mrs. J. B. Grant, Washington, D.C.

24. A good account of early Chinese public health activities is in The Association for the Advancement of Public Health in China, *Memorandum on the Need of a*

The earliest modernized public health agency was the North Manchurian Plague Prevention Service, established under the direction of Wu Lien-teh in 1911, when a severe outbreak of plague threatened the entire Asian continent.[25] In 1919, the Central Epidemic Prevention Bureau (*Chung-yang fang-i chü*) was established by Ch'ien Neng-hsun, Minister of Interior, on the grounds of the Temple of Heaven in Peking. This bureau was primarily responsible for the manufacture and distribution of serum and vaccines, and it did enjoy a steady income throughout the turbulent warlord era of the twenties.[26]

These governmental organizations were primarily concerned with preventing epidemics; the day-to-day sanitation measures necessary for eradicating many of China's communicable diseases were beyond their reach. Following the Revolution of 1911, some missionary and Chinese doctors began to recognize that preventive medicine would be far more beneficial to China than individual curative care. The China Medical Missionary Association (CMMA) and the Chinese National Medical Association (NMA) both set up committees to organize public health activities. In 1918 they sponsored a Joint Committee on Public Health. Among the most prominent early public health propagandists were W. W. Peter and S. M. Wu.

The health campaigns sponsored during those early days were ingenious displays of visual medical persuasion. A city stricken with cholera or typhoid would be inundated with large parades of poster-waving, role-enacting participants. Floats showing the correct and incorrect ways to cook and handle fresh foods, coupled with ominous coffins, wound up and down the narrow streets. Health themes conveyed by pamphlets, brochures, and lantern-slide displays attracted curious crowds. The message was forceful, but as Grant remembered, these exhibitions lacked follow-up:

> I mean, when they put on a publicity campaign it was memorable. Goodness, parades, meetings, I don't know what all. But after the short interval that they could remain there, two or three weeks and they departed,

Public Health Organization in China, Presented to the British Boxer Indemnity Commission (Peking: n.p., 1926).

25. Carl Nathan, *Plague Prevention and Politics in Manchuria, 1910–1931* (Cambridge, Mass.: East Asian Research Center, 1967).

26. National Epidemic Prevention Bureau, *A Report, Being a Review of Its Activities from Its Foundation in March 1919 to June 1934* (Peiping: n.p., 1934). After 1925, the Central Epidemic Prevention Bureau was known as the National Epidemic Prevention Bureau.

they left nothing permanent behind. By and large, the whole thing would collapse.[27]

There were some activities during the early twenties of more enduring quality. In 1920, Canton set up a municipal health department with the authority to supervise public markets and register physicians, as well as having the traditional responsibility for street cleaning and night-soil collection. Although the powers exercised were more supervisory than regulatory, the notion of a modernized municipal public health department was at least established.[28] In addition to general programs, a few child health projects were initiated, such as the Better Babies Campaign in Hangchow.

These plans lacked coordination and were but isolated efforts during a decade of political turmoil and general uncertainty. Summarizing the state of public health in 1923, Grant wrote that there is "little markedly encouraging," although he commended the increased interest by missionary medical personnel in public hygiene. Grant agreed with his New York supervisors, Rose and Vincent, that these private efforts would be ultimately ineffective unless the government cooperated—"For public health, like education, is dependent upon government."[29] But, in contrast to them, he felt that private endeavors in China could train leaders and stimulate a national awareness that would eventually result in government action.

In the training of public health specialists, Grant felt that PUMC was "confronted with an opportunity that is unique in medical history." Unfettered by tradition, and "possessing a faculty in which there is the minimum of the conservatism of an old school," Grant was convinced that curative and preventive medicine could be combined at PUMC and a community approach to health care taught.[30] He had slowly been introducing preventive medicine into the PUMC curriculum, first with a course in educational hygiene, and second by encouraging C. E. Lim, Professor of Bacteriology, to include public health bacteriology in his required courses. Grant's concern with the inclusion of preventive medicine in the medical curriculum was based on a keen awareness of the environmental condi-

27. "Grant Reminiscences," pp. 131–132.

28. Wong and Wu, *Chinese Medicine*, p. 493; Li T'ing-an, "A Public Health Report on Canton, China," *NMJC* 11 (1925): 324–375. Li T'ing-an, PUMC '26, was a native of Canton, and this paper appears to have been written as part of his public health course under Grant.

29. Grant, "Public Health," *The China Yearbook*, 1923, p. 385.

30. Grant, "A Proposal for a Department of Hygiene for Peking Union Medical College," 1923, *PUMC Papers*.

tions of most of China: "It was felt . . . that a PUMC graduate should have enough background so that he could be a community leader to advise his own community as to what initial steps they should take to protect their health in an organized manner."[31]

In spite of his far-flung activities, by 1924 Grant was frustrated with these various piecemeal projects. Henry Houghton described the public health professor's discontent: "No one is going to be satisfied with confining preventive medicine to a few deadly lectures; Grant is becoming fed up."[32] In order to provide cohesiveness to his various public health efforts, Grant began to insist that PUMC support an urban health demonstration center. He explained to his fellow professors that curative medicine diagnosed individual ills, but "public health regards the community as its unit." He later justified his proposal:

> A good sample community of from 40,000–60,000 population is to a department of public health . . . what a 250-bed hospital . . . are to the departments of medicine, surgery and obstetrics. The Department of Hygiene of the Peking Union Medical College is acquiring a teaching community comparable to its teaching hospital.[33]

Designed as a practical place for student training, Grant's center was also intended as a viable municipal demonstration of health care.

Although he initially met opposition from both PUMC and the International Health Board, Grant's Health Demonstration Station opened in 1925.[34] Its organization revealed the results of Grant's multifarious activities. The Station was established by order of the Superintendent of Municipal Police, Chu She, for the purpose of "effecting a demonstration of modern health procedures adapted to local conditions."[35] The city government transferred authority for sanitation and hygiene in Peking's second left inner city ward to the Health Station and provided it with a former temple as head-

31. "Grant Reminiscences," p. 149.

32. Houghton to Greene, February 24, 1924, RGP.

33. Grant, "Permeation of the Curriculum with a Preventive Viewpoint," in Conrad Seipp, ed., Health Care for the Community: Selected Papers of Dr. John B. Grant (Baltimore: Johns Hopkins Press, 1963), p. 102. See also a paper by his grandson, James D. Grant, "An Analysis of the Objectives, Techniques, and Accomplishments of Dr. John B. Grant in Establishing the First Health Station of Peking, China," unpublished college term-paper, Harvard University, April, 1973.

34. "Grant Reminiscences," p. 173; W. G. Carter (RF staff) to F. F. Russell (Director of the IHB), December 14, 1925. This letter is in the possession of Mrs. Grant, Washington, D.C.

35. Chinese Medical Directory, 1932 (Shanghai: Chinese Medical Association, 1932), p. 22.

quarters. Additionally, the city agreed to transfer the sanitation budget for that area to the center, and to pay the salaries of the police sanitation officers. The Health Station, with funds from PUMC and the IHB, agreed to provide minimal health care to the city ward. Fifty-eight thousand people were resident in the Health Station district (later in the decade the area was enlarged to encompass nearly 100,000 persons). By 1927 the staff included 6 physicians, 17 nurses, 1 dental hygienist, 1 pharmacist, 3 sanitary inspectors, 1 secretary, and 3 clerks.[36]

The connection between police and sanitation was derived from the German and Japanese police systems, which included public health responsibilities. In Peking, for example, the police maintained a small office for sanitation and they attempted to regulate a few of the sanitary laws, primarily concerning burials and epidemics. As in other parts of China, the main sanitation activity was street cleaning. Maintaining harmonious relations with the police was important for the Health Station. It was for this reason that Fang Shih-san (Shisan C. Fang) had been named the first director. Head of the Metropolitan Hospital, medically trained in Japan and speaking no English, Grant recalled that "he agreed to serve as the first head, because of his ability to approach and get the approval of old-style officials to innovations that were being undertaken at the health station."[37]

There was, however, inevitable friction between the police and the public health station. One particular problem was whether authority belonged to Fang and the Health Station or to the police. Grant continually urged Fang "to swallow his pride," and let the police continue much of their *de facto* power.[38] The Health Station provided special medical services to the police and their families. It also offered the police short courses in sanitary inspection, which remained in their hands. But vital statistics and health services were controlled by the Station.

The gathering and maintenance of vital statistics may appear as a rather impersonal item, but its inclusion in the organization of the Health Station was of tremendous sociological importance. Heretofore, knowledge of the specific cause and rate of mortality

36. John Grant, "Department of Public Health and Preventive Medicine, Peking Union Medical College," *Methods and Problems of Medical Education*, Fourteenth Series (New York: Rockefeller Foundation, 1929), pp. 111–118; Rockefeller Foundation, *Annual Report, 1925*, p. 334. See also, Li T'ing-an, "The Health Station of the First Health Area, Peiping," 1930, FA (601/J/44).

37. "Grant Reminiscences," p. 173.

38. Grant to Fang, August 8, 1925, FA (601/IHB/55).

in China was only impressionistic: accurate statistics would provide a medical and social profile of the city ward. To assist in collecting their data, the Health Station staff persuaded coffin makers to list deaths and the apparent cause of mortality. Since the coffin makers described the fatal disease in traditional Chinese terminology, such as "witchy wind" for pneumonia, Grant and his staff began to develop a standard terminology to facilitate translation of these folk terms into a modern Chinese medical vocabulary.[39]

The vital statistics department gradually put together a profile of medical conditions in its city ward. Of the first 1,000 deaths investigated, 36 percent had received no medical treatment, 48 percent had received treatment by traditional doctors, and 16 percent had received modern treatment. The death rate per thousand was 22.2.[40] The impact of the Health Station by 1934 had become noticeable: 25 percent had died with no medical treatment, 50 percent had received treatment from traditional doctors, and 25 percent had received modern treatment. Furthermore, the death rate had declined to 18.2 per thousand. In the early thirties, the death rate in the United States was 10.9.[41]

In the fall of 1925 Victor Heiser again visited Peking. He spent several days observing the newly-established health station and noted the overriding influence of Grant:

> Apparently the Center is looked upon as purely Chinese and fully under their own control and management. It seems to be rather generally agreed that if Dr. Grant's push and energy were withdrawn, the project would soon collapse. The undertaking impresses one giving much promise of successful results.[42]

As Heiser noted, the first administrative staff of the Health Station was completely Chinese, and drawn largely from the National Epidemic Prevention Bureau. In fact, in a history of its work printed in 1934, the NEPB claimed full responsibility for the Health Demonstration Station: there is no mention of cooperation and financing from PUMC.[43]

39. J. B. Grant, T. F. Huang, and S. C. Hsu, "A Preliminary Note on Classification of Causes of Death in China," NMJC 13 (1927): 1–23.

40. Grant, "Department of Public Health," p. 114; Association for Public Health, Memorandum on the Need for Public Health, p. 35.

41. Tsai Fang-chin, "American Standards of 'Good Medical Care' per 100,000 Population and Their Comparison with the Present Medical Facilities in the First Health Area, Peiping," in Transactions of the Ninth Congress, Far Eastern Association of Tropical Medicine (Nanking: National Health Administration, 1935), pp. 823–832.

42. Victor Heiser, Notes #27, October, 1925, pp. 9253–9254.

43. National Epidemic Prevention Bureau, Report, pp. 107–111.

This is exactly what Grant had intended, and this assumption of leadership by Chinese was to bear remarkable fruit. Three members of the first staff deserve particular mention: Huang Tse-fang, P. Z. King (Chin Pao-shan), and Hu Hou-ki. The latter was the first Chinese recipient of an International Health Board fellowship in public health to Johns Hopkins. Hu returned to China to become Chief of the Division of Vital Statistics in the Peking Health Station. Huang Tse-fang, who had received his M.D. from the University of Chicago, was appointed Chief of the Division of General Sanitation. Prior to working with the Health Center, Huang had been associated with the National Epidemic Prevention Bureau,[44] as had P. Z. King, who had been its director. King, who had an M.D. from a Japanese university, had also served as a professor in Peking's National Medical College. At the Health Station, King was Chief of the Division of Medical Services.[45] In time, both P. Z. King and Huang Tse-fang also received IHB fellowships for advanced study in public health in the United States.

In the late twenties, when municipalities as well as the national government began to organize urban health centers, those who had been members of Peking's First Health Demonstration Station were in great demand. In 1927, when Ting Wen-chiang became Mayor of Shanghai, Hu Hou-ki became the first Commissioner of Health for the Municipality of Shanghai.[46] In 1928 P. Z. King became Health Commissioner for Hankow; and in 1929 Huang Tse-fang became Commissioner of Health for the Municipality of Peking. The second director of the Health Station, S. H. Chuan (Chuan Shao-ching), former Surgeon General and Director of Tientsin's Army Medical College, later became Director of Public Health for Tientsin.

Not only did the Health Station provide a training ground for urban health administrators, it also served as a model for other efforts. As early as the fall of 1925, Heiser noticed its visible impact on other agencies within Peking. Under Mayor Hsueh Tu-pi, the city government had set up a metropolitan health demonstration station similar to the one sponsored by PUMC.[47] From the outset

44. See his discussion of collecting data for the NEPB, Tsefang F. Huang (Huang Tse-fang), "Communicable Disease Information in China," *NMJC* 13 (1927): 92–108. For biographical data see *China Year Book, 1929–30*, p. 951.

45. For biographical data on P. Z. King, see *China Year Book, 1929–30*, p. 934.

46. Hu Hou-ki, "The New Department of Health, Port of Shanghai and Woosung," *CMJ* 41 (1927): 429–438; C. S. Kim, "A Brief Survey of the Public Health Activities in Shanghai," *CMJ* 42 (1928): 162–180. Hu Hou-ki died in an automobile accident in 1934.

47. Hsueh Tu-pi was active in other urban reforms, see Charles W. Hayford,

it was this *demonstrative* aspect of the Station which interested Grant most. Of particular concern was the economic applicability of the health services provided, for "unless you planned your activities within the economic practicability of the community in question, you didn't get to first base."[48] As various experimental extension services were planned, a primary goal was to hold the cost to a minimum level.

One of the first programs was an industrial health service organized for the Yenching Rug Factory in the health district. This enterprise, which employed about 1,000 workers living in dormitories, agreed to pay the salary of a nurse and police sanitation inspector, and to equip a health room. The Health Station provided for free medical care, and the half-time service of a physician. During three years, a dispensary treated ordinary illnesses, the latrines and sanitation facilities were remodeled, first aid and health classes were held, and special study was made of diseases caused by industrial conditions. A high susceptibility to xerophthalmia was discovered, but inexpensive treatment with cod-liver oil proved to be successful. Wu Hsien, Professor of Biochemistry at PUMC, studied the food provided by the factory, and recommended a number of inexpensive changes which added vitamins and minerals to the daily diet. The cost of these services came to Mex.$2,600 a year, or Mex.$2.60 per capita.

Articles by two PUMC graduates, Li T'ing-an, '26, and Yao Hsun-yuan, '25, described the factory health program and urged the need for national legislation to provide adequate working facilities for industrial workers.[49] These were but two of an increasing number of PUMC students who specialized in public health. In 1926 the PUMC faculty required that all students serve a clerkship in the Health Station, and many subsequently went on to specialize in public health. In time, PUMC graduates became the backbone of the PUMC-affiliated health station.

A second experimental health program provided medical services for public and private schools in the special health area. From a total of fifty schools in the vicinity, eight representative ones were selected for a demonstration program. The schools agreed to pay Mex.$1 per capita to the Health Station for health care. All students

"Rural Reconstruction in China: Y. C. James Yen and the Mass Education Movement" (Ph.D. Thesis, Harvard University, 1973), p. 68.

48. "Grant Reminiscences," p. 159.

49. Li T'ing-an, "Danger from Nutritional Diseases in Modern Industrialization," *NMJC* 13 (1927): 377–382; Yao Hsun-yuan, "Industrial Health Work in the Peiping Special Health Area," *CMJ* 43 (1929): 379–387.

received physical examinations upon registration. Trachoma clinics at the schools treated this widespread disease. Inoculations were given for smallpox and typhoid, and a program of health education in the classrooms was undertaken. When physical exams revealed illness or deficiencies, a nurse notified the parents and recommended treatment at any one of the several hospitals in the area. If no action was taken, nursing teams visited the families and urged treatment. Li T'ing-an was again involved in this program, as well as Fang I-chi, PUMC '27.[50]

A third undertaking—assistance in maternal care and child-welfare—was located within the Station itself. Marian Yang (Yang Chung-jui), a PUMC assistant in gynecology who had received her M.D. from the Union Medical College for Women and had also done advanced work at Johns Hopkins, was the prime mover in this project. Prior to the creation of the Health Station, thirty local midwives had serviced the area. Their lack of knowledge about germs, particularly highly infectious *tetanus neonatorium*, directly contributed to the high infant mortality rate. The first maternal health services bypassed these traditional midwives. Three modern clinics were inaugurated: prenatal, obstetrical, and child health. Over a three-year period, 484 women were cared for at the prenatal clinic, 298 women were assisted at delivery, and the child health clinic recorded 17,516 treatments.

Although this modern center had begun to make an impression on child health in the vicinity, it was clear that it was only a beginning. Accordingly, Marian Yang proposed to retrain the traditional midwives, upon whom most of the population continued to rely for prenatal and childbirth assistance. With the cooperation of the midwives, health care could be vastly expanded. Accordingly, in 1928 the Municipal Health Department, in conjunction with the Health Station, established a two-month course for retraining old-style midwives.[51] This initiated a midwifery program which became the most successful experiment in medical education during the Republican period. (It will be considered in more depth in the next chapter.)

Grant's emphasis on the community as the primary health unit had led to the creation of an urban health demonstration station. It was inevitable that in time he would turn to the dominant com-

50. Fang I-chi and Li T'ing-an, "School Health in the Peiping Special Health Area," *CMJ* 43 (1929): 697–706.

51. Marian Yang, "Child Health Work in the Peiping Special Health Area," *CMJ* 43 (1929): 920–925.

munity unit in China—the rural village. The date of Grant's first acquaintance with James Y. C. Yen's Mass Education Movement is uncertain, but it appears probable that from the outset Grant and others at PUMC were aware of the nearby Ting Hsien rural program. By the late twenties, Grant was a close associate of Yen, a frequent guest in his Ting Hsien home, and an advisor to the MEM.[52]

In 1929 Grant arranged for Yao Hsun-yuan, already involved in a variety of public health activities, to be appointed Director of Public Health at Ting Hsien, and from that time PUMC cooperated extensively with Ting Hsien officials in the health work. Grant, Roger Greene, Marian Yang, and Wu Hsien, among others, served as advisors for the rural health program.

In 1932, an arrangement was made whereby the Mass Education Movement formally provided PUMC with teaching facilities for rural health. PUMC became the base hospital for the rural health work, and PUMC students regularly attended seminars at Ting Hsien.[53] For example, in 1934, 14 third-year PUMC students spent three days at Ting Hsien, and three of them selected Ting Hsien for their internship program. C. C. Ch'en, PUMC '29, who succeeded Yao as Director of the Ting Hsien program in 1932, described the rural experiences of PUMC students: "Most of these students were born and brought up in cities. Before they came to Ting Hsien, they had no idea of what the villages of their own country looked like."[54] C. C. Ch'en himself was to provide the leadership which transformed the concept of an urban health care delivery system into what Grant called "the first systematic rural health organization."[55] It became the basis of "state medicine" under the Nationalist government.

During the mid-twenties, sporadic governmental health projects were initiated, but nothing long-lasting was accomplished. As the Northern Expedition sought to unify China, hopes were expressed that the new government would establish a national ministry of health. In 1926 Roger Greene wrote to Welch, expressing his con-

52. "Grant Reminiscences," pp. 247–248.

53. Yao Hsun-yuan, "The First Year of the Rural Health Experiment in Ting Hsien, China," *Milbank Memorial Fund Quarterly Bulletin* (hereinafter *MMFB*) 9 (July 1931): 61–77; C. C. Ch'en, "The Rural Public Health Experiment in Ting Hsien, China," *MMFB* 14 (January 1936): 66–80; "Grant Reminiscences," pp. 326–332.

54. C. C. Ch'en, "Scientific Medicine as Applied in Ting Hsien," *MMFB* 11 (April 1933): 126.

55. "Grant Reminiscences," p. 177 A.

fidence that Grant and his public health associates would be involved in any nationwide public health program:

> Dr. Grant's efforts of the last six years are beginning to bear fruit in a surprising way. He has with him a group of young men, paid for the most part by the government, who are becoming highly enthusiastic about the experimental health station which has been started under the auspices of the police. These young men are digging themselves in, and I think we shall find them strong enough to survive any political upheavals that are likely to occur, especially since the friends of the work include representatives of practically every strong party.[56]

The Health Station was increasingly seen as a springboard to more extensive governmental involvement in public health. Industrial health, child health, and midwifery training all raised the larger national problem of the ways and means for extending modern health care throughout China. Every Friday night the staff of the Health Station and PUMC's public health students met in Grant's home, and their discussions ranged over the political future of medical care in China. Victor Heiser attended one of these Friday night sessions in the spring of 1928, and recorded:

> We discussed various problems until midnight. They wanted views as to whether they should encourage the development of State Medicine or whether they should endeavor to develop along opposite lines. Told them of [Ludwig] Rajchman, who after an extensive study of poor countries came to the conclusion that State Medicine is the only solution for the application [sic] curative and preventive medicine.[57]

Grant himself had already outlined his views on the subject of state medicine in an address given before the National Medical Association of China in January of the same year. The speech was entitled, "State Medicine—A Logical Policy for China." In it, Grant unreservedly advocated a system of state-supervised medicine for China. Grant noted that control of sanitation and communicable diseases had already been widely accepted internationally as a governmental function. More vital health responsibilities included early diagnosis and preventive medicine. There was a relationship between health care and economic conditions. Therefore, Grant argued, governments should develop "social machinery to ensure standards of living adequate for the maintenance of health."[58] Non-

56. Greene to Welch, April 8, 1926, *WWP*.
57. Heiser, *Notes #33*, April, 1928, p. 2590.
58. John Grant, "State Medicine—A Logical Policy for China," *NMJC* 14 (1928): 74.

medical components, such as education and economic development, ultimately determined a nation's medical health.

In Grant's eyes, a system of curative medicine which was largely
dependent upon private practitioners perpetuated disadvantageous
non-medical factors. Rural communities were insufficiently serviced, and most hospitals were located in cities. Arguing for a state
medical system which would supervise the distribution of medical
personnel, Grant foresaw a day when all Chinese would be within
one mile of a simple health station. This vision included agrarian
China: "One could confidently expect the rural area to be so served
that each village in the . . . hsiens would have dispensary facilities
within a mile at least once a week and there would be simple
hospital facilities in every hsien."[59]

After a decade-and-a-half of wars and warlords, the consolidation
of the Nationalist government in Nanking held out a hope that such
social visions might become reality. Grant's 1928 report to the
Rockefeller Foundation was certainly his most optimistic. He spoke
of the crystallization of a new social order in China and of the
Foundation's role in contributing to "the architect's plans."[60] It is
questionable whether even the foundations were laid for a new
order during the Nanking decade, but Grant continued to be involved in drawing the blueprints.

In the spring of 1928, Grant, Fang Shih-san, the first Director
of the Health Station, and J. Heng Liu, Vice-Director of PUMC,
prepared a memorandum proposing a Ministry of Health in the
Nanking government. Grant himself knew all but two individuals
in the first Nanking Cabinet on a personal basis; and J. Heng Liu,
a classmate of T. V. Soong at Harvard, was on even closer terms.
Hsueh Tu-pi, a former mayor of Peking and an admirer of the First
Peking Health Station, was a protegé of Feng Yü-hsiang, and had
been named Minister of Interior in the coalition cabinet. Grant's
proposal was to create a health department under Hsueh Tu-pi
in the Interior Department. The petition was designed to be impressive. Grant described it as a "museum document," prepared
carefully "in the old Empire style . . . the Chinese writing in [it]
was elegant. It was bound. Oh. I mean, it was a work of art."[61]

Hsueh Tu-pi informed Grant, Fang, and Liu that the request was
premature. But just six weeks later Grant received a telegram declaring that a separate Ministry of Health had been established

59. Ibid., p. 77.
60. Grant, "China—April 1928, General Situation," FA (601/4).
61. "Grant Reminiscences," p. 262.

with Hsueh Tu-pi at its head. Political reshuffling to accommodate Chiang Kai-shek's erstwhile opponent, Yen Hsi-shan, had necessitated Hsueh's removal as Interior Minister. Feng Yü-hsiang, however, persuaded Chiang to create a new ministry, Health, and to reinstate Hsueh as its Minister. In this ambivalent way, in the fall of 1928, China embarked on a program of government involvement in medical care.[62]

Well aware that political relationships primarily determined staff appointments, Grant was afraid that the new Ministry of Health would be staffed by non-professionals. Recollecting that Feng Yü-hsiang had been treated at PUMC, and that his second wife, Li Te-ch'üan, was well-known by many in the PUMC community for her social work, Grant decided to approach Mrs. Feng. Armed with a list of competent people, primarily those trained in the Health Station or being groomed at PUMC for leadership positions, Grant and George Char, the urologist who had treated Feng, went to call on Madame Feng. Grant later recalled the episode:

> We suggested that she send her husband a wire naming certain people to certain positions. She asked us to draft the wire, which we did. She sent the wire to her husband, and each of the men named in the wire was appointed to the position that was indicated.[63]

The most important position, Vice-Minister of the Ministry of Health, was allocated to J. Heng Liu, then Vice-Director of PUMC, and P. Z. King was named his second in command. Li Te-ch'üan's initial influence over the organization of China's first Ministry of Health was to stand her in good stead; over twenty years later, in 1950, she was named the first Minister of Public Health in the People's Republic of China. One of the men, P. Z. King, she had originally proposed for the Nationalist Health Ministry, she named once again to her own ministry.

As a result of his friendship with J. Heng Liu, Grant's impact on the policies of the Ministry of Health was to be considerable.[64] From the outset, this Western advisor anticipated political vicissitudes undermining the health program. He perceptively noted

62. *Ibid.*, p. 263; Tien Hung-mao, *Government and Politics in Kuomintang China, 1927–1937* (Stanford: Stanford University Press, 1972) pp. 23–24.

63. "Grant Reminiscences," p. 271.

64. J. Heng Liu always acknowledged his indebtedness to Grant; see Boorman, ed., *Biographical Dictionary*, 2:403. There were other observers who noted Grant's impact on the Ministry of Health; see Prentiss Gilbert, "The Work of the League Health Organization," November 15, 1932, p. 14, Correspondence, Nanking, American Consulate General, Part 21, Class 8, 812, Record Group 59, NA.

that his own influence, associated with American and Rockefeller Foundation support, could at times be detrimental to national health policy. He realized that he was identified with the Anglo-American group of Chinese medical personnel, and that other Chinese doctors, who had trained in Japan or Germany, constituted factions vying for influence at this time.[65]

To counteract this divisiveness, Grant recommended that a neutral force—the League of Nations—be interjected into Chinese medical policy. He believed this international group would tend to unite or at least obviate the contending cliques. Even more critically, their stewardship would insure that competent medical personnel were maintained in administrative and technical positions. Accordingly, late in 1928 or early in 1929, Grant cabled Ludwig Rajchman, then Director of the League of Nations' Health Organization and at that time visiting Japan, asking if he would be willing to stop over in China: "When he cabled that he would, there was no difficulty in getting an official invitation to him, and he came over, with the result that thereafter the League of Nations' Health Organization was quite actively associated with the Ministry of Health in Nanking."[66]

In a 1929 letter to J. Heng Liu, Grant reiterated the necessity of utilizing the League of Nations, stressing the importance of administrative continuity:

> You will recall my views as to why the League could become the chief stabilizing factor, especially if it possessed an integral interest in the more strategic activities. If the League had a representative in the country, no matter how complete the political change, this individual would felicitate the new group and as a matter of course get them to carry on with the same personnel.[67]

Grant urged Liu to announce that the League would not cooperate with China unless qualified people were appointed. He also spelled out a variety of possibilities for League assistance to China: quarantine survey, provincial health departments, educational commission, and technical advisors. These became the basis for the first formal agreement between the League and the Republic of China.[68] Concluding this candid and forthright letter of advice, Grant reassured

65. A recurrent theme in Grant's writings is the conflict between the Anglo-American and Japanese-trained Chinese doctors. Grant was continually trying to work with the Japanese group. Fang Shih-san is a good example of his efforts.

66. "Grant Reminiscences," p. 250.

67. Grant to J. Heng Liu, December 3, 1929, RGP.

68. League of Nations, "Proposals of the Nationalist Government of the Republic of China for Collaboration with the League in Health Matters," Annual Report for the Health Organization, 1930 (Geneva: League Series, 1931), pp. 15–22.

his Chinese colleague: "In all your criticisms remember all of us are interested only in one objective—RESULTS. This requires Stability." [69] Grant's personal role extended far beyond mere counsel with Liu. At the special meeting of the Health Committee of the League of Nations in March of 1930, which determined the specifics of League–Chinese cooperation, an American observer reported: "Dr. Grant, Professor of Hygiene at the PUMC, was also present in a private capacity." [70]

As a result of this agreement, a number of League advisors were sent to China over a period of years. Eventually, their responsibilities extended to social and economic reform as well as public health. Andrija Stampar, Knud Faber, and Ludwig Rajchman all came for short-term surveys. On the specific recommendation of Grant, Borislav Borcic, a Croatian, was assigned for a two-year term as medical advisor on the staff of the Central Field Health Station in Nanking. The Rockefeller Foundation loaned the services of Brian Dyer, a sanitary engineer, for a number of years in the 1930s.

There is some indication that League advisors did contribute stability to the medical administration during the Nanking era. [71] In 1930 the Ministry of Health was abolished as a separate cabinet department, but the staff was reincorporated, almost to the man, into the National Health Administration (*Weishengshu*) within the Department of Interior. Although this Department was to see twelve ministers from 1928 to 1937, J. Heng Liu retained his leading position as Director of the *Weishengshu*. For the most part, his staff continued to be well-trained personnel in various fields of medicine and medical administration. Frank Boudreau, a League of Nations health official in China, wrote in 1934 that "the efforts of the [League of Nations] Health Section had resulted in measurable progress in divorcing Chinese public health work from political factions and in setting up a separate Chinese governmental organization for purely public health work." [72]

The close connections between J. Heng Liu and the Rockefeller Foundation staff, including not only John Grant but also Victor Heiser, inevitably brought financial requests from the Chinese

69. Grant to Liu, December 3, 1929, *RGP*. Emphasis in original.

70. Frank Boudreau to Surgeon General Cumming, March 19, 1930, 893.12/4 League Survey, Record Group 59, *NA*.

71. For brief discussions of the League of Nations in China, see Dorothy Borg, *The United States and the Far Eastern Crisis of 1933–1938* (Cambridge, Mass.: Harvard University Press, 1964), pp. 56–62; Thomson, *While China Faced West*, pp. 15–16.

72. Conversation, Frank Boudreau with M. M. Hamilton, October 10, 1934, 893.12/12 League Survey, Record Group 59, *NA*.

health organization to the Foundation. In 1929, Liu concluded an article on the Ministry of Health in the *National Medical Journal of China* with an appeal to the Rockefeller Foundation: "After all, is not the aim of all of us to promote the well-being of mankind by making use of the modern science of preventive medicine and public health."[73] The phrase "to promote the well-being of mankind" was carefully chosen: it was the stated mission of the Rockefeller Foundation. In 1930, Liu approached Victor Heiser with requests for aid to the National Health Administration. In time the International Health Board of the RF contributed to the First Midwifery School and to metropolitan and rural health programs in and around Shanghai. Sixteen fellowships for public health specialists to study in the United States had been provided by 1932. But by 1934 the financial contributions from the Foundation to the National Health Administration were still relatively small: only US$200,000 had been appropriated to the government agency or its programs.[74]

In a draft of a letter to Max Mason, then President of the Foundation, Roger Greene partially explained the rationale for these limited financial contributions: "As far as China is concerned, there seems reason to believe that more effective co-operation with the government could be secured through the League of Nations than by direct relations between the Foundation and the national or provincial governments."[75]

The Foundation's ties with the National Health Administration were relatively loose, but PUMC staff and graduates dominated the government's medical hierarchy under the Nanking regime. With J. Heng Liu, still nominally Director of PUMC, serving also as the Director of the National Health Administration, employment possibilities were greatly enhanced. Although personal access greatly facilitated employment, it should also be recognized that these appointees had received extensive training in public health administration under Grant and in the First Health Station. A few examples from the Nanking Central Field Health Station will suffice: P. Z. King became Vice-Director under Liu; Marian Yang was Chief of the Department of Maternity and Child Health; Yao Hsun-yuan, Chief of the Department of Medical Relief and Social Medicine; and Chu Chang-keng, Chief of the Department of Health Educa-

---

73. J. Heng Liu, "The Chinese Ministry of Health," *NMJC* 15 (1929): 148.

74. Victor Heiser, "On the Present Status of Work in the East," September 12, 1934, p. 3, *VHP*.

75. Greene to Max Mason, January 4, 1930. A penciled note indicates that this version of the letter was not sent. *RGP*.

tion.[76] Service in the government had been a goal of the traditional Confucian literati. According to Grant, that pattern persisted in the vocational plans of PUMC students:

> P. Z. King said to me one day, although he was not a PUMC graduate, [that] in their ancestral line they like to be able to refer to their forebears who had held this position and that position and this position in government. That was the acme of success, rather than money or anything else in those days. . . . The generation at the PUMC . . . knew that getting in on the ground floor of public health, they would be given relatively high positions, which would be a very pleasant thing to be able to report to their families.[77]

That it became possible during the 1930s for these well-trained Chinese medical men and women to attempt solutions to China's health problems was due in large measure to the political pragmatism of John Grant. Some of their most innovative programs will be discussed in the following chapter.

The late twenties and early thirties found Grant increasingly involved in political affairs, and in hobnobbing with Chinese officialdom. But he was also concerned with the nature and direction of PUMC. In a 1930 letter to RF President Max Mason, Grant expressed his dissatisfaction with PUMC's role in medical education. Stressing the shortage of practitioners and the scarcity of trained personnel in China, Grant urged that the Foundation remedy this deficiency by urging PUMC to cooperate with others in establishing a new experimental medical school: "It is suggested that all preconceived conceptions as to hours should be disregarded and that experiments should be made to devise a curriculum based solely on consideration of the demands that will be made on a general practitioner under Chinese economic conditions."[78] Roger Greene, on Grant's behalf, also urged expansion of the public health teaching program at PUMC itself.[79]

These pleas for increased Rockefeller Foundation support to PUMC for public health education, or new innovative medical colleges, came at an inopportune time: by 1930 retrenchment was the order of the day. Much to Grant's disappointment, Chinese gov-

---

76. *First Report of the Central Field Health Station* (Shanghai: North China Daily News and Herald, 1934).

77. "Grant Reminiscences," pp. 300–301.

78. Grant to Max Mason, May, 1930, *RGP*. This appears to have been a draft and there is no indication as to whether the letter in this form was actually sent to Mason, if at all.

79. Greene to Mason, March 13, 1930, *RGP*.

ernment plans for an experimental medical school were also slow in materializing. Finally, in the fall of 1937, the school, built at Nanchang as a part of the rehabilitation of the former Communist provincial stronghold in Kiangsi, was scheduled to open. But the Japanese invasion of the same year nullified the long-awaited efforts.

Grant was increasingly disenchanted by the failure of both PUMC and the Nationalist government to utilize what he saw as a golden opportunity. His annual reports of medical conditions in *The China Year Book* grew increasingly pessimistic. In 1933 he recorded: "As far as is known, none of the provinces or special municipalities have complied with the order of June, 1931, relating to the establishment of medical schools which was reported in the last year book." [80] During his last years in China, Grant was to become associated more closely with non-medical and non-governmental aspects of China's social and economic progress. Principally, this was the rural reconstruction movement.

John Grant had undoubtedly known Selskar M. Gunn, Vice-President of the Rockefeller Foundation in Europe, before the latter made his first trip to China in 1931, for both were members of the RF's International Health Board. Whatever their previous relationship, Grant came to serve as Gunn's primary guide to medical, agricultural, economic, and public health projects in Nationalist China. [81] When Gunn proposed a creative interdisciplinary approach to China for the Foundation, Grant elected to participate:

> Well, I felt that if Gunn was going to survey or review opportunities throughout the world for a multi-disciplined R.F. program, that China would probably offer him as good an opportunity as any other country he could visit. Knowing that was in the offing, I felt that if such a potential developed, I would play a more useful role with him than continuing within the narrow confines of the PUMC itself. [82]

The China Program, inaugurated formally by the Foundation in 1935, bears the stamp of John Grant almost as much as it does

---

80. Grant, "Public Health and Medical Events," *China Year Book, 1933*, p. 172.

81. Heiser, *Notes #41*, November, 1932, pp. 8198–8215, describes Gunn's arrival in Peking and Grant's organization of Gunn's itinerary. It is curious that James Thomson, in his chapter on the RF China Program, does not mention John Grant, see *While China Faced West*, pp. 122–150. Franklin Ho (Interview, July 22, 1970) emphasized that Grant provided the data and ideas regarding specific Chinese institutions for Gunn's program. Marshall Balfour (Interview, February 15, 1972), who succeeded Gunn as Director of the China Program in 1939, emphasized the role of Grant in maintaining contacts with Chinese universities and rural reconstruction projects. The RF archives substantiate Grant's role in the China Program, see *FA* (601/12–14).

82. "Grant Reminiscences," pp. 321–322.

that of its principal author, Selskar Gunn. Grant's critique of earlier Rockefeller programs contributed to the *raison d'être* for the new program:

> The large investment already made by the Rockefeller Foundation toward the development of medical education in China has thus far been applied almost entirely to the traditional type of education which had already grown up in other parts of the world. It is fair to ask how much this investment so applied is capable of assisting in the attainment of the objective of a new social order. If in the midst of significant social changes the established system of medical education is found to be incapable of adapting itself to changing conditions, then the investment of $38,000,000 will have produced only mediocre results.[83]

He outlined an alternative medical policy which would be directly related to the non-medical aspects of Chinese life he had so frequently mentioned:

> The development of such a medical policy is, however, so dependent upon the progress in other fields of community activity, such as industry, agriculture, education and transportation, that it should be closely coordinated with a program of national planning. Future Foundation medical policy therefore should be limited to those projects which are a part of a unified medical program which in turn should constitute one aspect of a larger plan of social reconstruction.[84]

Grant specified a number of health projects which should be included in the proposed interdisciplinary Rockefeller program. These included support of public health activities of the Mass Education Movement, teaching sanitary engineering at Tsinghua University, selected provincial health organizations, and experimental medical education programs of the National Health Administration.

All of these were incorporated into the China Program which was launched in 1935. It also included support to university programs in agriculture and economics, notably the University of Nanking's Department of Agriculture and Nankai's Institute of Economics. In 1936, the North China Council for Rural Reconstruction was formed under the auspices of the China Program. It provided for experimental training of university students in public health, agriculture, economics, and public affairs, first at Ting Hsien, and later in the experimental *hsien* surrounding Tsining. Grant was the only Western member of this Council, which also included Robert Lim, pro-

83. Selskar Gunn, in his 1934 report, "China and the Rockefeller Foundation," included portions of a paper by Grant on new ideas for Rockefeller medical policy. This quote is from pp. 9–10.

84. *Ibid.*, p. 9.

fessor of physiology at PUMC, and several of Grant's former public health students.[85]

James Thomson later described this Council as "the most promising fruition of a generation of foreign and Chinese efforts toward an effective response to the rural crisis."[86] But war with Japan, and the diminishing possibilities for progressive educational alternatives in Republican China, led Marshall Balfour, Gunn's successor as Director of the China Program from 1939 to 1943, to describe this hopeful experiment—in retrospect—as a "splendid failure."[87]

Grant was transferred to India in 1938 to become Director of the All-India Public Health Institute. He thus ended over seventeen years of prodigious activity in China. Grant resembles in some ways two noted nineteenth century Western advisors who also began their China careers in Ningpo—Thomas Hart and W. A. P. Martin.[88] Like both Hart, who became the Inspector General of the Chinese Customs Service, and Martin, who became President of the T'ung-wen Kuan, the first Chinese modern school, Grant's primary approach to progressive change in China was through elite training and officialdom. Like Hart and Martin also, Grant hoped for efficacy in the government he served, and again like them he became increasingly disenchanted. In a 1938 letter to his children, he described the capricious conduct of Generalissimo and Madame Chiang Kai-shek.[89] In his reminiscences many years later, he recalled the progressive reforms proposed by the League of Nations: "They gave top priority—I mean, it was not included as 1, 2, 3, it was a priority by itself: land reform. Now if that land reform recommendation had been carried out, I don't believe the Kuomintang would have ever dissolved."[90]

Grant's career bears some resemblance to that of both Hart and Martin, but his unique role in China was also markedly different. Martin and Hart themselves became officials within the Chinese government. Hart presided autocratically over his own Chinese bureaucracy. Grant never joined the government. It was not merely that times had changed by the 1930s. Grant really had confidence

---

85. Marguerite Atterbury, "A Study of Some Phases of Chinese-American Co-operation in Promoting China's Agricultural Extension" (Ph.D. Thesis, Columbia University Teachers College, 1961), p. 160.

86. Thomson, *While China Faced West*, p. 142.

87. Interview with Dr. Balfour, February 15, 1972.

88. For essays on their lives, see Spence, *To Change China*, pp. 112–128, 129–140.

89. Grant to Jim and Betty, October 22, 1938, letter in possession of Mrs. J. B. Grant.

90. "Grant Reminiscences," p. 233.

in his Chinese colleagues; and he worked diligently for their success in political roles, not his own.

Hart stayed in China long enough to become an anachronism. Martin's whole career was consumed by the Middle Kingdom. Grant left China in his late forties. His ideas for the expansion of social medicine—the integration of curative and preventive medicine, a community teaching unit, and a rural health delivery system—had matured in China, and were to be applied with more tangible success first in India, later in Europe, and finally, at the end of his life, in Puerto Rico. For example, as International Health Board Director for the RF in Paris following World War II, Grant's concepts of health organization greatly influenced Western European governments, which were in the midst of overhauling their health systems.

Grant was not immune to the superiority assumed by Western advisors in China, and quite obviously he enjoyed the power which accrued to representatives of the Rockefeller Foundation. But he seems to have exercised his importance judiciously, with more thought for his ideal—public health in China—than for personal accolades. Perhaps it is because Grant worked so diligently to overcome the institutional encumbrances of Western medicine that one reflects favorably upon his career. But perhaps more revealing is the fact that he did not make himself indispensable to the programs which he started. Therein lies the measure of his success.

SEVEN

Barefoot Doctors and Midwives

The problem for the Chinese Government in this generation is how to establish a workable machinery that will introduce scientific medicine, curative and preventive, gradually, correctly, and continuously into the everyday life of the Chinese people.

Ch'en Chih-ch'ien,
"A Proposed Basic Medical Curriculum," 1935

JOHN GRANT's legacy was insured by the revolutionary programs of two of his Chinese colleagues, Ch'en Chih-ch'ien and Marian Yang. Grant's design for an urban health service, his interest in innovative medical training, and his advocacy of state medicine were carried several steps further by both Ch'en and Yang. Ch'en modified the metropolitan health model so that it would meet the needs of rural China. Yang set up midwifery training programs across China. Each worked tirelessly amid the vicissitudes of the Republican interregnum to make state medicine a reality. Pioneers in adapting Western medicine, they were a part of a small coterie of progressive Chinese medical leaders who challenged the blind transfer of the American structure of medical practice—private practitioners, standardized medical degrees, professional nurses—to China.[1] Not all of their recommendations were adopted, and many of their programs were implemented only in part. Nonetheless, their efforts are significant. Their lives indicate that some members of China's new professional elite could become a reintegrative force,

1. While medical educational curricula in China were based on many different systems—Japanese, German, French, and British, as well as American, the latter system was dominant. Likewise, until the 1930s at least, the general organization of medical practice was patterned after the United States.

and that their creative approach to medical education and rural health care would herald the widely acclaimed medical system of the People's Republic of China.

C. C. Ch'en might well be called the father of China's rural health care delivery system. A native of Szechwan, Ch'en specialized in public health and graduated from PUMC in 1929. In 1935, six years after matriculation, fifteen out of sixteen members of the class of 1929 were located in either Peking, Nanking, or Canton; all, that is, except Ch'en. Returning to China after receiving his M.P.H. from Harvard University, Ch'en elected to "go down" to the countryside. He became Director of Public Health for Jimmy Yen's Mass Education Movement at Ting Hsien. Ting Hsien was a county in northern Hopeh, about 200 miles from Peking, in which the MEM was demonstrating its social and educational reforms. As the foremost model *hsien* program, it attracted many Western visitors, and enlisted social-minded Chinese economists and educators among its leaders. Ting Hsien thus provided a unique opportunity to organize a rural medical program.[2]

Ch'en began his first public analysis of health care in Ting Hsien with a scathing denunciation of the existing state of modern medicine in China. He decried:

> Instead of working out solutions of our health problems on the basis of experimental studies, we have drifted into an imposition of the Western pattern of private practice upon the millions of people whose social and economic conditions are entirely different from those of the West.[3]

Turning immediately to the basic population unit of China—the rural village—Ch'en deplored the dearth of health consciousness among China's farming population: "In the delivery of newborns, mud is often used to stop the bleeding of the cord. People drink unboiled water from wells only a few feet from unprotected latrines. Cases of diphtheria and scarlet fever lie in the same bed with the healthy children of the family."[4] Well-trained Chinese doctors had been unable and unwilling to accept responsibility for solving the problems of rural health. They preferred to remain in Peking and the major coastal cities.

Not minimizing the difficulties ahead, Ch'en proposed a dramatic

2. For a contemporary description of Ting Hsien, see Sidney D. Gamble, *Ting Hsien: A North China Rural Community* (Stanford: Stanford University Press, 1968); for an evaluation of the Ting Hsien experiment see Hayford, "Rural Reconstruction."

3. Ch'en Chih-ch'ien, "Scientific Medicine," p. 98.

4. *Ibid.*, p. 100.

reversal for Ting Hsien's experimental health program: "First, we must solve our problems in health as in other phases of the people's life according to our social and economic limitations." He also outlined a notable aim: "the methods of approach here must, to a large extent, be applicable in other parts of the country." Ch'en eschewed taking advantage of the favorable conditions of the experimental *hsien* to create a rural health utopia, for "we would have defeated our own purpose on account of the fact that no other district could afford to duplicate it, and what we had created would amount to nothing more than an ornament."[5]

When C. C. Ch'en arrived in Ting Hsien in 1931, the health program had already been a part of the MEM for two years. It will be recalled that John Grant had recommended Yao Hsun-yuan, PUMC '27, as Ting Hsien's first director of public health activities. The programs undertaken by Yao reflected the application of procedures tested at Peking's First Health Station to the rural experimental district. Curative and preventive clinics were held in Ting Hsien city. A school health service was organized in twenty-four of the Mass Education schools. Vital statistics were collected. Also, training projects were established to provide auxiliary medical personnel. Five boys and nine girls from local middle schools were enrolled in a three-year training course for public health workers, and plans were made for a six-month sanitary inspectors course and a midwifery training school.[6]

Physical facilities and medical supplies for the health program were based on local resources. The 25-bed health center was constructed of sun-dried mud bricks and erected by native workmen. Teams of students were taught to vaccinate each other, provided with inexpensive kits, and then sent back to their schools and villages to inoculate others. Their equipment included sewing needles, cotton balls soaked in Chinese wine, vaccine tubes, towels, pencils and report forms. In one month, the teams vaccinated 21,605 people.

These teams are one fine example of the extension of medical services from the *hsien* capital into the surrounding countryside. Other efforts included biweekly clinics held in two central villages. In each of these, the active participation of local people was encouraged. Yao wrote:

5. *Ibid.*, pp. 101, 102.
6. Yao Hsun-yuan, "The First Year of the Rural Health Experiment in Ting Hsien," *MMFB* 9 (July 1931): 61–77; "The Second Year of the Rural Health Experiment in Ting Hsien, China," *MMFB* 10 (January 1932): 55–66.

Rural vaccination team, Ting Hsien, c. 1932.

> Since the health service is a demonstration and not a philanthropy, the people must take an active part in supporting it, or the work is not going to take root in the community. From the beginning, we were able to get the villagers to provide the building and furniture for the clinic. The patients were charged for the drugs and a charge of six coppers (less than 2 cents) was made for registration.[7]

By 1931, health care activities had a solid foundation in the city of Ting Hsien, but the biweekly clinics in two towns, vaccinations, and scattered school health projects had done little to extend health care into the homes of 400,000 village farmers. In his study of the Mass Education Movement, Charles Hayford observes that Yao's programs were too conventional, and that "the failure was in not developing an organized and organizational approach which would be self-supporting and self-generating."[8]

When C. C. Ch'en assumed the directorship in 1931, a new emphasis was introduced into the *hsien* health program—organization. With the systematic organization of different levels of medical personnel, health care would reach into rural homes. This PUMC graduate's writings are infused with an almost mystical belief in the importance of organization. In 1932, he blamed the maldistribution problems of China's medical personnel on a "total lack of organization."[9] In 1937, describing the inadequacies of some health work-

7. Yao, "Second Year," p. 59.
8. Hayford, "Rural Reconstruction," p. 126.
9. Ch'en, "Scientific Medicine," p. 98.

ers, he suggested that a "humble organization" would transform their efforts.[10]

Ch'en travelled in Eastern Europe and the Soviet Union, and his model for Ting Hsien's rural health system benefited from experiments he saw there. But his health stations were not welfare centers like the *zadrugas* in Yugoslavia; nor were his village aides second-grade physicians as the *feldschers* in the Soviet Union. His rural health structures were circumscribed by the economic and social limitations of the Chinese village, and differentiated so as to diffuse medical care throughout the region. Their geographical configuration conformed to the ecological contours of the Chinese countryside.

The organization design for medical services in a *hsien* included three basic units: a district health center located in the *hsien* capital; a sub-district health station located in various central villages; and small health units in all villages.

DEPARTMENT OF PUBLIC HEALTH[11]

District Health Center

Hospital Laboratory	Control of Epidemics	Administration	Health Education	Educational Training

Sub-district Health Station

Preventive Vaccinations	Supervision of Health Workers	Popular Health Education	Daily Clinics

Village Station

Smallpox Vaccination	Reporting of births and deaths	First Aid	Disinfection of Drinking Water	Free Service

The functions of the District Health Center differed little from the urban Peking Health Station, or, in fact, from Yao's original plan. Innovations included the network of sub-district and village stations necessary for the dispersal of medical care to China's basic population unit—the village. The revolutionary element were the lay workers, forerunners of today's "barefoot doctors," charged with the responsibility of staffing health stations in every village.

C. C. Ch'en's organizational model was based on his perception of the actual *possibilities* for medical care in China's rural areas. Surveys of the Ting Hsien area indicated that the average village government budget was less than $300, most of which went to

10. Ch'en, "Some Problems of Medical Organization in Rural China," *CMJ* 51 (1937): 805.
11. Ch'en, "Scientific Medicine," p. 103.

maintain small schools. A farmer spent roughly 30¢ a year for all kinds of medical relief. Acknowledging the continuing appeal of traditional medicine, Ch'en concluded that only 10 cents of this, during the present generation, could be expected to be diverted into modern medical service. Thus, a village of 1,000 could only afford $100 worth of modern medical care. The salary alone of a professional doctor—even were he available and willing, which was not likely—would be $600 a year.

Others during this period would lament this situation, and continue their training programs designed to produce enough physicians for a more affluent society at some indefinite time in the future. But Ch'en accepted the existing state of affairs and proposed immediate solutions. Local, lay participation was absolutely necessary if medical care, admittedly at a very basic level, was to be available to each individual village. Accordingly, Ch'en created "a new type of personnel who under proper conditions will serve as the most primitive and yet effective agents of health protection." This was the village worker.[12]

In Ting Hsien, this lay medical aide was a farmer who had graduated from one of the MEM people's schools. Recommended by his village elders, the lay worker attended a ten-day training session at the closest sub-district health station. There he was provided with a first-aid kit for use in treating minor ailments. This box contained skin cream, an eye ointment, castor oil, calomel, aspirin, and sodium bicarbonate. The drugs were selected on the basis of "inexpensiveness, safety, effectiveness, and need." It also contained locally made instruments: scissors, bandages, equipment for smallpox vaccinations, and record forms. The total cost of the box was $3.00, and it was paid for by the local Alumni Association of the MEM.[13]

Obviously, a ten-day training period was very minimal, and the first-aid services provided by this peasant-medic were but a token introduction of modern health care. Indispensable to the success of the lay worker was supervision for the sub-district health station. This pivotal center, regarded as a "strategic location where a community health physician may render the maximum service,"[14] was staffed by a graduate from a Grade B medical school, such as nearby Hopeh Medical College. A Grade B graduate would expect about

12. Ch'en, "A Proposed Basic Medical Curriculum," *CMJ* 49 (1935): 862.

13. Ch'en, "Scientific Medicine," pp. 114–116; Ch'en, "The Development of Systematic Training in Rural Public Health Work in China," *MMFB* 14 (October 1936): 374–375.

14. Ch'en, "Scientific Medicine," p. 119.

Village health worker, Ting Hsien, c. 1935.

$600 a year (graduates of Grade A schools such as PUMC would
expect much more, and were generally regarded as too specialized
for such a post). The primary responsibility of these sub-district
doctors was to train and supervise the village lay workers. The ten-
day course for these paraprofessionals was only the beginning of
their medical training, the most important aspect of which was

the continuing weekly supervisory visit from the sub-district doctor.

The District Health Station at Ting Hsien city was designed to coordinate all of these activities, to supervise epidemic control, and to provide hospital and laboratory facilities for the more serious cases. Just as the sub-district station served as a training center for the village workers, the larger district station served as a training and refresher station for the physicians isolated in the sub-district centers. As the Ting Hsien experiments received national recognition, this central station expanded to provide more than merely services for its immediate *hsien*: it became a training center for rural medical personnel throughout China.

In 1932, there were but two sub-district centers and only 15 medics. By the end of 1934, the village lay workers had expanded to 80, supervised by eight sub-district stations. Map 2 illustrates the extension of health services in just three years. Even more important than the numerical expansion of village lay workers and sub-district stations was the increasingly sophisticated view of the potential and limitation of their services.

Historically, a main objection to paramedical personnel has been that partially trained medics would attempt to do too much. Accordingly, several controls were built into the selection and supervision of the Ting Hsien village lay worker. The first involved employment in their own villages: an elder of the town nominated a member of the local Alumni Association of the MEM school. Writing in 1934, Ch'en noted the significance of these community controls:

> They realize, and their neighbors, the limitations of their training; their membership in an organized group, the Alumni Association, subjects them to group opinion and censure; and they could easily be replaced if they should prove incompetent or should attempt too much.[15]

A second control was the supervisory physician at the relatively nearby sub-district station. Difficult cases could be held until his weekly visit, and emergency ones referred to the daily polyclinic at the larger sub-district station.

A third check was psychological, and one is struck by its universal implications. At first the village health workers were remunerated locally for each treatment or vaccination. The charge was infinitesimal, but that practice was rather quickly abandoned: it had only encouraged the medical workers to treat as many cases as possible:

15. Ch'en, "Public Health in Rural Reconstruction in Ting Hsien, China," *MMFB* 12 (October 1934): 372.

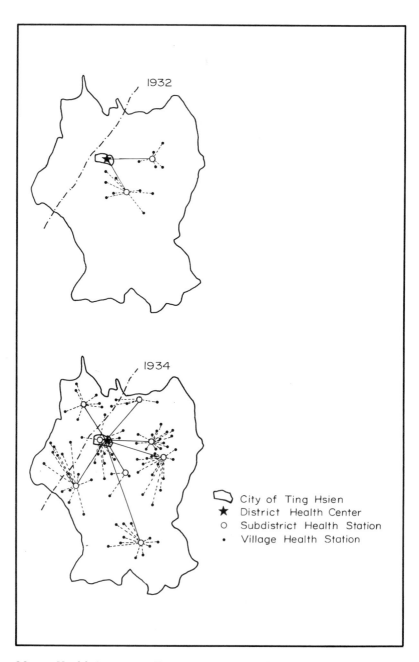

MAP 2. *Health Services in Ting Hsien, 1932 and 1934*

SOURCE: Ch'en, "The Rural Public Health Experiment in Ting Hsien, China," *MMFB* 14 (January 1936): 68

Experience has shown that the workers must not be allowed to collect fees from village people. No fees obtainable today will satisfy their greed, if aroused. A special remuneration, more or less nominal, to be given at the end of each year by the local government will surely encourage them to make greater efforts.[16]

With these kinds of restrictions, the village aides proved to be remarkably effective: over 95 percent of their treatments were found to be accurate. Villagers were enthusiastic about their services. In one instance, a bicycle was contributed to facilitate transportation to the sub-district center. In another, food and lodging were provided. Even more significantly, by 1935, 25 percent of those attending the daily sub-district station clinic had been referred by their village aide: diffusion of medical services was beginning to become a reality.[17]

Successful diffusion of medical care was partially dependent upon the relative distance between small villages and their supporting sub-district station, which was usually a market town. From the beginning, Ch'en had recognized variation in the village groupings, even within the relatively limited geographical confines of Ting Hsien. Two patterns were dominant: a small number of large villages with long distances between them, and a large number of small villages separated by short distances. The first two sub-district stations were set up in each kind of these areas, with the acknowledged possibility "that these two stations will yield different results, with regard both to the population they can serve, and to the readiness with which they may become self-supporting."[18]

Unfortunately, specific contrasts between these two areas were apparently never published. But in 1934 the addresses of 10,000 patients who had attended the sub-district health stations revealed that the average distance travelled to attend the local clinic was eight to nine *li* [three *li* approximate one mile]. Thus, an ideal geographical unit for the sub-district center would be a rural area with a diameter of approximately 15 *li*. In Ting Hsien county this would encompass approximately 25–30 villages with a population of around 25,000 people. Ch'en maintained that one sub-district doctor could "supervise about fifteen village health workers, conduct a daily clinic for diagnosis and treatment, carry on health education in the community, and last [sic] give preventive vaccinations."[19]

16. Ch'en, "A Proposed Curriculum," p. 862.
17. Ch'en, "Public Health in Rural Reconstruction," p. 371; Ch'en, "Systematic Training," p. 373.
18. Ch'en, "Scientific Medicine," p. 117.
19. Ch'en, "Rural Public Health Experiment," p. 78.

Health station clinic: district physician supervising village health worker,
c. 1935.

Although creating sub-districts for roughly every 25,000 people or
less was an ideal, Ch'en felt that for the next fifteen years this would
be an impractical standard. He recommended establishing them in
the larger market towns, where *ch'ü* government and higher primary schools were maintained, even though *ch'ü* districts were
generally much larger than 25,000 people. The main reason for this
was to insure a cross-fertilization between political and medical
leaders.[20]

Ch'en's realization that a successful Chinese health program, or
any social or educational program for that matter, must begin with
the smallest geopolitical units, the villages, is significant. Charles
Hayford cites the rural health organization as one of the only really
effective programs in Ting Hsien: "Perhaps the greatest innovations
which the MEM made in Ting Hsien were those which sought to
build organizations which would tie the villages together."[21] The integrated district/sub-district/village pattern of medical care was the
foundation of Ting Hsien's experimental rural health program. But
it encompassed other projects as well, the most important being
midwifery training.

Modern midwifery in Ting Hsien had its origins, as did all mid-

20. Ch'en, "Systematic Training," p. 375.
21. Hayford, "Rural Reconstruction," p. 252.

wifery education during the Republican period, in the vision of Dr. Marian Yang. Her first published call to a revolution in women's medical training came in a letter to the editor of *The China Medical Journal* in 1928.[22] Apparently in reaction to some of the experimental training programs of the Peking Health Station, the Nurses Association of China had passed a resolution stating: "That the N.A.C. cannot participate in any scheme which prepared to train non-nurses in the science of midwifery." This was not the first time that the highly trained nurses—at the PUMC School of Nursing they were taught in English and had completed several years of college —had opposed lower standards for other kinds of nurses, e.g., public health nurses. Victor Heiser repeatedly recorded discussions with Miss Ruth Ingram, Director of Nursing at PUMC, about the need for more public health nurses: she "apparently is not much concerned over increasing the number of pupils in the school and believes waiting will do it."[23]

Marian Yang's retort to the concept that the Nurses Association of China could reserve to itself the responsibility for safely delivering nearly 12 million Chinese babies a year was a bold call to legitimize the midwifery profession:

> By what logic is the conclusion reached that only in China can the midwifery problem be solved through demanding that candidates for qualification must possess a nurses' training in addition to middle school education before undertaking midwifery courses. There are approximately 12 million births a year in this country. Practice in countries possessing as high midwifery standards as England . . . and Denmark . . . estimate that one midwife can handle adequately 150 and 120 deliveries respectively a year. On this basis, reckoning that for another two generations the supply of physicians and economic conditions will require at least eighty per cent of deliveries to be done by midwives, the problem is to produce 64,000 of the latter. *Is this to be accomplished through establishing requirements at the outset not yet attained by other countries?*[24]

This plea for professional recognition of the status of midwives was sympathetically received by the editors of *The China Medical Journal*: the next several issues contained historical summaries of international midwifery programs and outlines of Marian Yang's own approach at the First National Midwifery School.[25]

22. Marian Yang, "Letter to the Editor," *CMJ* 42 (1928): 554.
23. Victor Heiser, *Notes* #33, April, 1928, p. 2598.
24. Yang, "Letter to the Editor," p. 554.
25. For summaries of international midwifery programs, see *CMJ* 42 (1928): 374–375, 444–446, 591–594, 914–927.

Marian Yang came to the Department of Hygiene at PUMC as an instructor after receiving her M.D. from Union Medical College and advanced training in obstetrics and midwifery in the United States, England, and Scandinavia. Her expertise was desperately needed. In his oral history, John Grant poignantly describes a trip with the redoubtable Yang to a village outside Peking. They had been invited by the magistrate to investigate an unusually high infant mortality rate—80 percent! Grant and Yang discovered that all births were assisted by one traditional midwife with extremely unsanitary techniques. Simple aseptic procedures would have prevented the vast majority of these deaths. Grant repeatedly urged Marian Yang to take up the task of training effective midwives in China. He prodded Victor Heiser and the Rockefeller Foundation's International Health Board into assisting by providing funds for a midwifery school in Peking.[26]

As a result, Yang became the Director of the Peking Midwifery School which opened in 1928 in a converted Chinese house provided by the Peking municipal government. As with other Grant projects, efforts were made to obtain Chinese sponsorship of the midwifery program. In 1929, the National Health Administration in Nanking appointed a Midwifery Commission with Dr. Yang as Chairman, and Mesdames Chiang Kai-shek and Feng Yü-hsiang as members of the board. Grant explained the warlord wife's interest: "Mrs. Feng is extremely interested in this question and already had started a midwifery school last spring in Kaifeng, Honan."[27]

The Midwifery Commission reconstituted the Peking Midwifery School as the First National Midwifery School, and the National Health Administration agreed to share responsibility with the Rockefeller Foundation for its operating expenses.[28] In 1931 the facilities were expanded to include a new school and maternity hospital with living quarters for 40 students and 45 hospital beds.

During its first years, the First National Midwifery School conducted three different courses. The first was a two-month training program for traditional midwives; the second, a six-month course to train younger, modern midwives; and the third was a more extensive two-year course designed for high school graduates who

26. Grant, "Reminiscences," pp. 217–219; Grant to Heiser, September 20, 1926, FA (601/45).

27. Grant to Heiser, October 3, 1928, FA (601/L/45).

28. The discussion of the midwifery program which follows is drawn from the annual reports of the First National Midwifery School, 1928–1937, FA (601/stacks). For published sources see, Marian Yang, "Midwifery Training in China," CMJ 42 (1928): 768–775; Yang, "Control of Practising Midwives in China," CMJ 44 (1930): 428–431; Lily Tseng, "Midwifery," CMJ 44 (1930): 431–445.

Graduates of the two-month course of the First National Midwifery Training School, Peking, 1928.

would become supervisors and leaders in the midwifery program. It also operated a Child Health Institute, conducted prenatal and postnatal clinics, and published numerous popularized pamphlets on maternal and infant care..

Since the Han Dynasty, midwifery had been an honorable Chinese profession, and it was estimated that in 1928 there were 240,000 practicing midwives in China. Therefore, the two-month course to retrain traditional midwives is of special interest. The first class opened in late 1928 with 30 women. Their average age was 54 and they were all illiterate. Yang described her teaching goals: "There are only three main points we are trying to get across in their minds: Namely, aseptic methods of conducting normal delivery, the proper way to dress a cord, lastly to recognize the danger signals and to refer the abnormal cases to physicians."[29]

A simple exam was required to graduate from this two-month course. Each midwife had to demonstrate three practical techniques—washing hands before assisting at deliveries, tying the cord properly, and bathing the newborn with special attention to

29. Yang to Grant, November, 1928, *FA* (601/L/45).

Midwifery class demonstration: cutting fingernails, washing hands, giving a baby's first bath, tieing the cord, and administering prophylactic eye drops, c. 1929.

Visiting bag with equipment for prenatal and postnatal care, First National Midwifery Training School.

cleaning the eyes. Additionally, each woman had to explain orally how to watch for hemorrhaging and fever, and describe the difference between normal and abnormal labor. Twenty-six of the original thirty took the exam, and nineteen of the twenty-six, or 73 percent, passed. A make-up exam was scheduled for those who failed.

Upon successful completion, each midwife was given a "delivery basket." Yang solicited donations from wives of Peking officials to help defray the $5.00 cost of each basket. Included were: an apron and cuffs, towel, sterile cord, scissors, eyedroppers, soap, brush, lysol, boric acid, alcohol and silver nitrate. Supplies for each delivery cost about thirty cents. The midwives were instructed to keep their fees low, charging a maximum of $2.00 per birth. By 1932, 268 traditional Peking midwives had successfully completed this course.

Annual reports of the First National Midwifery School were mailed out in Chinese to educational officials across the country. One result was that Peking's midwifery program quickly attracted national attention. In 1932, Yang wrote that she had received numerous requests from local gentry groups in the surrounding province of Hopeh, as well as from Chekiang and Kiangsu, for additional information on her programs. In 1934, J. Heng Liu, Director of the National Health Administration, announced that priority was being assigned to maternity and infant welfare. A second national midwifery school was established in Nanking in conjunction with the Central Hospital and Central Field Health Station there. While maintaining her position as Director of the Peking school, Marian Yang also became head of the Maternal and Infant Care Division of the Central Field Health Station in Nanking, spending several months a year there.

By 1935, the progress of these programs in Peking and Nanking could provide a glimpse of the gradual penetration of modern medical care into urban China. In the Peking demonstration area which had been set up by John Grant, the maternity program had been in operation since 1926. In 1935 Winston Yung, PUMC '32, charted the ten-year growth of its modern maternity service. Prenatal clinic attendance had almost doubled from 993 in 1926–1927 to 1,856 in 1934–1935. Delivery service provided by the health station midwives, which included supervised old-style midwives, had quadrupled from 170 in 1927–1928 to 679 in 1934–1935. These figures include some expansion of the zone serviced, but also indicate a remarkable increase. Table 8 compares the kinds of delivery services received for all births in the area in 1926–1927 and 1934–1935.

In Nanking the Maternity and Child Care Department of the Municipal Health Administration was established in 1930, and it worked in close conjunction with the Central Midwifery School. The main objective was to provide free maternity treatment for all pregnant women in the entire Nanking municipal area. At least three PUMC graduates, all women who had specialized in obstetrics or maternity and child welfare, were instrumental in organizing and directing its program. Li Jui-lin (Mrs. Yang Chi-shih), PUMC '29, served as Chief of the Maternity Department from 1933 to 1934. T'ang Han-chih (Mrs. C. P. Li), PUMC '28, succeeded Li Jui-lin as department chief. Huang Huai-hsin (Mrs. Hsu Chi-ho), PUMC '32, served as a maternity and child health officer from 1935–1937, as well as dean of the maternity and child health training course at the Central Field Health Station.[30]

By 1935, the maternity service had grown to include six urban and ten rural or suburban stations. The urban centers included two doctors, one supervising midwife, 12 midwives, and five part-time public health nurses. The rural–suburban stations were staffed by four midwives and five nurse-midwives. Total first visits to these clinics had grown from 604 in 1931–1932 to 10,288 in 1934–1935, and the number of deliveries attended by supervised personnel had grown from 327 in 1931–1932 to 2,564 in 1934–1935. In spite of the rapid expansion, this latter figure represented only 14.1 percent of the 18,143 births in Nanking in 1934–1935. Cost per delivery by a trained midwife was calculated to be $4.53. It was estimated that private physicians averaged a charge of about $9.00 per delivery in the same district. It is interesting to compare the maternity outreach in the far-flung Nanking municipal area with the more constricted Peking demonstration area for the year 1934–1935 (see Table 9). The large percentage, 20.9 percent, who went to hospitals for deliveries in the Peking area, reflects the existence of a number of nearby hospitals, including one maternity hospital.

Marian Yang believed that an overall program of maternal and infant care must include birth control. But this subject was taboo in early 20th century China, even for members of the medical profession. Some impetus to family planning does seem to have come from a visit by the American Margaret Sanger in 1922, but the first organized birth control clinic does not appear to have been established until 1930. During three subsequent years, the Peiping

30. PUMC *Annual Announcement*, 1932–1937.

TABLE 8

Maternity Services at Childbirth in Peking First Health Demonstration Area, 1926–1927 and 1934–1935

	Trained Midwives and Physicians	Untrained Midwives	Others, Family
1926–1927	17.1%	54.3%	25.8%
1934–1935	43.3%	38.5%	18.2%

SOURCE: W. W. Yung, "Child Health Work in Peiping First Health Area, 1925–1935," *CMJ* 50 (1936): 564. The figures for 1926–1927 appear to be slightly inaccurate in the original table, which is reproduced here, for they total only 97.2%.

TABLE 9

A Comparison of Maternity Services at Childbirth: Peking and Nanking, 1934–1935

	Peking	Nanking
Total births in area	2,836	18,143
Delivery assisted by:		
Health Station midwives	22.4%	14.1%
Hospitals	20.9%	5.9%
Private physicians	.0%	3.6%
Old-type midwives	38.5%	26.8%
Family members, others	18.2%	49.5%

SOURCE: H. H. Huang and T. H. Wang, "A Survey of the Maternity and Child Health Work in Nanking," *CMJ* 50 (1936): 556. Information on Peking's program in this article appears to be derived from W. W. Yung's ten-year survey cited in Table 8.

Committee on Maternal Health, spearheaded by Marian Yang, members of Yenching's Department of Sociology, and PUMC's Department of Public Health, conducted an intermittent clinic. Only 99 women were advised and the kinds of birth control devices available, primarily diaphragms, frequently proved unreliable.[31] The Chinese Medical Association organized a contraception committee, and by 1937 a regular birth control clinic was conducted at PUMC by Kha-t'i Lim (Lin Ch'iao-chih), PUMC '29.[32]

The National Health Administration never seems to have organized a concerted program on birth control, but in 1934, J. Heng Liu

31. Marian Yang, "Birth Control in Peiping: First Report of the Peiping Committee on Maternal Health," *CMJ* 48 (1934): 786–791; *Round the World for Birth Control with Margaret Sanger and Edith How-Martyn* (London: Birth Control Information Center, 1936), p. 34.

32. *CMJ* 59 (1936): 284; *Round the World for Birth Control*, pp. 38–41.

did include the promotion of "the mother's health by regulating the number of children," among the guidelines for maternity health centers.[33] In Nanking, the implementation of this policy proved difficult for two main reasons: first, "because the present, recognized, reliable articles used in birth control are expensive," and second, because "only intelligent or well-to-do seek advice on this matter."[34] In Peking, nearly all of the 99 cases came from well-educated families. Likewise in Nanking the University Hospital had by 1936 provided information to 122 women on birth control, 90 of them from the upper class.[35]

By the late thirties, the incursion of modern ways into the private, familial enclave of childbirth in Nanking and Peking was still very limited. It did appear that modern midwives had proved a practical answer to the more equitable distribution of medical services. Furthermore, the retraining and supervision of traditional midwives were crucial in swelling their numbers. But Peking and Nanking were relatively modern, urbanized centers. Well supplied with medical personnel, hospitals, and private physicians, they were not at all characteristic of most of China. In Ting Hsien, the attempt to utilize many of the principles of midwifery training which had emerged from these urban centers became a frustrating aspect of C. C. Ch'en's rural health program.

If modern, aseptic delivery procedures were needed in urban China, they were of even more consequence in preventing unnecessary deaths at childbirth or in early infancy in rural China. Since most infant deaths[36] are deemed preventable, infant death rates are considered the most critical social indicator of overall health conditions in a country. The contrast in the mid-1930s between urban and rural China is well demonstrated by a simple comparison. Naning and Peking had an infant death rate of approximately 120 per 1,000 live births.[37] The death rate in a rural county near Shanghai was a staggering 200 per 1,000 births.[38] Aseptic delivery habits and inoculations against smallpox and diphtheria are relatively

33. J. Heng Liu, "Some Phases of Public Health Work in China," *CMJ* 48 (1934): 71.

34. Huang and Wang, "Maternity and Child Health," p. 559.

35. Yang, "Birth Control in Peiping," p. 789; Huang and Wang, "Maternity and Child Health," p. 559.

36. Infant mortality is considered the percentage of deaths sustained during the first year of life.

37. S. C. Chu and T. H. Wang, "A Study of Infant Mortality in Nanking," *CMJ* 50 (1936): 573–580.

38. Chang Tsze Shen, Daniel G. Lai, and Hsi Ju-chu, "A Note on the Infant Mortality Rate in Kao-chiao, Shanghai," *CMJ* 50 (1936): 581–582.

simple medical techniques. However, introducing them into the tradition-bound rural countryside was to prove difficult.

Marian Yang had been a friend of C. C. Ch'en's since they had both worked together in Peking's Urban Health Demonstration Station. She made a number of trips to Ting Hsien during the early 1930s to advise in setting up a rural maternity service. Ting Hsien's first step was to bring an obstetrician and a well-trained professional midwife to the District Health Center. At the same time, training sessions for old-style midwives, along the lines pioneered in Yang's Midwifery School, were begun.[39]

Each of these first programs encountered social obstacles. In 1935 Ch'en frankly admitted:

> Without the guidance of any precedent, the first effort was to introduce a midwife and a fairly experienced physician of obstetrics. This soon failed because the community would not accept a girl only twenty-five years old as a trustworthy midwife and the number of abnormal cases of labor were so few that the physician was a luxury.[40]

Not only was the young midwife socially unacceptable, her cost per delivery turned out to be at least $5.00. For either Nanking or Peking, this figure would have been tolerable, but in the rural budget envisioned by Ch'en the cost of modern midwives would have rapidly drained all the county health funds. Even more disappointingly, retraining of old-style midwives proved to be less effective in the rural areas than it had in the city. In 1934, Ch'en observed with uncharacteristic pessimism: "Out of the forty [old-style] midwives trained by members of the District Health Center not more than three are today working honestly without special supervision."[41] And he lamented again in 1935:

> It was practically impossible to correct the habits of a lifetime, or even to enforce cleanliness. The emergency nature of labor made sufficiently early notification for field supervision and assistance difficult, and even when it was possible the lack of quick and easy transportation was an insurmountable handicap. Thus the second phase was ended.[42]

The next step taken at Ting Hsien was to train younger relatives of the older, traditional midwives to work as their assistants. It was

39. Ch'en, "Systematic Training," pp. 381–384, summarizes the various steps taken in midwifery training.

40. *Ibid.*, p. 382.

41. Ch'en, "Rural Public Health Experiment," p. 76. This report was for 1934, although it was not printed until 1936.

42. Ch'en, "Systematic Training," p. 383.

thought that if they worked together in teams, the more flexible younger women would influence their older kin in adhering to aseptic procedures. This training concept also failed because the young women were too busy with their own families to undertake this extra work. Another project provided short courses in child care and cleanliness to classes of housewives in scattered villages. Training of midwives continued, but Ch'en reluctantly concluded that in rural China, "The improvement of midwifery practice seems to be a question of two or three generations, even provided continuous education is carried on." [43]

Although C. C. Ch'en's forays into the limited arena of maternal and child health proved discouraging, the overall results of his rural health programs were encouraging. His network of health stations had been designed to create a health service that could be duplicated in other parts of China. From the outset, a major concern had been to hold the expenditures to a level that most areas could afford. By 1936, Ch'en was ready to summarize his findings of the cost per capita for these services: it was calculated to be 9.08 cents (see Table 10). Ch'en had held the cost to his original goal of 10 cents a person.

Ting Hsien was not the only county which had conducted experiments in rural medicine. Health programs were included in many of the scattered model *hsien* programs of the rural reconstruction movement. In 1934, the Chinese Medical Association commissioned Li T'ing-an, Commissioner of Health for Shanghai, to review rural health centers. He located and described 17 rural health programs in the provinces of Hopeh, Shantung, Anhwei, Kiangsu, Chekiang, and Kwangtung. It is quite clear that none of them matched Ting Hsien. Outreach beyond the *hsien* capital itself, the key to Ch'en's program, had been minimal. [44]

Even while private organizations were attempting piecemeal to provide health care in a few, selected rural areas, Nanking's National Health Administration was studying guidelines for rural health programs. Yao Hsun-yuan, who had been Ch'en's predecessor in Ting Hsien, headed up the government's Rural Health Service. It is thus not surprising that when the National Health Administration announced its guidelines in 1934 for state medicine, Ting Hsien became the prototype for national medical care. Its description of a *hsien* health program follows closely the Ting Hsien model:

43. *Ibid.*, p. 384.
44. Li T'ing-an, "Summary Report on Rural Health Practice in China," *CMJ* 48 (1934): 1086–1090.

TABLE 10
Cost of Ting Hsien Health Services, 1936

Village Health Station	
Average annual remuneration	$ 6.00
Average cost of drugs and vaccine per worker	10.00
Posters and others	.50
Total cost per worker per annum	16.50
Subdistrict Health Station	
Average salary per station	$600.00
Drugs and other supplies	150.00
Wage of attendant	120.00
Miscellaneous	100.00
Total cost per subdistrict per year	970.00
District Health Center with a hospital of 45 beds	
Salaries	$12,000.00
Drugs and supplies	2,000.00
Coal, light, and water	2,400.00
Wages	1,600.00
Food for patients	2,000.00
Miscellaneous	1,000.00
Total cost of District Health Center	21,000.00

The per capita cost to the general population may be calculated in the following manner:

For village work—$16.50 per 1,000 people	1.65 cents
For subdistrict health station—$970.00 per 30,000	3.23 cents
For District Health Center—$21,000 per 500,000	4.20 cents
Per capita cost per annum	9.08 cents

NOTE: This chart appears on page 77 of Ch'en, "Rural Public Health Experiment." All currency figures are in Mex. $.

"The health activities of a *hsien* are: medical relief, including the establishment of a base hospital in the *hsien* city, clinics in the subdistricts, and first-aid stations in the villages."[45] Their outline duplicates Ch'en's organizational chart:

> *Hsien Government*
>   *Hsien* Health Committee
> *Hsien Health Center*
>   *District Health Station*—polyclinic
>   *Commune Health Station*—including first aid.[46]

During the years remaining in the Nanking decade, state medicine was increasingly identified with a national network of *hsien* health centers. The Ting Hsien model was expanded to include provincial health units. These would supervise the county health

45. *The First Report of the Central Field Health Station*, p. 23.
46. *Ibid.*, p. 24.

centers; establish basic medical schools for physicians, nurses and midwives; and maintain hospital and technological laboratories for use by the entire provincial network of health centers.[47] In 1936, the National Health Administration reported that provincial health administrations had been established in 12 provinces, with a total of 181 *hsien* health centers, supervising 76 sub-stations.[48]

It is difficult to evaluate these figures. Compared with Li T'ing-an's survey of 1934, which found only 17 *hsien* health programs, the increase seems phenomenal and perhaps exaggerated. However, a 1935–1936 survey by Andrija Stampar confirms most of the government's statistics.[49] Conceding that some form of health program may have existed in 181 rural counties of 12 provinces, this was after all only one-eighth of all the *hsien* in these provinces, and population in each *hsien* ranged from 200,000 to nearly 1 million. Furthermore, the degree to which sub-district stations had been established and village aides had been trained is even more questionable.

Variations in intensity of rural penetration were graphically presented by contrasting the effectiveness of two Shensi rural centers mentioned in Stampar's 1936 report. The first center was based at a former mission 60-bed hospital with a budget of Mex.$1,200 a month. It was staffed by two graduate doctors and three nurses. Conditions were favorable for an energetic program, but Stampar concluded that the opportunity had been aborted: "the root error has been to pay too much attention to the population of the *hsien* city."[50] No study of the villages had taken place, and only with an urgent summons did the doctors venture forth into the countryside. The free clinical center had been changed into one with charges for services; ironically, this had resulted in an unused budget surplus. In a tradition-bound area, the midwives had waited at the hospital for deliveries; very few pregnant women had come to them.

On the other hand, at another health center in Shensi, Dr. Stampar found that "doctors are conducting vigorous health programs and are training selected villagers to co-operate with them as help-

47. For examples of the widespread acceptance of the provincial–county health scheme, see Wu Lien-teh, "Fundamentals of State Medicine," *CMJ* 51 (1937): 773–780; T. F. Huang, "The Development of Health Centres," *CMJ* 55 (1939): 546–560.

48. For a chart which locates each of these, see R. Cecil Robertson, "Public Health," *The China Year Book, 1938* (Shanghai: North China Daily News, 1939), p. 132.

49. Stampar, "Health and Social Conditions in China," pp. 128–134.

50. *Ibid.*, p. 132.

ers in their programme."[51] The one midwife herself sought out pregnant women, and vaccinations and preventive inoculations were given free. All of this was being conducted on a budget of only Mex.$900 a month.

No one had been more cognizant of the difficulty in applying his system of rural medical care than C. C. Ch'en himself. He was deeply concerned about the ease with which provincial or *hsien* health centers could end up serving only themselves. In 1937, in an article by Ch'en and Robert Lim on "State Medicine," Dr. Stampar's observations on the failures of some rural centers were echoed:

> The *hsien* centre, *ch'ü* centre and provincial centre are technicalized in degrees culminating in the highest specialized services and the largest establishments in the provincial center, but as Dr. Stampar rightly insists, the provincial center is established primarily not to provide the urban population with medical service (this is merely one of its responsibilities) but to control and direct the rural centres and units—"without the rural centres, the provincial centre has no raison d'etre."[52]

Ch'en had recognized that even if financial support were available, the favorable community environment at Ting Hsien would not be easily duplicated in other rural areas. He was well aware of the support given to the health programs by the local Mass Education Movement schools, and the degree to which their participation facilitated the extension of medical service beyond the *hsien* city. But in a decade when social and economic conditions were crumbling, the MEM schools were hardly characteristic of most of rural China. Ch'en had always believed that finding village peasants capable of becoming medical aides would be possible, but he also perceived that the existence of a supportive community was extremely uncertain. Conditions which had existed in Ting Hsien, that is, far-sighted leadership and widespread community support, simply did not exist in other parts of China during the latter part of the 1930s.

The depressing realities of contemporary China were also mirrored in Marian Yang's annual reports of visits to struggling offshoots of the First National Midwifery School. Although midwifery schools had been established from Kansu in the northwest to Kiangsi in the southeast, Yang found nearly all of them inadequately housed, staffed, and funded. Her courses, which had already reduced obstetrics to its fundamentals, frequently had become so di-

51. *Ibid.*
52. R. K. S. Lim and C. C. Ch'en, "State Medicine," *CMJ* 51 (1937): 787.

luted as to be nearly worthless. Furthermore, most of these schools were located in, and served, urban areas such as Shanghai, Soochow, and Nanchang.

It is beyond the scope of this study to describe the fate of the various medical programs undertaken during the Nationalist era. What is important here is that, despite the problems in implementation, Ch'en and Yang had designed programs that were clearly adapted to China's needs. Furthermore, Yang's midwifery training courses and Ch'en's rural health organization were both well known and widely emulated during this period. Yang and Ch'en were equally tireless in their efforts to publicize their programs, travelling extensively throughout China. In her 1932 report Yang names ten midwifery schools she had visited, and nine more which she planned to investigate during the coming year.[53] *The National Medical Journal of China*, *The Chinese Medical Journal*, and the reports of the Central Field Health Station and National Health Administration repeatedly describe and advocate the acceptance of these programs.

It seems especially significant that the concept of paramedical personnel—lay village workers and midwives—was well-established during this period, well-established enough to provoke debates over the most effective means of training. For example, Chu Chang-keng (C. K. Chu), PUMC '29 and Commissioner of Medical Education from 1935–1937, proposed among other things that the village worker attend classes for two years instead of ten days.[54] This concept of expanded training was also echoed by Julius Tandler, an eminent Austrian public health specialist, who suggested that China emulate the *feldscher* pattern of Europe which prepared medics for two years.[55] Ch'en chose to adhere to his policy of training village aides for only ten days, emphasizing the immediacy of the need, as well as their continuing education through supervision. He maintained that it was possible to find village farmers capable of fulfilling this function.

Much more overwhelming was the problem of preparing enough physicians to staff the sub-district stations, which were usually located in small market towns. At Ting Hsien, Ch'en had found that securing well-rounded physicians for these mid-level stations was

53. Yang's travel diary is appended to each annual report. For a list of these schools, see *Annual Report of the First National Midwifery School*, 1932, p. 2., FA (601/stacks).

54. C. K. Chu, "The Training of Personnel for State Medicine," *CMJ* 51 (1937): 373–380.

55. J. Tandler, "Medicial Protection and Medical Education in China," *People's Tribune*, N.S. 8 (March 1935): 383–399.

extremely difficult. Not only did these doctors have the responsibility to train and supervise a score of lay workers, they also presided over a daily polyclinic confronting the gamut of China's medical problems. Chinese medical colleges with their Western-oriented medical curricula, whether they be PUMC or a Grade B school like Hopeh Provincial Medical College, did not train doctors for leadership in rural areas.[56] Accordingly, in a 1935 educational issue of *The Chinese Medical Journal*, Ch'en submitted a proposal for a basic medical curriculum which would train Chinese physicians for rural service. Since this program also represents the first attempt to design an integrated educational system for both rural doctors and medical researchers, it deserves close attention.[57]

Graduates of normal schools or junior high schools would first attend a three-year premedical course. Heretofore, premedical curricula had been primarily theoretical. Ch'en would now require that each student spend the summer in either urban or rural public health activities. Upon completing their training, each student would have also studied parasitology, bacteriology, and pharmacy— surely the three subjects most needed by any medical worker in rural China. The graduates of this premedical course could either become medical assistants, or they could proceed with regular medical school.

While instruction during the next three years was more traditional, the emphasis continued to be placed on common maladies in China. For example, during the second year one covered skin, parasitic, nutritional, and infectious diseases. The internship year which followed these three years was *not* to be spent in an ordinary urban hospital. Rather, each student would work in a municipal health administration and a rural health center, and would be required to become familiar with veterinary medicine. Ch'en felt that graduates of this program would be well-equipped, and not overly specialized, to serve as medical supervisors in vital rural centers.

Himself a graduate of PUMC, Ch'en was also well aware of the need for medical teachers and researchers. However, he felt that these professional elite needed to be familiar with the medical realities of contemporary China. Therefore, Ch'en's educational scheme would retain institutions of higher medical learning, such as PUMC, but primarily as postgraduate schools. Those training to be medical specialists would have *first* graduated from these more practical programs. This would insure that *all* medical personnel would have

56. Ch'en, "Systematic Training," p. 376.
57. Ch'en, "A Proposed Curriculum," pp. 861–867.

worked on sanitary surveys, conducted epidemic campaigns in rural areas, and assisted at municipal polyclinics. Any graduate of any level could also return at a later date for advanced training, insuring an opportunity for upward professional mobility. Ch'en believed that if this program was adopted on a national scale, it would not only train doctors for rural China, it would also eliminate elitism in medical circles. Unfortunately, as we have already seen, plans to demonstrate this curriculum in an experimental medical school at Nanchang in Kiangsi never materialized. Medical schools continued their traditional training, with only an occasional nod to rural experience.

Marian Yang was more successful in having her curriculum for training various kinds of maternal and child health workers nationally approved. At the request of the Ministry of Education in 1933 a syllabus for each of her courses was prepared and published. In 1934 all registered midwifery schools (there appear to have been about ten) were ordered to follow its outline. In a 1937 letter to an RF official Yang observed that: "Requests have continually been received for complete sets of detailed lecture notes and at the present time they are in use as the guide in the majority of registered schools." [58]

In addition to standardizing the innovative curriculum, a national plan for training rural midwives, supervisors, and teachers was drawn up and approved by the National Health Administration. Yang's First National Midwifery School in Peking would serve as a "higher normal school," primarily training teachers. By 1936 it was already performing this function. Of 189 graduates of the two-year course, 87.3 percent were in either public health or educational institutions in 44 different locations in 16 different provinces. Yang proudly noted: "As many of them hold positions as instructors or deans in midwifery schools their reproductive power is inestimable." [59] At the next level down, there would be national schools, primarily training teachers for the third level, provincial schools. These provincial schools would be primarily responsible for training practicing midwives.

Yang increasingly realized the difficulty of extending this comprehensive system (which remained largely on paper) into the rural areas. In late 1936 she organized two national conferences which discussed the problem of training rural maternity and child health

58. Yang to W. A. Sawyer, January 21, 1937, FA (601/L/45).
59. Ibid.

workers.[60] And, in her 1937 letter which summarized her activities of the past decade, she continued to ponder this problem, wondering if ". . . considering the present state of China, we give too thorough training to maternity and child health officers and workers."[61] Nonetheless, Yang did not give up advocating relatively high standards for midwives. She maintained that to cope with transportation difficulties and economic limitations, the rural health centers must be strong and self-sufficient.

There is a contemporary ring to the educational questions addressed by both Ch'en Chih-ch'ien and Marian Yang in the waning days of the Nanking decade. How do you begin to bring quality medical care to five hundred or eight hundred million rural Chinese? What kind of curriculum will insure the availability of both rural medical workers and medical scientists? Ch'en and Yang may have trained only a handful of people, but in their experimental programs they tackled one of the most difficult and pressing problems of the twentieth century—immediate and equitable distribution of the fruits of modern science and technology. They also represent a new breed of Chinese elite, technologists who themselves participated in the adaptation and assimilation of Western medicine in China.

Both Ch'en and Yang lived to see the successful implementation of their programs, Ch'en in his native province of Szechwan and Yang in Peking. The barefoot doctors of Mao's China are descendants of Ch'en's village health workers. And present-day China's impressively low infant mortality rate owes a great deal to the pioneering programs of Marian Yang's First National Midwifery School.

60. Minutes, "Discussion of Rural Maternity and Child Health Workers," December 15, 1936, Nanking; Minutes, "Discussion on Midwifery and Nursing," December 12, 1936, Nanking; both in *FA* (601/L/45).
61. Yang to Sawyer.

EIGHT The Challenge of War

The more I live, the more I believe that PUMC was not China. . . .

Ch'en Chih-ch'ien to Marshall Balfour, 1942

T HE SINO-JAPANESE WAR began in earnest in 1937. Its onset naturally curtailed the public health programs of the Nanking decade and ultimately forced the closing of Peking Union Medical College. The chaos of the subsequent era of conflict presents the historian with one of those peculiar segments of time when everything is uprooted—when the mettle of a people is tried and tested. There are, however, few surprises in the reactions of our PUMC protagonists; their leadership and elitism both continued.

Before discussing the fate of PUMC and pursuing a few individual careers, however, it is well to touch briefly on the Rockefeller Foundation's involvement in China at the end of the Nanking era and on its institutional response to the war. By the late thirties, there were many indications that the Foundation's programs and PUMC itself were becoming increasingly responsive to Chinese realities. The gradual modification of PUMC's curriculum and increasing Sinification of the faculty has already been chronicled. The North China Council for Rural Reconstruction, formed in 1936 as the primary institutional vehicle for the interdisciplinary China Program, was beginning to flourish in both Ting Hsien and Tsining. Its primary purpose might be said to have been "sending educated youth to the countryside." In these two counties, university students and faculty from Tsinghua, Nankai, Yenching, and Nanking Universities, as well as PUMC, lived and worked in rural areas. By studying local needs and undertaking projects as varied as sanitary engineering and cotton pest control, they sought to fulfill the Council's major objective of training university students for rural service.[1]

A secondary purpose of the China Program had been to "conserve and revivify the work that has already been done through the Peking Union Medical College."[2] This was to be pursued primarily by supporting two government medical programs: the Commission on Medical Education, and the Public Health Training Institute. The latter was the technical education arm of the Central Field Health Station in Nanking. It was the only institution in China training sanitary engineers, public health officers, and sanitary inspectors. While not exactly a public health school of the type John Grant had envisioned, it did provide the technical training necessary to support any effective national health program.[3]

Aid to the Commission on Medical Education reflected the Foundation's desire to see PUMC integrated into a nationwide system of medical education. It will be recalled that it was this Commission that began urging PUMC in the mid-thirties to expand its enrollment, to use Chinese as a medium of instruction, and to include more emphasis on the specific medical problems of China. The Commission also sought to set standards for other institutions, and to plan systematically for teacher education. Seizing the initiative which should have been exercised by PUMC itself, this government commission sought to utilize PUMC as a teacher-training center to supply medical colleges throughout China. It operated a fellowship program which identified potentially good instructors at Chinese or missionary medical colleges and then sent them to PUMC for one or two years of postgraduate training. The Rockefeller Foundation was especially pleased with the activities of this Commission, and with the thoughtful studies on medical education in China produced by its Director, Chu Chang-keng, PUMC '28.[4]

Support of these two government programs reflects the maturation of the Foundation's medical policy in China. Quality training had not been abandoned, but it was now tempered with an aware-

1. North China Council for Rural Reconstruction, "Announcement for 1936–1937," *FA* (601/10).

2. Committee on Appraisal and Plan, "Mr. Gunn's Program for China," December 21, 1934, pp. 105–106, *FA* (601/12).

3. Correspondence and reports related to the Public Health Training Institute will be found in *FA* (601/5).

4. Correspondence and reports related to the Commission on Medical Education will be found in *FA* (601/2–3). See especially C. K. Chu's "Initial Year of the Medical Education Program."

ness of the perils of ivory tower elitism. PUMC's original objective of
training medical leaders was still valid, but only if these leaders
became an integral part of a nationally responsive medical system.
Other lessons learned in the Foundation's nearly quarter-of-a-cen-
tury presence in China included the value of local as opposed to
foreign fellowships, the importance of giving only partial financial
support to any institution and in decreasing sums, and the significance of supporting Chinese rather than foreign projects even if,
as Grant had put it so well, they are only 60 percent as efficient.

Peking Union Medical College had been a highly visible symbol of an American foundation's beneficence in China. Subsequent
activities, such as the China Program, had a noticeably lower profile. Comparing the role of the Rockefeller Foundation with that
of other American charitable enterprises during the war and immediate post-war period provides a good example. While other medical organizations, notably the American Bureau for Medical Aid
to China (ABMAC), United China Relief, and the American Red
Cross, greatly increased their donations, the Rockefeller Foundation's contributions to China steadily declined.

There were several reasons for this. From the outset the Foundation had pledged itself not to be a mere relief agency. Rather
than donate funds for what it considered palliative remedies, even
in the face of overwhelming disaster, the RF had always tried to
channel its support into long-range solutions. Secondly, the RF's
China Program had disintegrated during the war period; it is to their
credit that they did not attempt to prolong unduly a dying program.[5]

The Rockefeller Foundation did make a few grants which might
be considered in the relief category. The Associated Board for Christian Colleges in China received US$425,000 from 1937 to 1945
for aid in their wartime education programs. The Division of Humanities and Medical Sciences made small grants to a variety of

5. Marshall Balfour, "Memorandum on Rockefeller Foundation Activities in China
(1935–1944) for the Inter-Divisional Committee," April 3, 1944, copy was in Balfour's possession. This important document summarizes and evaluates Rockefeller
Foundation programs during this period. Financial support from the RF to the China
Program dwindled from a peak of US$293,789 in 1936–1937 to US$75,000 in 1944–
1945. This latter figure covered grants for fellowships and token support to the few
surviving institutions of the North China Council. The China Program might have
been discontinued by the Foundation even without the disruption of war. It represented the only attempt ever made by the Foundation to coordinate its contributions to one country in a single program, and was not very popular among most
Foundation officers. The traditional divisional interests of the RF began to reassert
themselves, resulting in separate post-war International Health Board, Medical Sciences, Humanities, etc. policies toward China. Interview with Marshall Balfour,
February 14–15, 1972.

Chinese institutions. Some funds were donated through the China Foundation for support to scientific and medical personnel. The International Health Board made contributions to the National Institute of Health and the Szechwan provincial health program. The only new thrust in the RF program was an attack on malaria mounted by the IHB in 1939. This was undertaken to cope with a serious problem in the Yunnan area of the Burma Road. It was administered during the war with the cooperation of the Chinese and the United States governments.[6]

Although the wartime role of the Rockefeller Foundation as an institution was minimal, the activities of the Chinese doctors trained at PUMC or supported by RF fellowships provides a fascinating glimpse of China at war. Furthermore, a composite picture of PUMC colleagues during the war years illustrates very well the variety of their endeavors during the entire Republican period.

In 1937 PUMC witnessed the patriotic trek of Robert Lim, Lee Chung-en, Chang Hsiao-ch'ien, and a few other professors to wartime training programs in unoccupied China. In 1942, with the closure of the College by the Japanese, others, including Wu Hsien and Yuan I-chin, PUMC '27, made their way to Chungking to assist the Nationalist cause. But the majority—probably three-fourths—of the former PUMC community remained in Peking, Shanghai, or Tientsin throughout the war. The First Health Station, which remained open throughout the Japanese occupation, provided employment for some PUMC medical and nursing graduates.[7] Some alumni joined the staff of local hospitals, while others retreated into private practice or research. A few, like Chu Fu-t'ang, '27, and Teng Chia-tung, '33, founded their own medical facilities, such as the Peking Children's Hospital.[8]

The School of Nursing, led by its first Chinese director, Vera Nieh, did move *en masse* to southwest China, reopening in Chengtu in the fall of 1942.[9] One should thus ponder for a moment the absence of such a mass migration by PUMC itself. For one thing, charismatic leadership was missing. Henry Houghton, Director of PUMC, was incarcerated by the Japanese in Peking for the duration of the war. The senior Chinese professors who had remained past

6. Balfour, "Memorandum," pp. 8–13; *Diary*, p. 78. Balfour's personal record of his years in China remained in his personal possession, Chapel Hill, N.C.

7. Marshall Balfour, "A Report on the Peiping First Health Station during the Years 1942–1945," *PUMC Papers*.

8. Stephen Chang [PUMC '35] to Claude Forkner [Director CMB, 1943–1945], July, 1943, *RFA*.

9. Bowers, *Medicine in a Chinese Palace*, includes a chapter on the School of Nursing, pp. 199–214.

1937, C. E. Lim, Wu Hsien, and J. Hua Liu, all lacked both the requisite leadership qualities and sufficient motivation. Inasmuch as PUMC had never been politically oriented, it is not really surprising that its affiliates chose to respond to the war through private retreat. There were few like Robert Lim who combined medical scholarship with zealous patriotism. Also, one might suspect that there were some who had not been enamored of the Kuomintang cause in the first place.

While most of the PUMC community maintained a low profile in occupied China, the minority who left for the southwest became highly visible in wartime medical programs. The two directors of the *Weishengshu* during this period, Yen Fu-ching and P. Z. King, were friends of PUMC, so PUMC alumni continued to dominate the ranks of their institutes. In fact, although there were some notable exceptions, those who joined the KMT government in exile were generally those who had been active in its public health programs during the Nanking era.

For those who left eastern China for the isolated west, primitive conditions challenged their medical adaptability. The response was as varied as PUMC itself. C. C. Ch'en administered rural health programs while living in a peasant's house in Tingfan *hsien*, Kweichow.[10] Chou Chin-huang, '34, translated his medical notes from English into Chinese in order to teach at the amalgamated Kweiyang National Medical College.[11] Marian Yang dispiritedly managed Madame Chiang Kai-shek's "warphanages."[12] Thirty PUMC students transferred to West China Medical College grumbled because their facilities were inadequate.[13] And an unnamed group of former PUMC students clamored for a PUMC-type graduate research institution in Chungking.[14]

There were reports that PUMC alumni contributed little to the demands of wartime conditions. Both of the American representa-

10. Marshall Balfour, *Diary*, May 25, 1939, p. 24.

11. Chang Yao-teh, a 1934 graduate of Cheeloo Medical College, assisted Chou Chin-huang in translating his notes and lectures, Interview, October 23, 1972, Washington, D.C.

12. John B. Grant to his children, Betty and Jim, October 22, 1938, noted: "The most pessimistic individual was Marian Yang. She had been transferred to head up Madame Chiang's war orphans (many thousands) and cannot cope with either Madame's superficialities or the vagaries of her entourage." Letter in possession of Mrs. John Grant, Washington, D.C.

13. Claude Forkner, "Report of the Chairman to the Meeting of the China Medical Board, Inc.," January 28, 1944, p. 2, *RFA*.

14. Claude Forkner, "Report of the Chairman to the China Medical Board, Inc.," May 19, 1943, pp. 5–6, *RFA*. The CMB steadfastly resisted the idea of creating a research haven for PUMC graduates and encouraged its former colleagues to participate in other wartime institutions.

tives of the Rockefeller Foundation in China during the war years, Marshall Balfour for the International Health Board and Claude Forkner for the China Medical Board, were critical of the stand-offish attitude of some former members of the PUMC community. Balfour, in a 1968 letter to Dr. Harold Loucks evaluating the impact of PUMC, made numerous favorable comments, but he also wrote:

> Of the students and teachers who emigrated to S.W. China, both before and after the closure of the College, it seemed to me that some of them were reluctant to join other medical schools or to participate in government services. Apparently they wished to save themselves for the reestablishment of the PUMC either in S.E. China or in Peking. This criticism does not apply, of course, to many PUMC graduates of earlier years, such as Drs. C. C. Ch'en, T. A. Li, C. K. Chu, and I. C. Fang, who were already an integral part of other medical schools and national institutes before Pearl Harbor.[15]

In his 1944–1945 report to the China Medical Board, Forkner stressed that in addition to "playing leaders," the PUMC graduates had been too Americanized, over-isolated from social conditions, and unable to adapt to problem situations.[16]

Undoubtedly, service in southwest China forced many of them to learn how to modify their superior training to the realistic problems of everyday life. Accounts of medical institutions with which PUMC graduates were associated during World War II are full of records of makeshift equipment and improvised techniques. At the orthopedic centers of the Army Medical Relief Corps, surgical bandages were made of reusable cloth, instead of disposable paper materials.[17] The National Epidemic Prevention Bureau's list of locally manufactured drugs and serums expanded yearly.[18]

Some practitioners of modern medicine gained a new perspective on the difficulties involved in integrating scientific medicine into the life of ordinary Chinese people. Miss Ching-ho Liu described the reaction of the Szechwanese people to her transplanted alma mater, the PUMC School of Nursing:

> We nurses are looked up to because we can speak English, and not many people can do that. We have attended college, and not many

15. Marshall Balfour to Harold Loucks, July 31, 1968, copy in possession of the author.

16. Claude Forkner, "Defects in the Former PUMC and Suggestions for Their Correction," 1945, pp. 3–7, *RFA*.

17. Agnes Smedley, *Stories of the Wounded: An Appeal for Orthopedic Centers of the Chinese Red Cross* (n.p.: n.p., 1941), pp. 27–28.

18. "List of Locally Manufactured Drugs and Serums," 985.08, American Red Cross Archives, Washington, D.C. Hereinafter referred to as *RCA*.

people have had the opportunity of attending college. We are immaculate. We have starched uniforms pressed by American laundry machines, which people admire. But it is not because of the nursing profession. We see that. We can see it in the fact that in the recruitment of students in Chengtu, when the School of Nursing of the P.U.M.C. was re-established there. I met on the campus the applicants coming to the nursing profession. They were all from Peking, not one from Chengtu. Not one of the applicants came from Chengtu, the local place.[19]

Mary Ferguson, sent back to China by the China Medical Board in 1946 to assess opinions on PUMC, echoed the re-appraisals of many when she wrote:

The dispersion of our graduates and staff members during the war years has convinced many who had never paid much attention to other institutions of the importance of closer ties between the College and other medical schools. . . . There is a general recognition of the fact that formerly there was a tendency toward keeping too closely within our walls, described by some as "monastic" isolation, and a definite conviction that this must not be allowed to develop again.[20]

Wartime experiences were a rude shock for some of the former ivory tower graduates. For others, the disruption brought challenging situations which cried out for leadership. Progressive guidance was at a premium in Republican China; the score-or-more PUMC colleagues who managed the medical programs of the war period exercised an influence far greater than their numbers. Most of these men and women were inheritors of John Grant's mantle— dedicated to adapting medical training and care to the Chinese people at large. Their efforts in the war period, as in the thirties, began with a burst of enthusiasm. But by 1943 the prolongation of the war and the concomitant discouragements of waiting, runaway inflation, and an increasingly corrupt government had taken their toll. It is easy to list all the failures of their programs, but one must also recognize that their concepts of modern medicine's public responsibility heralded a new age.

Kweiyang in heretofore isolated Kweichow province became the center for several medical programs.[21] Chu Chang-keng was appointed Health Commissioner of Kweichow province and actively encouraged former classmates and professors to bring their medical expertise to this region. In 1937, he reported that there were only

19. The American Bureau for Medical Aid to China, "Conference on Medical Situation in China," 1946, p. 18.
20. Mary Ferguson, "Report to Trustees of the PUMC," March 13, 1946, RFA.
21. Balfour, Diary, pp. 20–30.

seven modern doctors of any kind in the entire province. By 1940, at least thirty-five PUMC graduates were assisting in various projects. For example, an amalgamated medical college, the National Kweiyang Medical School, headed by former PUMC professor Lee Chung-en, was established there. The National Health Administration also based its Public Health Training Institute, still partially funded by the Rockefeller Foundation's China Program, in Kweiyang. Several PUMC graduates were associated with this institute which graduated 234 students between 1938 and 1941. It was moved to Chungking in 1941, but a branch institute continued the Kweiyang instruction courses.

The most ambitious medical project in Kweichow was undertaken by the Kweichow Provincial Government with the cooperation of the Rockefeller Foundation's National Council of Rural Reconstruction. This Council, formerly known as the North China Council for Rural Reconstruction, had changed its name when it moved from Shantung to Kweichow province at the outset of war. A five-year plan, outlined by this Council, the National Health Administration, and the provincial government, aimed at extending health care to all 84 counties in Kweichow.[22] In 1941 the NHA reported that 76 *hsien* had created health centers.[23]

It is difficult to substantiate these statistics, but the National Council for Rural Reconstruction did briefly operate a model *hsien* program in Tingfan county, some sixty miles from Kweiyang. C. C. Ch'en, who had been on the Board of Directors of the North China Council, resigned from Jimmy Yen's Mass Education Movement, and became Director of the National Council's Rural Training Institute.[24]

The Department of Social Medicine at Tingfan was organized in a Buddhist temple with a small 15-bed hospital, run by Ch'en and two other PUMC graduates. Marshall Balfour, who was then still new to medical programs in China, reflected on Ch'en's approach to social medicine: "It is obvious that medicine and public health are interlocking and with no private doctors in the district there is no discussion of pros and cons of social medicine. There will be no such debate in China."[25]

22. F. C. Yen, "China's War-Time Public Health Administration," *China Quarterly* 4 (Spring 1939): 253.

23. "Public Health and Medicine," *China Handbook, 1937–1943* (New York: Macmillan, 1943), pp. 667, 674.

24. For Ch'en's goals at Tingfan, see C. C. Ch'en, "Memorandum on the Program of Work of the National Rural Service Training Institute, 1938–1939," *FA* (601/10).

25. Balfour, *Diary*, p. 24.

The activities of the National Council for Rural Reconstruction in Kweichow province were to be short-lived. In May 1939, C. C. Ch'en submitted his resignation as Director of the Rural Training Institute. Ch'en had decided to accept the position of Provincial Commissioner of Health in Szechwan, his native province. Although they had been active in east China, the rest of the Chinese leaders of the National Council had now assumed other positions in the wartime capital, Chungking. Furthermore, the institutions which had originally constituted the North China Council, such as the Mass Education Movement, Nankai Institute of Economics, and Nanking's School of Agriculture, had been widely dispersed during the retreat to the west. Leadership attrition and the overriding impact of war were the major factors contributing to the early demise of the National Council for Rural Reconstruction.[26]

The fate of the National Council was probably duplicated by other well-meaning medical and social programs in southwest China. It is significant, however, that on paper at least China's wartime medical leaders continued to emphasize the adoption of C. C. Ch'en's *hsien* health organization. Both of the wartime directors of the National Health Administration, Yen Fu-ching and P. Z. King, repeatedly stressed the growth of the *hsien* system. For example, in 1938 and 1939 Yen described eight new health centers in Hupeh, nine mobile units in Hunan, eleven new health stations in Kwangsi, twenty new facilities in Yunnan, and so forth.[27] The government's claim in 1945 that 978 *hsien* in Free China had health centers was undoubtedly highly inflated.[28] The same must be said of reports which implied that each center corresponded in outreach to the original Ting Hsien model.[29]

There does appear to have been an expansion of medical programs during this period, but epidemic control rather than extensive health care service was their main focus. A severe cholera outbreak in 1938 spurred some of the provincial governments to make larger allocations for public health. Whatever the actual extent of the provincial health system, PUMC graduates did provide

26. *Ibid.*, pp. 30–31; Rockefeller Foundation, *Annual Report, 1939*, p. 283.
27. F. C. Yen, "The National Health Administration during War-time," *People's Tribune* N.S. 23 (October 1938), pp. 45–48; Yen, "Some Problems of Public Health," *People's Tribune* N.S. 23 (November 1938): 113–119; Yen, "War-Time Health Administration," pp. 243–258.
28. *China Handbook*, p. 493.
29. Discussions of the *hsien* program appear frequently in medical literature of the 1940's. See, for example, G. H. Woo, "Medical Progress in China," *Asiatic Review* 5 (April 1942): 179–187; Sun Kee-wong, "China's War-Time Health Work," *China Quarterly* 6 (Summer 1941), pp. 288–295.

leadership throughout the war for some of the more effective programs. Provincial commissioners of health included Yao Hsun-yuan in Yunnan, Fang I-chi in Kiangsi, and C. C. Ch'en in Szechwan.

The activities of C. C. Ch'en in his native province of Szechwan are best documented. As to be expected, the building of a provincial network of county health centers became his primary goal. In 1944, five years after taking office, he was able to report that 116 of the 140 provincial *hsien* had some form of health facility. Initially supported by grants from the Rockefeller Foundation and the provincial government, the health programs had witnessed a dramatic increase in financial support from the counties themselves: from nothing in 1939 to $782,000 in 1942, to $19,530,000 in 1945, although inflation must also be taken into account.

Marshall Balfour wrote in 1944 that he felt Szechwan's expansion had been too rapid. For example, in 1939 each of the *hsien* centers had at least one qualified doctor, but by 1944 only 52 percent had qualified physicians and the other 40 percent relied totally on paramedical personnel. Ch'en's emphasis on local leadership in Ting Hsien had been carried over to his work in Szechwan, for Balfour also observed: "Of his staff, 80–90% are Szechwanese, which maybe sacrifices in quality, but it signifies acceptance by local people."[30]

For all its problems, Ch'en's Szechwan medical organization is one bright spot amid the disintegration of the war years. The military medical training programs of his former professor, Robert Lim, are another. Lim, the Scottish-trained son of Lim Boon-keng, President of the University of Amoy, had always been PUMC's most outspokenly patriotic professor. Most of Lim's life prior to becoming Assistant Professor of Physiology at PUMC in 1924 had been spent abroad; it even included a stint in the English army in France during World War I.

One of the few at PUMC to become zealous in the cause of China's resistance to imperialism, Lim himself had personally led PUMC students in a protest march against the British in 1925. Following the Manchurian Incident of 1931 and partial Japanese occupation of north China, Lim organized PUMC students and hospital residents in teams of medical assistance to the Chinese wounded. Lim's identification with the struggle of the Chinese nation *vis-à-vis* imperialist intrusions of any kind compensated for his own British background. His patriotic sentiment was well represented in the closing line of his presidential address to the Chinese Medical Asso-

---

30. Balfour, *Diary*, 1944, p. 155. For the annual reports of the Szechuan Provincial Health Administration, 1942–1945, see *FA* (601/IHB/203).

ciation in 1930: "This is the only way to keep our White Sun blazing in the blue sky!"[31]

Robert Lim's Western ways were to embroil him eventually in repeated personality clashes with his superiors, the generals of the KMT. But in 1937 he appeared in Changsha, during the retreat of the KMT government, with some much needed answers to the problems of providing medical care for the Chinese army. This was a subject to which Lim had already given much thought. In 1930, foreseeing a period when China would be at war and would need army medical officers, he had outlined a curriculum for them, and also spoken of their potential peacetime contributions:

> When peace finally comes, could not these men be in turn drafted to training centres and there given instruction in rural health control so that on their return they could undertake the work of health officers for the districts in which they are stationed?[32]

Lim had also been closely associated with C. C. Ch'en in planning an experimental medical curriculum; many of Ch'en's concepts of medical education were to become incorporated into Lim's Medical Relief Corps (MRC) and Emergency Medical Service Training School (EMSTS).

Established initially as private organizations in 1937, the MRC was soon merged into the activities of the Red Cross Society of China, and the EMSTS was governed by the Army Medical Administration. The purpose of the relief corps was "to give medical aid to the Chinese troops, supplementing the work of the Army Medical Corps, but it also cares so far as possible for the civilian population in the places where its units are stationed."[33] The EMSTS started a series of short courses for army medical officers: "A policy of 'stage education' is being followed whereby the education of such subsidiary personnel can be so organized in stages, intervening between periods of field service, that it will be possible for them eventually to gain a complete medical education."[34] Three two-year stages were created: medical subordinate, assistant medical officer, and qualified medical officer.

As the Nationalist government retreated further west into Szechwan, the medical training programs were also moved, eventually

31. Lim, "Presidential Address," p. 120.

32. *Ibid.*, p. 119.

33. Roger Greene, "Medical Relief Corps of the Red Cross Society of China," 1942, p. 1, 989.08, RCA. When he wrote this report, Greene was a special consultant on Chinese medical affairs at the State Department.

34. Sze Sze-ming, *China's Health Problems* (Washington, D.C.: The China Medical Association, 1943), p. 32.

being located for the duration of the war near Kweiyang, Kweichow. By 1941, the MRC had a staff of 153 doctors, 314 nurses, 940 medical assistants, plus numerous mechanics, technicians, and drivers. The 150 medical relief teams were divided into units of about 18 people, with each paramedical military group accompanied by a qualified doctor and nurse. In 1942 the EMSTS reported it had trained 5,000 paramedical personnel and had launched five branch schools and several orthopedic centers.[35]

Many of the reports by American medical advisors to the Chinese army were discouraging; Robert Lim's organizations appear to be a major exception. In 1942 Robert Barnett, Director of ABMAC, described Tuyukwang where Lim's training took place:

> There is a community life there which is very complete, I think. They are building up to something very energetic and productive in the community in Kweiyang and then spreading it out into the country. That may not make much sense, but when they moved to Kweiyang there was nothing there. In time they build their water supply, their roads. They have their own dynamo. The self-sufficiency of Kweiyang makes it a real community.[36]

There were a number of reasons for the initial success of Lim's programs. The semi-official character of the organization, coupled with Lim's practical yet professional leadership, enticed a number of well-trained medical graduates who would have been loathe to serve as medical officers in the poorly organized Chinese army. Lim had been a popular professor at PUMC, and a number of his former students joined him in Kweichow.[37]

By 1943, nevertheless, discord with army personnel and the Chinese Red Cross itself had undermined Lim's authority. General Ho Ying-ch'in was irate that Robert Lim had been awarded the Order of Merit by the United States at the same time as himself and Chiang Kai-shek. Red Cross personnel accused Lim of hoarding supplies and juggling financial accounts. Much more damaging, however, was the accusation made by jealous, competing army medical personnel that Lim and some of his subordinates were Communists. After 1943 Lim was removed from the EMSTS and the MRC. Holding only a nominal position as a Supervisory Com-

35. Greene, "Medical Relief Corps," pp. 1–2; J. Blaine Gwinn, "American Red Cross Activities in China, 1937–1943," pp. 15–17, 895.08, *RCA*.

36. Robert Barnett, *ABMAC Bulletin* 4 (August–September, 1942): 5. For other favorable reports see Agnes Smedley, *Stories of the Wounded*, and Walter Wesselius, "Medical Relief Corps of the National Red Cross Society of China," June 1, 1941, 985.08, *RCA*.

37. For example, P'eng Tah-mou, '33; Thomas Ma, '35; Loo Chih-teh, '29.

missioner for army medical activities, his influence was greatly diminished.[38]

The Army Medical Relief Corps, the National Medical College of Kweiyang, the Tingfan county demonstration, a variety of provincial health programs—these are but a few examples of the projects to which PUMC associates contributed wartime leadership in southwest China. The National Health Administration itself, and its subsidiary, the National Institute of Health, continued to be dominated by PUMC alumni or former faculty. The intent of these health organizations was to extend health care and training in unoccupied China. But war conditions and a graft-ridden government cast an inevitable web of failure around their efforts.

Monetary inflation had perhaps the most destructive impact on wartime relief programs. By 1943, most of the funds donated to the NHA from the RF, ABMAC, and the Nationalist government itself were primarily used to maintain the livelihood of the NHA staff and their families—not for the expansion of medical care. Some NHA employees were discovered to be drawing double or triple salaries—from the NHA, RF, and ABMAC. American Red Cross investigators uncovered tremendous caches of drugs in Kweiyang, hoarded by the Medical Relief Corps.[39] Jessie Lutz, in her discussion of the role of the Christian colleges during this period, has described the atmosphere well: "As the elementary task of securing food and shelter grew more difficult in interior China, many resorted to a kind of privatism. Day-to-day survival became the preoccupation of many."[40]

While waiting for the war to end, many who had been active in the College planned for the reestablishment of PUMC. Their comments parallel Mary Ferguson's 1946 report which emphasized the integration of PUMC personnel with other medical practitioners, but they also reflect a new confidence in the nature of the old PUMC. In mid-1945 a contingent of PUMC colleagues and Chinese medical leaders met at the home of Trustee Y. T. Tsur in Chungking to discuss the educational aspects of a resurrected PUMC. Attending were P. Z. King, James K. Shen, Marian Yang, Chu Chang-keng, I. C. Yuan, Robert Lim, and Loo Chih-teh, among others. It should be noted that there were no Americans present at this meeting—

---

38. Gwinn, "American Red Cross Activities in China"; Wesselius, "Medical Relief Corps"; Dwight Edwards, *et al.*, "Confidential Notes on an Interview with General Ho Ying-ch'in," August 16, 1943, 985.08, *RCA*.

39. Claude Forkner, letter to the author, October 25, 1971; Balfour, *Diary*, 1943, pp. 43–44, tends to confirm Forkner's accusations. See also, Gwinn, "American Red Cross Activities in China," pp. 17–18.

40. Lutz, *China and the Christian Colleges*, p. 361.

Chinese were asserting their own leadership. Most of these medical doctors generally adhered to the policy of perpetuating PUMC as a first-rate medical college. A number, including Y. T. Tsur and, at a later meeting, C. C. Ch'en, still felt that instruction should be in English while efforts to develop a Chinese medical vocabulary resumed. P. Z. King argued for the continuation of high standards, coupled with the expansion of the student body to about 50 students per class. He and several others also argued for increased public health instruction.

In reports of these meetings and others, no apologies were offered for stringent standards.[41] Kuomintang educational and political leaders, including T. V. Soong and Vice-Minister of Education K. L. Chu, urged that the institution be restored as a top-notch school. One may speculate on the rash of reinvigorated enthusiasm for PUMC in the mid-forties. The leadership exercised by some PUMC graduates during the war had proved PUMC's worth to some observers. War had severely curtailed the medical programs of other institutions. China was desperately in need of the professors which only PUMC could produce. Even those most active in paramedical training, C. C. Ch'en, Marian Yang, and Chu Chang-keng, had always envisioned PUMC at the apex of a national medical system. Finally, the excellence of PUMC would, it was assumed, continue to be funded by American dollars.

When the war ended, most of the national health departments returned to Nanking. Ambitious plans were made with cooperating American relief agencies for extensive national medical programs. For a brief time there was a flurry surrounding the medical reconstruction of China. ABMAC, United China Relief, and the new United Nations Relief and Rehabilitation Administration (UNRRA) all contributed funds, advisors, and ideas. J. Heng Liu, who had spent most of the war in the United States as the Medical Director of the China Defense Supplies Corporation, became a medical coordinator of UNRRA. Robert Lim, whose American connections now became an asset, was appointed Surgeon-General to oversee all medical work in the armed forces.[42]

The optimism which accompanied the end of World War II was

41. "Minutes of Two Meetings Called by Dr. Y. T. Tsur for Exchange of Views on the Future of the P.U.M.C.," June 9, 1942; "July 10, 1945 at Dr. T. A. Li's House," both in *RFA*. Harold Loucks to Richard Pearce, October 5, 1945, *RFA*, describes conversations with several PUMC Chinese faculty; Ferguson, "Report to the Trustees," 1946.

42. For brief biographical sketches of Liu and Lim, see Magnus I. Gregersen, "Dr. J. Heng Liu," *ABMAC Bulletin* 20 (May 1959): 1, 4; George E. Armstrong, "Robert Kho-seng Lim, Ph.D.," *ABMAC Bulletin* 30 (July 1969): 1–3.

soon vanquished by the onset of civil war. There may have been ambitious American medical relief programs during these last years of the 1940s, but the Chinese medical profession itself turned inward. The spirit of public health, which had been a progressive sign in the mid-thirties and even during the early years of the Japanese conflict, was not rekindled during these last years of the Republican era. Inflation and corruption, combined with the ever-prevalent problem of sheer survival, turned many doctors away from national or institutional service into more lucrative private practice. Disenchanted by the Kuomintang and ambivalent toward the Communists, the medical profession, like much of the rest of China, awaited the outcome of civil war.

This was the pessimistic situation in which plans for the reconstitution of PUMC were made. The interdisciplinary China Program of the mid-thirties had temporarily diverted RF attention away from its primary beneficiary, the Peking Union Medical College. Even during the war, John D. Rockefeller, Jr. was still considering the possibility of "some day moving the PUMC into the interior and reestablishing it on far simpler and less expensive foundations."[43] But when the conflict ended, in the closing years of Raymond Fosdick's tenure as president, the Rockefeller Foundation refocused its attention on the prestigious medical college.

Transfer of power from the Rockefeller Foundation to the ostensibly independent CMB Inc. had been incomplete during the prewar years. Likewise, devolution of authority from the CMB to the PUMC Trustees remained ill-defined. In a 1945 report, Claude Forkner described the tensions which had existed between the Rockefeller Foundation, CMB, and PUMC in former years, and then quoted C. C. Ch'en, elected in 1944 as a PUMC Trustee, as saying: "Unless some change is made in the organization . . . anybody who wishes to help out would get into unnecessary trouble. In other words, the present organization of the CMB and the PUMC only speaks favorably for those who will not say or do a thing."[44]

Nonetheless, a number of individuals began to voice their opinions for a more responsive and effective postwar administration. C. C. Ch'en himself suggested combining the China Medical Board and the PUMC Trustees into one body.[45] C. E. Lim recommended that the PUMC Trustees should include more medical experts instead

43. Rockefeller Jr. to Raymond Fosdick, November 23, 1942, *RFA.*

44. Claude Forkner, "Memorandum on Planning for the Postwar Program of the China Medical Board, Inc. and the PUMC," 1945, p. 2, *RFA.*

45. C. C. Ch'en to Claude Forkner, March 12, 1945, *RFA.*

of enrolling prestigious statesmen.[46] Marshall Balfour proposed gradually transferring American funds to the PUMC Trustees.[47]

In New York, however, post-war planning for PUMC continued to be plagued by the triangular relationship between the Rockefeller Foundation, the China Medical Board, and Peking Union Medical College. There was a growing recognition of the need for the PUMC Trustees to have at least sole managerial authority, but even this commitment was hedged. One stands aghast at the reenactment of controversy surrounding the appointment of a postwar PUMC director. With echoes of the Roger Greene debacle in 1934, the RF and CMB refused to ratify the PUMC Trustees' choice for director. Only after considerable delay, politicking, and the sending of an American survey commission to China in 1946 was Dr. Lee Chung-en eventually appointed Director.[48]

In these postwar years, the Rockefeller Foundation did appear to be extricating itself, at least financially, from the CMB and PUMC. At a meeting of the RF in January of 1947, with the persistent encouragement of John D. Rockefeller, Jr., the Foundation allocated a final sum of US$10,000,000 to the China Medical Board; this increased the endowment of the CMB to US$22,000,000. The cable which conveyed this decision to Hu Shih, the new Chairman of the PUMC Trustees, also announced the end of Rockefeller Foundation involvement in PUMC:

> In voting this appropriation today the Trustees of the Rockefeller Foundation wish to record the fact that it represents the terminal contribution of the Foundation to the China Medical Board and thus toward the work of the Peiping Union Medical College. Insofar as the Foundation is concerned, it completes the task undertaken in 1915, when the creation of a modern medical school in China was agreed upon. The development of new departments in the Peiping Union Medical College or further support of existing activities must be left to other friends of the institution. The Rockefeller Foundation can do no more.[49]

One partner in the three-way management of PUMC had, perhaps finally, departed. The revised relationship between the two remaining members, the PUMC and the China Medical Board, did not last long enough to be evaluated. But the authority of the PUMC Trustees certainly remained nebulous. As an advisor to John D. Rockefeller, III, put it: the financial solvency of the CMB and the token addition

46. Isidore Snapper, "Interview, C. E. Lim," 1941, *RFA*.
47. Balfour, *Diary*, 1946, pp. 262–263.
48. Ferguson, *CMB and PUMC*, pp. 194–197.
49. Quoted in *Ibid.*, p. 200.

of one Chinese member to its Board in no way insured the transfer of power to China and the PUMC Trustees.[50] Financial control still remained totally in the hands of the American-based China Medical Board.

Still, the PUMC which finally reopened its doors in October of 1947, after having weathered occupation by both the Japanese and General George C. Marshall's Peace Commission, was more nearly a truly Chinese college. Director Lee and the PUMC Trustees were eager to resume the activities of the College, even at a much re- duced level. Hu Shih wrote to Philo Parker, the new Chairman of the CMB, laying forth the reasons for the immediate resumption of classes:

> The buildings are now free. Can we let them stand idle? . . . The PUMC has in the past been criticized as being too well off, its staff and students too comfortable, and too much separated from the life of the country. If we should defer reopening until it is possible to reproduce our pre- war working conditions, while at the same time others are carrying on the work of teaching and healing in spite of unfavorable circumstances, then indeed the imputation that the PUMC cannot face adversity would have some basis in fact.[51]

The entering class in 1947 had only 22 students. With but three exceptions (Harold Loucks, William Adolph and Reinhard Hoep- pli), however, the faculty was entirely Chinese, including 16 former PUMC graduates. Some who had been on the staff since the mid- twenties now became departmental chairmen: Chang Hsiao-ch'ien became the first Chinese head of the Department of Medicine; Chang Hsi-chun, head of the Department of Physiology; and Hsieh Chih-kuang, head of the Department of Radiology. One PUMC grad- uate, Lim Kha-t'i, was also among the heads of the departments, hers being Obstetrics and Gynecology.[52]

Only a little more than a year after the PUMC reopened, Peking was occupied, in January 1949, by the Communist forces. During the first year under Communist government, the Western faculty remained in Peking and, for the most part, the activities of the College continued. Four unions had been organized within the Col- lege by the summer of 1949—the Students' Union, Clerical Union, Workers' Union, and Professors' Union—although there was no interruption in medical instruction. Mary Ferguson, who was still in Peking at the time, later recorded the atmosphere in the College

50. Webb (?) to John D. Rockefeller III, January 9, 1947, RFA.
51. Hu Shih to Philo Parker, April 30, 1947, RFA.
52. Ferguson, CMB and PUMC, pp. 202–204.

on October 1, 1949, when the People's Republic of China was officially proclaimed:

> Students and staff had instructions through their respective unions to get gray cotton uniforms following the accepted pattern, to be ready to participate in the city-wide parade and mass demonstration in front of the T'ien An Men on October 1. . . .

> Excitement mounted among the students. Detailed information on organization of the parade came from the Central Labor Union. All schools were closed so that everyone could take part. The PUMC contingent which included students, workers, clerks and some professional staff (but not Dr. Lee), gathered in San T'iao Hutung between the Auditorium and "C" Court. While waiting for the signal to move, squad leaders taught them slogans to shout as they marched. It was evening before the last of the workers saluted Mao Tse-tung and the other party leaders who stood on the balcony of the great red "Gate of Heavenly Peace" with its crown of imperial yellow tiles. This was the regime under which the future of the PUMC would have to be worked out.[53]

While PUMC accommodated itself to Communist rule, other medical institutions and personnel closely associated with the Nationalist regime fled from the mainland. The National Defense Medical Center, the peacetime successor to the Emergency Medical Service Training School (EMSTS), had been reestablished in Shanghai under the direction of Loo Chih-teh at the end of the war. A number of former PUMC colleagues who had been associated with the military medical programs formed the nucleus of this institution, including P'eng Tah-mou, Thomas Ma, and Shih Hsi-en. When the Nationalist government withdrew to Taiwan, this medical institution also migrated across the Formosa Straits.[54]

Many of the public health leaders of Republican China chose neither to retreat to Taiwan nor to remain in mainland China. Although they were disenchanted with the Nationalist government, their long service in its health programs made them politically suspect to the new regime. A number joined the World Health Organization of the United Nations, including Fang I-chi, Yuan I-chin, and Chu Chang-keng. Two of the older members of the faculty, Robert Lim and Wu Hsien, as well as a number of their students, left for haven in the United States.[55]

A few former leaders of public health remained in the People's

53. *Ibid.*, p. 214.
54. T. M. P'eng [P'eng Tah-mou], "A System of Medical and Allied Education at the National Defense Medical Center, Taipei, Taiwan," *Journal of Medical Education* 37 (1962): 463–472.
55. Interview with Yuan I-chin, October 12, 1971.

Republic. C. C. Ch'en had become Dean of the Chungking Medical College during the late forties; he stayed in this institution.[56] P. Z. King became an official in the new health ministry. Others, such as Yao Hsun-yuan, faded into obscurity. It was slightly ironical that these PUMC colleagues, who had been most progressive and most active in the adaptation of modern medicine in the Republican period, were no longer to be symbols of PUMC's leadership. Since 1949, representatives of PUMC in high places have primarily been medical scientists who had remained aloof from politics or social change in earlier decades.

The outbreak of the Korean War in the summer of 1950, and the subsequent participation of Chinese forces, brought an end to any American involvement in PUMC. All Western staff, except Reinhard Hoeppli, a Swiss citizen who remained until 1952, withdrew from China, although the China Medical Board continued for a time to send operating funds to the College. When American financial transactions with China were frozen in December of 1950, officers of the CMB attempted to continue remitting some funds to China. It was to no avail. The era of American participation and of private colleges had terminated. On January 23, 1951, Dr. Lee Chung-en sent his last cable to the China Medical Board: "Referring your 51001 [telegram number] College Nationalized January Twentieth."[57]

56. For a brief glimpse at Ch'en's life during the 1950s, see his letter to Philip Drinker, December 21, 1956, PUMC PAPERS. During the years 1945–1950 Szechwan was the scene of a number of medical programs which received direction from Ch'en. See "Minutes of Founder's Meeting of the Anti-Tuberculosis Association (Chengtu), March 30, 1946," 985.5, RCA; Chang Kwei, Studies on Hookworm Disease in Szechwan Province, West China (Baltimore: Johns Hopkins University Press, 1949).

57. Quoted in Ferguson, CMB and PUMC, p. 225.

NINE

Epilogue

With you, I deeply regret that the Peking Union Medical College should have passed out of the hands of the China Medical Board and been taken over by the Peking Government. . . . We must not feel that this necessarily means a curtailment of the College's usefulness, but rather only a change in its management attended very probably by certain limitations in its ideals and standards. But who are we to say that this may not be the Lord's way of achieving the intent of the founders, although it be a way so wholly different from what has been in our minds.

John D. Rockefeller, Jr., to Mary Ferguson, 1951

IN 1972, NEARLY a quarter of a century after the nationalization of PUMC, the People's Republic of China sent its first medical delegation to the United States. A lively gray-haired woman from Capital Hospital, Dr. Lin Ch'iao-chih, better known to her former American friends as Kha-t'i Lim, was one of the emissaries of China's new medicine. She was eager to learn of new developments in American cancer research, a direct reflection of her own important contributions to studies of cancer in China.[1] But at a press conference in Washington, D.C., she also declared confidently, "We don't have so many new things [in medicine] but we are able to push care out [deliver service to the people]."[2]

Over fifty years earlier, in 1921, Dr. Lin had been but a first-year premedical student at PUMC. It is doubtful that she even attended the dedication exercises. The thoughts that were expressed that day were a mixture of American confidence in the supremacy of their medical institutions, and latent Chinese hope for their ultimate Sinification. The participants were the American benefactors

1. Kha-t'i Lim, *et al.*, "Mass Survey for Cancer of Cervix Uteri in China," *CMJ* 81 (1962): 705–712; Lim, "Obstetrics and Gynecology in the Past Ten Years," *CMJ* 79 (1959): 375–383.
2. Stuart Auerbach, "China Doctors Take A Look at U.S. Medicine," *Washington Post*, 14 October 1972, 2:1.

and the Chinese recipients. Since that time the Chinese recipients, under several governments, have become creative, innovative adapters of scientific medicine. While problems remain, the figurative image of China as the "sick man of Asia" is an anachronism. Today there is national pride in China's medical accomplishments, and the West looks to the East for instruction in the distribution of medical services.

To trace the careers of PUMC alumni, such as Kha-t'i Lim, since "liberation" is to discover that China's recent medical gains have been cumulative, based in part on the prior training and experience of a core professional contingent. It is to follow the continuing debates regarding elites and scientific medicine in modern China. And, it is to realize that the question of "standards" with which the early Rockefeller educators wrestled is not easily resolved.

Graham Peck, in his masterful account of China during World War II, *Two Kinds of Time*, describes a journey from sultry, foggy Chungking to the clear, desert air of northwest China. The weather contrast between the Nationalist bastion in Szechwan and the Communist enclaves north of the Yellow River was frequently cited by KMT leaders as a reason for the more favorable journalistic reports emanating from the North.[3] The chronological journey from the Sino-Japanese and civil wars to the present time is somewhat similar to Peck's geographical one; the chaos and decadence of the war period stand in sharp contrast to the Promethean organization of the People's Republic of China.

A definitive history of medicine and public health in twentieth century China has yet to be written, but it will have to include a discussion of the problems faced by the People's Republic in creating a medical profession that was both "red" and "expert," both politically conscious and technologically competent. It will also describe the steps taken to distribute medical care more equitably throughout the far-flung rural regions of China. The PUMC community constituted a nationally recognized Western-oriented medical elite. As such, they were "expert," not "red," and were frequently singled out to demonstrate the mistakes of pre-Communist medical policies. They were simultaneously enlisted as spokesmen for new policies. Information is not available on their personal views of the dual roles or of hardships that might have been incurred. But the published words and recorded actions of the PUMC community during the past three decades provide a revealing record of the changing medical priorities of the People's Republic of China.

3. Graham Peck, *Two Kinds of Time* (Boston: Houghton Mifflin, 1967), p. 158.

During the fall of 1951 and spring of 1952, thought reform and ideological remolding sessions were held for the educators, scientists, and intellectuals of Peking. Generally, these lasted four months and resulted in personal statements castigating class origins, pro-American sentiments, anti-Russian suspicions, and previous political indifference. At PUMC, renamed the China Union Medical College, these ideological campaigns began in the fall of 1951, intensified in the spring of 1952, and culminated in an exhibition of U.S. crimes committed in the name of research at PUMC.[4] The anti-Americanism expressed in these years is new, but the charges of elitism, excessively high standards, imitation of Western curriculum, and luxurious living had been leveled against PUMC since its very beginnings.

One of the first of the published confessions was by Teng Chia-tung, '33. It concentrated on denouncing PUMC as an elite institution. Criticizing the "PUMC style and standard," Teng described the insidious impact of the College on Chinese students:

> Special were its construction, system, education, tradition . . . and almost everything. After at least five years' training here, the students considered themselves special, and they were truly special. . . . They thought that they were specially learned, wiser than others, wanted to do special work, and considered themselves special personages.[5]

PUMC was especially culpable for having copied the ways of the West: "When they [the educational standards and curriculum] were first established, after much careful study and consideration, they were based on the needs, not of China, but the U.S."[6]

Another confession by a graduate of the same class was that of Wu Jui-p'ing, who was Vice-Director of Peking Children's Hospital and a professor at Peking University Medical College. Wu described his more than nineteen years in imperialist organizations, concluding that "I was completely intoxicated by the American way of life with all its material comforts of a nice house, fine equipment, excellent food and luxurious life."[7] Wu further revealed his pride at being sent abroad for study, his lack of interest in expelling the

---

4. For simplification I continue to use the term "PUMC" to designate the medical institution. For general background on thought reform see Theodore H. E. Chen, *Thought Reform of the Chinese Intellectuals* (Hong Kong: University of Hong Kong Press, 1960); Chalmers Johnson, *Communist Policies toward the Intellectual Class* (Hong Kong: Union Research Institute, 1959), pp. 55–68; Lutz, *China and the Christian Colleges*, pp. 461–473. Events at PUMC seem to parallel those at Yenching.

5. *Jen-min Jih-pao*, November 16, 1951, in *Survey of China Mainland Press* (*SCMP*), No. 261, p. 23.

6. *Ibid.*, p. 24.

7. *Chin-pu Jih-pao*, May 27, 1952, in *SCMP*, No. 354, p. 31.

Japanese from China, his ignorance of Soviet medicine, and his preference for rich patients.

After recounting these personal shortcomings, the PUMC alumnus turned to analyze the Rockefeller Foundation's motive for creating PUMC. Depicting the medical college as "the greatest bulwark for cultural oppression," Wu affirmed that PUMC students were trained to be leaders so that from high positions they could spread imperialist doctrines, especially in the field of public health:

> The department of public health, headed by a big spy (J. B. Grant) offered the earliest opportunity to go abroad. Health centers were headed by PUMC graduates, and all the health services in colleges, middle schools and primary schools were dominated by PUMC graduates ... to spread the poison. . . . Through the public health work, the poison was spread to workers and the public in general.[8]

The most important of these deprecatory statements was that of Lee Chung-en (Li Tsung-en), Director of PUMC. On January 9, 1952, Peking's daily newspaper, the *Jen-min Jih-pao*, printed a rather long, personal exposé from PUMC's first *bona fide* Chinese director. At PUMC he had "remained in this little world for over ten years, teaching, doing research, enjoying the good name of a 'scholar,' receiving a nice salary, and living a comfortable life to my full satisfaction." Downplaying his role as wartime director of Kweiyang Medical College, Lee concentrated on the inadequacies in his educational philosophy: "I myself believed that the type of education I promoted exerted definite effects on the change of the social order, and that by raising the standards of my school I could foster the development of medical education." Lee had apparently resisted the earliest efforts under the Communists to modify the program at PUMC: "For quite a time after liberation, I persistently held that medical education should be kept up to international standards and observed the College's pure technical point of view. I did not realize the correct principle that technique must necessarily be integrated with politics."[9]

The PUMC Director, as had Wu Jui-p'ing, then turned to analyze the reasons for Rockefeller charity. Declaring that "the Foundation is a world organ for cultural aggression," he assigned two motives to the Foundation's program: first to "win the name of a larger philanthropist and thereby to enlarge its oil markets," and the other, "to evade taxes."[10]

8. *Ibid.*, p. 35.
9. *Jen-min Jih-pao*, January 9, 1952, in *SCMP*, No. 439, pp. 19–21.
10. *Ibid.*, p. 22.

A fourth ideological confession, by Professor Lin Ch'iao-chih is significant because, as reflected by her trip abroad in 1972, she was destined to become one of the more visible medical leaders under the PRC. Her article, titled "Open the PUMC Window and Take a Look at the Motherland," has more flair than the three preceding personal statements. It begins: "For the past 30-odd years I have observed the motherland through a closed window of the Peiping Union Medical College." She described her education as a young Fukienese girl at PUMC, her career as a junior professor, and blamed herself for lack of political consciousness during the Japanese invasion: "At the outbreak of the 'July 7 incident,' many patriotic people, leaving everything behind, got out of Peking to resist the Japanese. I, however, persisted in my work in the 'PUMC' because it was my little universe as well as my little kingdom." She stayed in Peking throughout the war, and after Liberation took a "wait and see" attitude toward the Communist regime.[11]

Now noting that many positive changes had been seen from her "window" at PUMC, Dr. Lin attributed her change in attitude to the *San-fan* ("Three-anti") movement at PUMC. The exposure of corruption, waste, and bureaucratism at PUMC in the early 1950s made her doubt the PUMC standard. After reading Chairman Mao, she learned that "technique is inseparable from politics." After the exhibition of U.S. imperialism staged at PUMC, and the discovery of germ warfare in Korea, her feelings toward America also reversed. Acknowledging that the United States was an imperialist nation, Lin Ch'iao-chih expressed her desire to learn instead from the Soviet Union. Her article concluded: "The window of the 'PUMC' is open and the five-star red flag of the Mao Tse-tung time is hoisted while the entire working personnel of the College have come to their own."[12]

The exhibit of U.S. medical crimes committed at PUMC was mounted at the former Rockefeller college in the late spring of 1952. The Shanghai newspaper, *Ta Kung Pao*, noted that ideological reconstruction had not penetrated deeply enough into the fabric of the PUMC community: "Since they had ideologically been so deeply influenced by U.S. imperialism, many of them are still unable to see immediately the serious extent to which they have been poisoned by such cultural aggression."[13]

The display of American crimes included letters and records from

11. *Jen-min Jih-pao*, September 27, 1952, in *SCMP*, No. 439, p. 29.
12. *Ibid.*, pp. 30–31.
13. *Ta Kung Pao*, July 26, 1952, in *SCMP*, No. 398, p. 8.

the PUMC files which purported to show the subversive nature of U.S. activities at PUMC. A letter from Roger Greene to John Grant concerning U.S.–China relations was featured to prove that "from the start the hospital and teaching college was seen by the imperialists as an instrument that fitted in with their plans for controlling China and the Rockefeller Foundation with all its tawdry benevolent trimmings was a useful cover for the purpose."[14] The indoctrination at PUMC had included teaching in English and introducing the American way of life. By exhibiting case histories from various medical files, the show also attempted to prove that Chinese patients had been experimented upon maliciously by American doctors.

The exposition of American medical crimes at PUMC was one way to neutralize American affiliations; participation in the exposure of American germ warfare in Korea was another. In July 1952, Fang Shih-san (Shisan C. Fang), who was the first director of the Peking Health Station, addressed an international congress in East Berlin, enumerating scientific data and eyewitness accounts of bacteriological warfare in Korea.[15] In September the normal publication of *The Chinese Medical Journal* was suspended, and a series of special issues on germ warfare in Korea was published. Chung Huei-lan, PUMC '29, Director of the People's Hospital in Peking and Editor of *The Chinese Medical Journal* at this time, became one of the primary investigators of germ warfare.

In addition to technical reports, the journal also published a special supplement, titled "Views of Chinese Scientists on U.S. Bacterial Warfare." The roster of authors included P. Z. King and James F. K. Shen, Director and Vice-Director, respectively, of the old NHA under the Kuomintang. PUMC professors who participated included C. U. Lee and Hu Ch'uan-k'uei. Director Lee's statement was typical: "The American aggressors with the collaboration of Japanese and Nazi germ war criminals launched bacterial warfare against Korea and Northwest China in flagrant violation of international law."[16] The support of these leading men gave authority to the charge of germ warfare; furthermore, it was indicative of the role they played as publicists in the mobilization of support for the new government's health program.

14. "Sordid Practices of U.S. Imperialists at PUMC Exhibition," *New China News Agency* (hereinafter *NCNA*), June 22, 1952, in *SCMP*, No. 361, p. 9.

15. Fang Shih-san, "On Bacteriological Warfare," *CMJ* 70 (1952): 329–332. Fang appears to have been a major spokesman on this issue to international groups; see also his address at the World Congress of Doctors at Vienna, "Effects of War on the Health of the People," *CMJ* 71 (1953): 321–327.

16. Lee Chung-en, "International Scientists Give Their Verdict," *CMJ* Supplement, 70 (1952): 37.

Ideological struggles abated during the years 1953–1956. For the most part, scientific institutions in China remained relatively stable during this period. As John Lindbeck has written:

> From the Communist viewpoint, there was, in fact, little need for change in the functional organization of science as it existed in 1949. On some points there were strong similarities in the outlook and policies of Nationalists and Communists. Both looked on science as a tool with which to develop China's resources and national strength.[17]

Medical education was, however, subjected to pressures to increase the number of graduating medical students. Courses were shortened to three or four years, although a wide variety of instructional programs continued. Training of secondary physicians, after the pattern of the Soviet Union, greatly increased the number of practicing medical personnel.[18]

In the midst of all this, PUMC, as the China Union Medical College, continued as an identifiable institution. In 1952, the enrollment was increased and the spacious facilities more fully occupied —the animal house, for example, became a hospital ward. Ample funds were available to support the medical work. In 1953, Dr. Harold Loucks, at this time the Chairman of the CMB Inc., observed from New York: "To give the devil his due, the Communists are more interested in education than any previous Chinese government."[19] C. U. Lee was retained as Medical Director, and former faculty and graduates continued to dominate the College. By the mid-fifties, some realignment seems to have taken place, for contemporary reports suggest that the College had become a specialized graduate research center with relatively few students, and that the hospital had become a separate entity.[20]

PUMC graduates and faculty began to reappear during the mid-1950s as the new China's medical elite. The Chinese Academy of Sciences, which elected to its membership the most eminent representatives of the various scientific fields, announced its member-

17. John Lindbeck, "Organization and Development of Science," in Sydney Gould, ed., *Sciences in Communist China* (Baltimore: American Association for Advancement of Science, 1961), p. 7.

18. Leo A. Orleans, "Medical Education and Manpower in Communist China," *Comparative Education Review* 13 (February 1969): 20–42.

19. The Rockefeller Foundation, "Confidential Monthly Report," No. 146, (March 1, 1953), p. 20, *RFA*. Also see "Chinese Union Medical College Expands," *NCNA*, December 17, 1954, in *SCMP*, No. 951, pp. 29–30.

20. "Some Professors of China Union Medical College Ask to Be Entrusted with More Apprentices," *Kwang-ming Jih-pao*, February 7, 1957, in *SCMP*, No. 1484, p. 18; T. F. Fox, "The New China: Some Medical Impressions," *Lancet*, November 9, 1957, No. 7002, p. 938.

ship in 1955. Of the nine medical members in the field of biomedical science, seven were either former PUMC faculty or graduates.[21]

The Chinese Medical Association also continued to be dominated by PUMC personnel, just as it had in earlier decades. Vice-Presidents of the CMA included Lin Ch'iao-chih, Chung Huei-lan, Hu Ch'uan-k'uei, Fang Shih-san, and Yen Fu-ching, the latter having been Vice-Director of PUMC in 1927–1928. The publications of the CMA, which included *The Chinese Medical Journal* and all other scientific medical periodicals, were primarily edited by PUMC colleagues. Chung Huei-lan was editor of the *CMJ* from 1950 until just before the Cultural Revolution, and his editorial staff was primarily composed of former professors and classmates. For example, in 1962 nineteen of the twenty-six editors were former PUMC faculty or graduates.[22]

In 1956–1957, the People's Republic outlined a twelve-year plan for scientific and medical research, and undertook a major reorganization of medical and scientific institutions. Among the new centralized research agencies, modeled after those in the Soviet Union, was the Chinese Academy of Medical Sciences. This institution assumed supervision over a number of colleges and hospitals, including the China Union Medical College and hospital. Its offices were located in the beautiful buildings of the former Rockefeller college. PUMC associates also dominated the leadership of this most prestigious academy.

Huang Chia-ssu, '33, and former professor at Shanghai First Medical College, distinguished himself in the mid-fifties by becoming the first Chinese to perform successful open-chest surgery. In 1959, he became Director of the Chinese Academy of Medical Sciences and remains in this position to the present day. Lin Ch'iao-chih became one of four deputy directors. Of the eight known directors of the participating specialized institutes, six were PUMC colleagues.[23] In addition to those who have been conspicuous in

21. The seven were: Chang Hsiao-ch'ien, Chu Fu-t'ang, Chung Huei-lan, Feng Lan-chou, Huang Chia-ssu, Lin Ch'iao-chih, and Ma Wen-chao; see Cheng Chu-yuan, *Scientific and Engineering Manpower in Communist China, 1949–1964* (Washington, D.C.: National Science Foundation, 1965), pp. 323–338.

22. A list of the officers and members of the CMA can be found in *CMJ* 74 (1956): 411. Also see, *Directory of Selected Scientific Institutions in Mainland China* (Stanford: Hoover Institution Press, 1970), pp. 206–208. For a short time during 1962, *CMJ* published a list of its editorial board in each issue; for example, see *CMJ* 81 (July 1962), inside the back cover.

23. Cheng, *Scientific and Engineering Manpower*, pp. 363–366; research institute directors included Hu Ch'uan-k'uei, Ch'en Wen-kuei, Chang Wei-shen, Chu Fu-t'ang, Teng Chia-tung, and Yang Chien. See also Richard P. Suttmeier, "The Academy of Medical Sciences," in Joseph R. Quinn, ed., *Medicine and Public Health*

research and education, the rank-and-file PUMC alumni also appear to have been quite productive. A cursory survey of Chinese medical journals from 1949–1965 revealed articles by at least 75 (24 percent) of the PUMC graduates. The topics ranged from kala-azar to cancer, from plastic surgery to neurology.

The dominant role of the PUMC community in medical sciences can be pointed to with a degree of confidence. It is somewhat more difficult to determine whether any PUMC affiliates were active leaders in the mass public health campaigns which dramatically improved health conditions in China. A few former public health officials were incorporated into Li Te-ch'uan's Health Ministry. P. Z. King (Chin Pao-shan) had joined the World Health Organization in the late forties, but in early 1950 he was invited by Li Te-ch'uan to return to China as one of her technical advisors.[24] During the Kuomintang era, King, who had served as Vice-Director of the NHA under J. Heng Liu and Yen Fu-ching before becoming director in his own right, was widely regarded as China's most competent technical expert in the field of public health. By 1953, he was reporting in glowing terms the vast advances made under the Communist regime.[25] Yen Ching-ch'ing, a 1932 PUMC graduate in public health, became Commissioner of Health for Peking, and served in that capacity from 1950 until the Cultural Revolution.[26] Although little is known of their activities, Marian Yang continued to live and work in Peking, and C. C. Ch'en was involved in health programs in Szechwan.

Perhaps even more important than attempting to trace the influence of specific people in official health agencies is to note that in the PRC many programs, which had existed in the KMT period in only embryonic form, now became realities. A major emphasis in the post-1950 writing of P. Z. King and of outside Western observers has been the expansion of *hsien* health programs. King reported—these figures are likely to have been exaggerated, as were those of earlier decades—that 92 percent of the counties had some form of modern medical care in 1952.[27]

---

in the People's Republic of China (Washington, D.C.: National Institutes of Health, 1972), pp. 173–190.

24. Interview with I. C. Yuan, October 12, 1971.

25. P. Z. King, "U.S. Imperialists Meet Double Debate in Their Bacterial Warfare," *CMJ* Supplement, 70 (1952): 47–49; "Health Services in New China," *People's China* 24 (December 16, 1953): 14.

26. See *CMJ* 70 (1952): 641; *CMJ* 74 (1956): 411. Also note Yen Ching-ch'ing and Liu Ch'ing-hsueh, "Death Rates in the City Districts of Peking," *CMJ* 78 (1959): 27–30, which is an important source of data for health conditions in Peking.

27. King, "U.S. Imperialists," p. 48.

A relatively recent study of the public health institutions in the PRC makes the statement: "The cornerstone for the development of rural health programs was a revived system of state-supported *hsien* (county) hospitals and health centers which had been established in China during the 1930's."[28] Their organization was noticeably similar to Ch'en Chih-ch'ien's original model: medical care flowed from highly specialized provincial centers to county hospitals with epidemic units, and on to smaller health facilities staffed by lower-level medical personnel.[29]

During the early 1950s the major thrust in health care had been the drive to eradicate the most debilitating parasitic diseases.[30] It will be recalled that a great deal of research at PUMC had been on parasitic diseases, especially kala-azar and schistosomiasis. For the most part these scholarly articles had not considered the mass organizational means necessary for disease control. There is one important exception—in January of 1949 *The Chinese Medical Journal* printed a very elaborate and specific program titled "Control of Kala-azar in China," which had been submitted by a 1946 kala-azar conference of the National Institute of Health in Nanking. Not only did this report name the specific *hsien* in which eradication measures should be undertaken, it also presented in detail the step-by-step technical and organizational procedures to be taken. For example, mobile teams of a specified size were to be trained in kala-azar prevention techniques for four weeks and their curriculum was outlined in this report. Chu Chang-keng was the chairman of the conference, and PUMC graduates participating in outlining these programs included Eutrope A. Ho, '37, Huang Chen-hsiang, '34, and Wu Chao-jen, '28.[31] From what is known of the kala-azar prevention campaigns in the early 1950s, the specific recommendations of this earlier report were implemented.[32]

There is little to indicate what PUMC colleagues thought of the

28. Susan B. Rifkin, "Health Care for Rural Areas," in Quinn, ed., *Medicine and Public Health*, p. 140.

29. William Y. C. Chen, "Medicine and Public Health," *China Quarterly*, No. 6 (1961): 135–169; Robert M. Worth, "Health Trends in China since the Great Leap Forward," *China Quarterly*, No. 22 (1965): 181–190; Worth, "Institution Building in the People's Republic of China: The Rural Health Center," *East-West Center Review*, 1 (February 1965): 19–34.

30. For one evaluation of their progress, see Kun-yen Huang, "Infectious and Parasitic Diseases," in Quinn, ed., *Medicine and Public Health*, pp. 239–262.

31. "Control of Kala-Azar in China," Report Submitted by the Kala-Azar Prevention Conference, held at National Institutes of Health, from November 15 to 18, 1946, *CMJ* 67 (1949): 24–46.

32. For example, see Chung Huei-lan, "A Résumé of Kala-Azar Work in China," *CMJ* 71 (1953): 421–464.

medical programs of the People's Republic of China until the brief dramatic outburst of intellectuals which took place in May of 1956 during the ferment of the Hundred Flowers Movement. On May 7, the *Kuang-ming Jih-pao* described a series of seminars and forums held at the former PUMC:

> The professors thought that at present the central problem of medical education was the contradiction between quantity and quality. There were insufficient qualified teachers at many medical colleges and the quality of the teachers was not high. . . .[33]

On May 20, the same newspaper again published the PUMC professors' evaluation of their college under the Communist regime:

> Many comrades say that the Union Medical College, in spite of frantic efforts in the last few years, shows very few results. What is the reason? Dr. Wu Wei-jan says that this is mainly due to leading comrades of the college failing to understand the feelings of the intellectuals and failing to come to grips with their work.[34]

Other criticism from the medical profession was directed at the Chinese Medical Association. Dr. Wu Ying-k'ai, long-time PUMC Professor of Surgery, "held that the program of the CMA was very vague. . . . He thought that although in name the CMA had various specialized associations, in actual fact these specialized associations were without substance."[35] Adding their agreement were a number of other PUMC personnel, including Lin Ch'iao-chih, Hu Ch'uan-k'uei, P. Z. King, and Lin Tsung-yang. The Ministry of Health was also castigated by King:

> Public Hygiene expert Chin Pao-shan [P. Z. King] said that for the past several years the Ministry had laid too much emphasis on medical treatment at the expense of preventive work which ensured the overall protection of the health of the people and prevented the spread of disease.[36]

Sometime later, when recriminations against those who spoke out during the "Hundred Flowers" ensued, Director Lee Chung-en became the scapegoat for all those at PUMC who had criticized the Party's program. Twelve debates were carried on at the College over a period of two months during the fall of 1957, designed to discredit both Lee and the ideas which had "bloomed" during 1956:

> . . . in opposing the leadership of the Communist Party in the medical and the public health undertakings, Li Tsung-en [Lee Chung-en] com-

33. Quoted in Roderick MacFarquhar, *The Hundred Flowers* (London: Stevens & Sons, 1960), p. 126.
34. *Ibid.*, pp. 126–127.
35. *Ibid.*, p. 126.
36. *Ibid.*, p. 127.

posed the "trilogy" of: exaggerating and distorting the mistakes and the shortcomings in the work of the Union Medical College, obliterating the achievements during the past few years, and attributing these mistakes and shortcomings to the leadership of the Party.[37]

Those PUMC colleagues who spoke out against Lee's apostasy re-affirmed their own political orthodoxy. Chow Hua-k'ang, '42, a son of former PUMC trustee Y. T. Tsur, affirmed, "the political move-ments were the fundamental safeguards to the tremendous achieve-ments which Union College had obtained since the taking-over by the People's government."[38] Tseng Hsien-chiu, '40, great-grand-daughter of Tseng Kuo-fan, declared that "Li Tsung-en intended to create the idea that the Party could not lead science, and from thence to overthrow the Party's leadership in scientific undertak-ings."[39] Others who attacked Lee's ideological mistakes were spe-cifically cited in the *Jen-min Jih-pao*, and they included the most renowned at PUMC: Chiang Hsiao-ch'ien, Hu Cheng-hsiang, and Wu Ying-k'ai—all professors at the institution prior to Liberation—and such notable graduates as Chu Fu-t'ang, Hu Ch'uan-k'uei, and Lin Ch'iao-chih. Well known to all in China's modern medical profession, their anti-rightist position was both a symbol and a warning.

Attacks on "rightist" medical personnel following the Hundred Flowers period were not limited to Peking. In Shanghai, Fan Jih-hsin, '34, professor at the Shanghai First Medical College and a member of the discredited Peasant-Worker Democratic Party, was denounced for his criticism of the Shanghai Department of Health when he said, in part, that "its leadership was ignorant but pre-tended to be learned," and that the "principal contradiction between the leadership and the masses arose from the disregard of expert opinion by lay people."[40]

During the first year (1958) of the Great Leap Forward, medical personnel continued to be involved in ideological struggles. Chang Ch'ing-sung, '32, head of PUMC's Ear, Nose and Throat Depart-ment, was charged with:

> the haughtiness of a self-styled expert who flouted the authority of the Party leadership. Instead of obeying the orders of the leadership, he per-sisted in his own chosen research with the chief purpose of writing

37. "Rightist Li Tsung-en of Union Medical College Defeated in Debate," *Jen-min Jih-pao*, October 6, 1957, in *SCMP*, No. 1671, p. 16.

38. *Ibid.*, p. 17.

39. *Ibid.*

40. "Meeting of Prominent Doctors in Shanghai Rebukes Rightists in Medical Pro-fession," *NCNA*, August 2, 1957, in *SCMP*, No. 1590, p. 28.

research papers to enhance his personal fame. He resisted co-operation with the herbists because he considered them ignorant of ear and nose diseases.[41]

The anti-expert bias during the Great Leap Forward was also reflected in the charge that Huang Chen-hsiang, '34, had disobeyed the party leadership in the prescribed reorganization of the departments of pathology and epidemiology: "He boastfully considered himself a foremost authority in pathology, and said, 'I do not fear anything. I have ability and the Party needs me.'"[42]

In spite of the conflicts between technological experts and party comrades, the Party and the nation did need the capable PUMC personnel. Perhaps one of the best ways to examine the role of PUMC graduates in the People's Republic of China is to examine the careers of a particular graduating class. At the present time, the class of 1933 offers the most complete historical record for analysis: of the 17 graduates, a generalized notion of the post-1950 locations of 15 are known (see Table 11).

This class is somewhat atypical in that all but one remained in China after 1950. (Sketchy data on the post-1949 careers of 173 of the 313 PUMC graduates has been gathered. Ninety-seven were in China, 76 were scattered mainly in Hong Kong, Taiwan, and the United States. Since those outside China have been fairly well traced, the majority of the remaining alumni are probably in China.)[43] The selection of this class is, however, not altogether arbitrary. These students graduated midway in the course of PUMC's history, and would have been roughly in their mid-forties in 1950. With a few very important exceptions, notably Lin Ch'iao-chih, Hu Ch'uan-k'uei, and Chung Huei-lan, the graduates of the very earliest years have practically vanished from sight. On the other hand, the more recent graduating classes were only in their mid-thirties or so at the time of Liberation. While they have published extensively in medical journals since 1950, this group has not achieved the same recognition as have graduates from the middle years, 1930–1936.

There are a number of interesting things about the class of '33. On the romantic side, it contained two married couples, Teng Chia-tung and Wang Yueh-yun, and Fang Hsien-chih and Wei Shu-

---

41. Quoted in Theodore Hsi-en Chen, "Science, Scientists, and Politics," in Gould, ed., *Sciences in Communist China*, p. 73.

42. *Ibid.*

43. In addition to the sources already listed for the post-1950 locations of PUMC graduates, Dr. Harold Loucks provided the author with a copy of his own record, "Peiping Union Medical College—Alumni in the Free World, 1972."

TABLE II
PUMC Class of 1933: Post-1950 Occupations

Name	Occupation	Source of Information
Ch'en Kuo-chen	Dean, Canton Medical College	*CMJ*, 74 (1956): 412
Chou Shou-k'ai	Vice-President, Chung-shan Medical College	*Directory of Scientific Institutions*: 214
Ch'u Ch'eng-fang		Information not available
Fang Hsien-chih	Department of Orthope-dics, Tientsin People's Hospital	*CMJ*, 82 (1963): 493
Hsu Hsin-an		Information not available
Hsu Yin-hsiang	Peking Research Institute of Ear, Nose & Throat	*CMJ*, 81 (1962): 127
Huang Chia-ssu	President, Chinese Med-ical University, and Chinese Academy of Medical Sciences	*Directory of Scientific Institutions*: 253
Huang K'eh-wei	Department of Pathology, Szechwan Medical College	*CMJ*, 80 (1960): 455
K'o Ying-k'uei	Municipal Central Hospi-tal of Obstetrics and Gynecology, Tientsin	*Ibid.*: 53
Li Hung-chiung	Department of Dermatol-ogy, China Union Medical College	*Ibid.*: 170
P'eng Tah-mou	Vice-Director, National Defense Medical Col-lege, Taiwan	*Journal of Medical Education*, 37 (1962): 463
Szutu Chan	New York	Loucks, "PUMC Alumni, 1972"
Teng Chia-tung	Peking	Jen-min Jih-pao (Nov. 16, 1951)
Wang Shao-hsun	Department of Radiology, China Union Medical College	*CMJ*, 74 (1956): 411
Wang Yueh-yun (Mrs. Teng Chia-tung)	Peking	Presumed to be with husband; see Teng, above
Wei Shu-chen (Mrs. Fang Hsien-chih)	Tientsin	Presumed to be with husband; see Fang, above
Wu Jui-p'ing	Tung Jen Hospital, Peking	Conversation with Mary Ferguson, Nov. 4, 1972

chen. More significantly, only two of these graduates, Huang K'eh-wei and P'eng Tah-mou, had been connected in earlier decades with the KMT's National Health Administration. Huang K'eh-wei's position after 1950 in Szechwan suggests that he perhaps went there during the Japanese war and remained. P'eng Tah-mou, on the other hand, left China for Taiwan, becoming the Vice-Director of the National Defense Medical College. Three of the graduates, Ch'en Kuo-chen, Chou Shou-k'ai and Huang Chia-ssu became especially prominent in China after 1950: Ch'en as Dean of the Canton Medical College, Chou as Vice-President of Chung-shan Medical College, and Huang as President of the Chinese Academy of Medical Sciences.

Leadership in medical colleges, however, was not limited to the class of '33: Hu Ch'uan-k'uei, '27, was President of Peking Medical College; Chu Hsien-i, '30, President of Tientsin Medical University; Wang Chi-wu, '34, Vice-President of Chekiang Medical University; and Li Wen-jen, '41, Vice President of Fukien Medical College.[44]

Returning to the class of 1933, the medical research of Fang Hsien-chih in Tientsin's People's Hospital has been widely described for its successful integration of traditional and modern medical procedures. Fang utilized modern X-rays and surgical procedures to rejoin fractured limbs, but flexible willow splints, instead of hard plaster casts, are used in his healing process. According to Fang, and other observers, bones knit much faster and regain the original strength more fully utilizing this technique.[45]

It is quite difficult to determine the degree to which traditional medicine has been genuinely incorporated into the medical techniques of China's erstwhile modernists. Certainly, in pre-Communist China, there was no indication that, for these people, such a synthesis had any merits at all. Yang Chi-shih, '26, probably expressed the feelings of all PUMC graduates when he wrote in 1925: "You worthies who promote Chinese medicine, what a responsibility you bear for the deaths of your fellow country-men!"[46]

Some at PUMC had been active in assessing the chemical properties of traditional Chinese drugs, and perhaps no one person contributed more to their understanding prior to 1950 than Bernard

44. See *Directory of Scientific Institutions*, pp. 266–267, 275, 247, and 255, respectively.

45. Fang Hsien-chih, *et al.*, "The Integration of Modern and Traditional Chinese Medicine in the Treatment of Fractures," *CMJ* 82 (1963): 493–504; NCNA, September 19, 1965, in *SCMP*, No. 3543, p. 20; Wilder Penfield, "Oriental Renaissance in Education and Medicine," *Science* 141 (September 20, 1963): 1157.

46. Quoted in Croizier, *Traditional Medicine in Modern China*, p. 79.

Roger Greene and the Peking Union Medical College class of 1933. From left to right: Chou Shou-k'ai, Wei Shu-chen, Teng Chia-tung, Fang Hsien-chih, P'eng Tah-mou, Szutu Chan, K'o Ying-k'uei, Wang Yueh-yun, Huang Chia-ssu, Greene, Li Hung-chiung, Wang Shao-hsun, Wu Jui-p'ing, Ch'u Ch'eng-fang, Huang K'eh-wei, and Ch'en Kuo-chen. (Missing are Hsu Hsing-an and Hsu Yin-hsiang.)

Read, Professor of Pharmacology. But the essential attitude at PUMC was well summed up by Robert Lim, writing from the United States in 1960:

> Legitimate research by scientific methods on the mechanism of the response to acupuncture and the pharmacology of herbs with demonstrated clinical utility can be carried out in the modern medical schools or institutes, but all other activities in connection with Chinese medicine must be regarded as political.[47]

The Communists have themselves been ambivalent with regard to traditional medicine, even since 1950.[48] Although institutes for traditional medicine were established in the early fifties, it was actually not until the Great Leap Forward that traditional medicine

47. Robert K. S. Lim and G. H. Wang, "Physiological Sciences," in Gould, ed., *Sciences in Communist China*, p. 347.
48. Croizier, *Traditional Medicine in Modern China*, see especially pp. 189–209.

received great emphasis. At Peking Union Medical College, two prominent herbal doctors were appointed to the staff in 1954, and one surgeon was sent to study acupuncture.[49] A few Western-trained professors published articles describing traditional medicine's approach to their own specialty.[50] Only in 1961 did reports start to claim extensive integration of traditional and modern techniques in clinical practice and research investigations at this former citadel of modern medicine. Sometime after 1958, seventeen senior professors at the old Rockefeller hospital were required to study traditional medicine for an extended period of time.[51]

From about 1958 forward, research articles published by PUMC faculty and graduates show some concern with traditional medicine. Somewhat typical is Chu Fu-t'ang's 1959 summary of ten years of pediatric work under the Communists. He first considers modern advances made in inoculation procedures, institutional expansion, and the creation of day care centers for children. But then he turns to cite specifically Chinese drugs which are useful in treating children's diseases such as bacillary dysentery. Chu acknowledges that the efficacy of the cheaper Chinese herbs is not always uniform in comparison with modern drugs, but he also notes that quality and consistency can be improved: "In short, the aim of pediatrics is the discovery of an economical and at the same time effective agent against bacillary dysentery."[52] Similar conclusions were reached by Feng Lan-chou in an article concerning parasitic diseases.[53] Both these authors list the Chinese herbs which are most effective in combatting particular ailments. Whatever their personal scientific judgments, forced familiarity with traditional Chinese drugs made these medical professionals more sensitive to the problems of expense and local availability.

Again returning to the class of 1933, whose activities are repre-

49. "Herb Medicine at CUMC," *NCNA*, September 8, 1954, in *SCMP*, No. 885, p. 12.

50. For example, see Lee T'ao, "Achievements of Chinese Medicine in the Sui and T'ang Dynasties," *CMJ* 71 (1953): 301–320; Pi Hua-teh, "History of Glaucoma in Traditional Chinese Medicine," *CMJ* 81 (1962): 403–416.

51. "CUMC Seriously Carries Out the Policy Concerning the Traditional School of Medicine," *Kuang-ming Jih-pao*, March 24, 1961, *Current Background*, No. 662, pp. 12–13; Tung P'ing-k'un, "Face of CUMC Changed with the Combination of Traditional and Western Schools of Medicine," in *ibid.*, pp. 4–8; Chang Chih-nan, *et al.*, "Chinese Medicine is Good and Western Medicine is Also Good, but a Combination of the Two is Better," in *ibid.*, pp. 9–11.

52. Chu Fu-t'ang, "Accomplishments in Child Health since Liberation," *CMJ* 79 (1959): 397.

53. Feng Lan-chou, *et al.*, "Research on Parasitic Diseases in New China," *CMJ* 80 (1960): 1–20.

sentative of many PUMC graduates, it should be noted that both Wang Shao-hsun and Ch'en Kuo-chen were delegates to international medical conferences in 1956: Wang attended the 5th International Conference on Radiobiology in Stockholm and Ch'en was a delegate to the 14th Congress of Therapeutists in the Soviet Union.[54] Medical delegations from China to other countries were relatively few during the fifties and sixties, but whenever they were sent, PUMC colleagues formed the majority of the contingent.[55]

At the dedication of PUMC in 1921, John D. Rockefeller, Jr., had declared that the purpose of the China Medical Board was to develop "a medical school and hospital of a standard comparable with that of the leading institutions known to Western civilization."[56] Forty or more years later the success of PUMC in achieving this aim served to enhance the status of the People's Republic at international medical conferences. The continued existence of a visible medical elite was obvious. There are indications that during the late 1950s and early 1960s these medical professionals began to exercise more influence in the shaping of medical education programs. In fact, in 1959 a new medical college, named the China Medical College (sometimes termed a university), was constituted on the old grounds of PUMC. Administered by the Chinese Academy of Medical Sciences, the president of this prestigious school was Huang Chia-ssu, and its vice-presidents were *all* former PUMC colleagues. The curriculum of the college was based on an eight-year medical program—three years premedical training and five years for the advanced medical degree,[57] all somewhat similar to PUMC's original design. At the opening, Li Te-ch'uan, Minister of Health, discussed the reasons why this eight-year medical course, the first of its kind in Communist China, had been created:

> We must popularize medical education with our maximum efforts and set up more medical schools and colleges and train various sorts of health workers. This is an indispensable "leg". . . . But attention should also be paid to raising the level. . . . The higher medical colleges should provide

54. *CMJ* 74 (1956): 412.

55. This conclusion has been reached from analyzing the material in *CMJ* pertaining to international meetings. Not one of the delegations listed from 1956–1958 (the only period when this kind of information was given) was without a PUMC graduate or former faculty member; in most cases all but one or two were PUMC colleagues; see *CMJ* 74 (1956): 412; *CMJ* 75 (1957): 1036; *CMJ* 76 (1958): 101, 516, 612.

56. *Addresses and Papers*, p. 59.

57. Suttmeier, "Academy of Medical Sciences," pp. 173–190; *Directory of Scientific Institutions*, p. 253; Penfield, "Renaissance in Chinese Medicine," pp. 1154–1155, includes photographs.

both four-year special courses and eight-year courses of this kind. If this "leg" is neglected, the raising of the level of medical science will be restricted.[58]

There was a need for higher medical institutions, but the Communist revolution, especially as interpreted by Mao Tse-tung, was a rural revolution. And, in the early 1960s, there were indications that in the field of medical care, as in other areas, the urban-rural dichotomy, which had plagued the modernization of China since the 19th century, continued to be evident. It was not that heroic efforts had not been made to train doctors, assistant doctors, and traditional doctors to serve the people of China. It was just that they still tended to congregate in the cities and there still were not enough.

A recent study of mortality rates in China suggests that in 1956–1957 the rural death rate was 33 percent higher than the urban one.[59] In 1960 Canton's *Nan-fang Jih-pao* printed a revealing critique of health services in rural areas:

A medical and health network has been basically set up in the rural districts of the province, and its quality is continually rising. The health work in the rural districts, however, is at present still far below the standard in cities and towns. Few doctors of either Chinese or Western medicine are working in the rural districts and skilled treatment cannot be easily obtained for serious cases of injury and illness.[60]

It is thus not surprising that a major thrust in the Cultural Revolution was to redistribute medical care to the countryside; or in Chairman Mao's words: "In health and medical work, stress the rural areas."

Nor is it surprising that PUMC colleagues became symbols of this major new emphasis. As China's medical elite, they remained institution-oriented, and they too had congregated in the cities.[61] Huang Chia-ssu, as President of the Chinese Academy of Medical Sciences and the prestigious China Medical College, was apparent-

58. "New Medical College Opened in Peking," *NCNA*, September 5, 1959, in *SCMP*, No. 2095, p. 13.

59. Janet Salaff, "Mortality Decline in the People's Republic of China and the United States," paper presented at the Annual Meeting of the American Public Health Association, Atlantic City, November 15, 1972, p. 19.

60. Chang T'ung-chiu, "Health Workers Must Energetically Support the Construction of Rural Districts," *Nan-fang Jih-pao*, August 6, 1960, in *SCMP*, No. 2329, p. 16.

61. Specific locations for all the 97 PUMC graduates thus far located in the PRC are not known; however, at least 45 were in Peking, 10 in Shanghai, 7 in Tientsin, and 4 in Canton.

ly one of the first to be sent to the countryside. In fact, according to his own report, he was sent alone to Hsiangyin *hsien* in Hunan in October 1964, antedating Mao's formal proclamation by nearly a year. In this report Huang described his earlier resistance to teaching medicine on a part-time basis and commented on his self-conceived importance: "I held that since I undertook full-time education in medicine the running of part-work, part-study . . . schools was no concern of mine." In Hunan, Huang was isolated from medical centers and modern drugs. Emerging as a newly converted rural physician, Huang reported that while in Hunan he had cured workers with just aspirin: "Without profound medical skills and complicated medical equipment, I could also relieve the poor and lower-middle peasants of much pain."[62]

In early 1965, Huang was joined in Hunan by the first team of Peking medical experts to be sent as a group to the country. Thirty doctors and nurses from the Chinese Academy of Medical Sciences, China Medical College, and Peking Union Hospital were sent for a period of about six months; included were the notables of China's modern medicine: Chung Huei-lan, Chang Hsiao-ch'ien, Hu Ch'uan-k'uei, and Lin Ch'iao-chih. Indeed, all of the participants named by newspaper reports were PUMC colleagues, with the exception of one traditional herbist. Altogether ten medical teams were sent from Peking in the early months of 1965, but only this eminent delegation went as far as Hunan; the others served in the nearby rural areas surrounding Peking.[63]

Some thirty-five years after C. C. Ch'en had begun the first concerted effort to train village lay people in the simple treatment of medical ills, his younger schoolmate, Huang Chia-ssu, now an elderly man, described the goal of the medical team in Hunan: "We want to foster rural doctors who are capable of curing diseases usually seen in the countryside and know the seriousness of diseases inflicting some people who need hospitalization without delay."[64] Huang prescribed a curriculum which was later even more simplified, of training village farmers six months out of each year; the other six months they would participate in agricultural activities. He predicted that after only two months of training these lay medical aides would be able to recognize the most common maladies.

62. Huang Chia-ssu, "We are Confident of Properly Running Part-Farming, Part-Study Medical Classes," *Kuang-ming Jih-pao*, May 11, 1965, in *SCMP*, No. 3471, p. 5.

63. "Peking Medical Experts Help Countryside Hospitals," *NCNA*, February 15, 1965, in *SCMP*, No. 3400, pp. 18–19.

64. Huang, "We Are Confident," p. 6.

Huang's description of medical conditions in this particular *hsien* indicated the paucity of medical treatment which had previously been available. The sophisticated medical scientists had first to treat the sick in order to prove the effectiveness of their remedies before they gained popular acceptance: "After we had gained their confidence by relieving them of their discomfort, we found them more receptive of our publicity about prevention. In our production team we made a general survey and gave many treatments for trachoma." When he returned to Peking, Huang described the revelation of living in the country: "For almost all of us in the team this was the first trip to the countryside. . . . Eleven of our doctors were over the age of 50, but all came back strong and healthy." [65]

As the Cultural Revolution proceeded, the attack on PUMC as an elite institution was revived. [66] More forceful than all the rhetoric, however, was a series of photographs published in December 1965 —Huang Chia-ssu, Chang Hsiao-ch'ien, Hu Ch'uan-k'uei, Lin Ch'iao-chih and others from the old PUMC community were seen in rice fields, rural villages, and peasant homes bringing modern medicine to the masses of China. [67]

During the decade since the Cultural Revolution, China's medical policies have continued to emphasize improved medical services for rural regions. In order to train more physicians, formal medical training programs were shortened to three years. Senior biomedical research scientists from medical research institutes or leading teaching hospitals spent considerable time in rural areas in a major effort to up-grade the quality of provincial and *hsien* health centers. As a result of these and other policies, most communes today have some form of health unit, and paramedical personnel of the type long envisioned by Ch'en Chih-ch'ien and Marian Yang are available in China's most remote regions.

China's health care delivery system has been widely acclaimed. But more recently there has been concern over the need to replenish the aging corps of highly trained biomedical scientists and professors. As China enters a post-Mao, post-Cultural Revolution era, it is becoming clear that there will be a new emphasis upon quality training in all scientific fields. And an aging, dwindling group of PUMC graduates is again being called into service. In June 1977, Huang Chia-ssu, still the President of the Chinese Academy

65. Huang Chia-ssu, "Our Medical Team in the Countryside," *CMJ* 84 (1965): 801.

66. For example, see "China's Khruschev Resurrected PUMC to Advance Revisionist Line in Education," *China's Medicine* 12 (December 1967): pp. 890–892.

67. *CMJ* 84 (December 1965), see pages preceding back cover.

Peking Union Medical College Hospital (now the Capital Hospital), May 1, 1975. Slogans read "Long live the invincible thought of Mao Tse-tung," "Long live our great leader Chairman Mao," "Long live the Chinese Communist Party."

of Medical Sciences, discussed China's new medical priorities with a visiting American delegation. He received the distinguished American scientists, including Dr. Philip Handler, President of the National Academy of Sciences, in the old Board Room of Peking Union Medical College. Many a heated debate over PUMC's curriculum, or the relationship between the PUMC Trustees and the China Medical Board, had taken place in this room. It is now the conference room for the Chinese Academy of Sciences. The teak paneling remains, and the chairs are still covered in deep red velvet. But portraits of Chairman Mao and Chairman Hua have replaced that of John D. Rockefeller, Sr.

With the quiet dignity of a man who has survived the many vicissitudes of revolutionary China, Dr. Huang described for his American guests the medical accomplishments of the past quarter of a century. He spoke with pride of the seven research institutes under the Chinese Academy of Medical Sciences, including institutes for clinical medicine, cardiovascular disease, cancer, health, epidemic diseases, *materia medica*, and pediatrics. He outlined the trends in medical training, noting that prior to Liberation there were fewer than 10,000 medical graduates, and that today there are 31 times that number. He talked about barefoot doctors, health aides, and the importance of traditional medicine. But as he gave credit to the educational policies of the recent past, Huang was also looking to the future:

> There is now a major debate about changing the educational period for physicians, to give more attention to quality in addition to maintaining the quantitative requirements. We are considering bringing back those who received three years of training for additional training. We are also considering initiating a longer period of training at the beginning. These steps are currently being debated.[68]

Huang's words, "quality training," evoked memories of the earliest Rockefeller educators. Events have come full circle. Today it is the Chinese medical leaders themselves who are evaluating their own vigorous hybrid of Eastern and Western medicine.

68. From notes taken by myself and Dr. John Bryant, Columbia University School of Public Health, June 15, 1977.

Occupations of PUMC Graduates (1924–1933) in 1937

	Class & Name	Position	City
	1924		
侯祥川	Hou Hsiang-ch'uan	Associate, Division of Physiological Sciences, Henry Lester Institute	Shanghai
梁寶平	Liang Pao-p'ing	Private practice	Tientsin
劉紹光	Liu Shao-kuang	Chief of Laboratory of Materia Medica and Chemotherapeutics, Central Field Health Station	Nanking
	1925		
劉士豪	Liu Shih-hao	PUMC Associate Professor, Medicine, study leave abroad	Abroad
劉書萬	Liu Shu-wan	Private practice	Chungking
穆瑞五	Mu Jui-wu	PUMC Assistant Professor, Dermatology	Peking
潘銘紫	P'an Ming-tzu	PUMC Associate, Anatomy	Peking
姚尋源	Yao Hsun-yuan	Director, Yunnan Provincial Health Center	Kunming

NOTE: Data derived from the PUMC *Annual Announcement, 1937–1938*, pp. 89–100. The romanization, here as in the text, is the form used by the individuals themselves in their published works and academic records. It does not always conform with the traditional Wade-Giles system.

1926

陳鴻達	Ch'en Hung-ta	Director, Pediatrics Service, Shanghai Hospital	Shanghai
賈　魁	Chia K'uei	Superintendent and Head of Department of Medicine, Hopei Provincial Medical College	Paoting
	Johnson, Hosmer F.	Superintendent, Shadyside Presbyterian Hospital	Weihsien
李士偉	Lee Shih-wei	Head, Department of Obstetrics & Gynecology	Nanking
李廷安	Li T'ing-an	Commissioner of Public Health	Shanghai
凌熾桓	Ling Chih-huan	Medical Officer, Chinese Maritime Customs	Shanghai
宋志望	Sung Chih-wang	Manchurian Plague Prevention Bureau	Harbin
楊濟時	Yang Chi-shih	Chief, Department of Medicine, Hsiang-Ya Medical College	Changsha

1927

陳舜名	Ch'en Shun-ming	Superintendent, Ch'angchow Red Swastika Hospital	Ch'angchow
諸福棠	Chu Fu-t'ang	PUMC Assistant Professor, Pediatrics	Peking
方頤積	Fang I-chi	Kiangsi Provincial Commissioner of Health	Nanchang
	Fernando, Felino C.	Private practice	Philippines
	Guna-Tilaka, Yai	Private practice	Bangkok
胡傳揆	Hu Ch'uan-k'uei	PUMC Assistant Professor, Medicine	Peking
倪飲源	Ni Yin-yuan	Superintendent, Municipal Infectious Diseases Hospital	Nanking
沈驥英	Shen Chi-ying	Chairman, Peiping Committee on Maternal Health, and Director, City Birth Control Clinic	Peking
萬福恩	Wan Fu-en	Private practice	Peking
袁貽瑾	Yuan I-chin	PUMC Associate Professor, Public Health	Peking

1928

張同和	Chang T'ung-ho	Chief surgeon, Kiaotsi Railway Hospital	Tsingtao
陳恒義	Ch'en Heng-i	Head, Department of Surgery, Central Hospital	Nanking
陳寶書	Ch'en Pao-shu	Not practicing	Shanghai
程玉麐	Ch'eng Yu-lin	Associate Professor, Neuro-Anatomy, Central University Medical School	Nanking
黄克綱	Huang K'e-kang	Superintendent, Kiangsi Provincial Hospital	Nanchang
康錫榮	K'ang Hsi-jung	Head, Department of Pathological Laboratories, Central Hospital	Nanking

李方邕	Li Fang-yung	Kiangsi Provincial Health Administration	Nanchang
凌筱瑛	Ling Hsiao-ying	Soochow Hospital	Soochow
柳安昌	Liu An-ch'ang	Chief, Department of Physiology, Army Medical College	Nanking
湯漢志	T'ang Han-chih	Chief, Division of Maternal and Child Welfare, Nanking Municipal Health Station	Nanking
王世偉	Wang Shih-wei	Technical expert, Shanghai Bureau of Public Health	Shanghai
王大同	Wang Ta-t'ung	PUMC Assistant Professor, Surgery	Peking
吳朝仁	Wu Chao-jen	PUMC Associate Professor, Public Health	Peking
吳烈忠	Wu Lieh-chung	Private practice	Shanghai

1929

張先林	Chang Hsien-lin	PUMC Assistant Professor, Medicine	Peking
陳志潛	Ch'en Chih-ch'ien	Superintendent, Ting Hsien Rural Health Station	Ting Hsien
陳元覺	Ch'en Yuan-chueh	Lingnan University staff	Canton
鄭榮斌	Cheng Jung-pin	Instructor, Kwong Wah Medical School	Canton
朱章賡	Chu Chang-keng	General Secretary, Commission on Medical Education, Ministry of Education	Nanking
鍾蕙瀾	Chung Huei-lan	PUMC Associate, Medicine	Peking
榮獨山	Jung Tu-shan	Chief Roentgenologist, Central Hospital	Nanking
李瑞麟	Li Jui-lin	Head, Department of Obstetrics and Gynecology, Hsiang-Ya Medical College	Changsha
黎文娥	Li Wen-e	St. Elizabeth's Hospital	Shanghai
林巧稚	Lim Kha-t'i	PUMC Assistant Professor, Obstetrics and Gynecology	Peking
林元英	Lin Yuan-ying	Staff, National Medical College	Shanghai
盧致德	Loo Chih-teh	Director General, Military Medical Services, study leave abroad	Abroad
白施恩	Pai Shih-en	Assistant Professor, Bacteriology, Hsiang-Ya Medical College	Changsha
施錫恩	Shih Hsi-en	PUMC Assistant Professor, Surgery	Peking
湯澤光	T'ang Tze-kuang	Lecturer, Hackett Medical College	Canton
汪國錚	Wang Kuo-cheng	PUMC Assistant Professor, Medicine	Peking

1930

| 卞萬年 | Bien Wan-nien | PUMC Associate, Medicine, study leave abroad | Abroad |

張茂林	Chang Mao-lin	Superintendent, Isolation Hospital	Shanghai
陳美珍	Ch'en Mei-chen	American Baptist Mission Hospital	Shaohsing
秦光煜	Ch'in Kuang-yu	PUMC Associate, Pathology	Peking
朱憲彝	Chu Hsien-i	PUMC Instructor, Medicine	Peking
鍾世藩	Chung Shih-fan	Central Hospital	Nanking
潘作新	P'an Tso-hsin	Head of Eye Department, Army Medical College	Nanking
王叔咸	Wang Shu-hsien	PUMC Assistant, Medicine, study leave abroad	Abroad

1931

查艮鍾	Cha Liang-chung	Head, Bacteriological Laboratory, Kiangsi Provincial Health Administration	Nanchang
張紀正	Chang Chi-cheng	PUMC Associate, Surgery, study leave abroad	Abroad
張去病	Chang Chu-pin	PUMC Instructor, Radiology	Peking
鄭兆齡	Cheng Chao-ling	Kiangsi Provincial Health Administration	Nanchang
裘祖源	Ch'iu Tsu-yuan	PUMC Assistant, Public Health, study leave abroad	Abroad
范權	Fan Ch'uan	PUMC Associate, Pediatrics, study leave abroad	Abroad
金顯宅	Kimm Hyen-taik	PUMC Associate, Surgery, study leave abroad	Abroad
李鉅	Li, Richard C.	Army Medical College	Nanking
李文銘	Li Wen-ming	Municipal Health Department	Nanking
林景奎	Lin Ching-k'uei	PUMC Associate	Peking
盧鴻典	Lu Hung-tien	Asia Life Insurance Co., physician	Shanghai
左雪顏	Tso Hsueh-yen	Dean of Nursing School, Kwong Wah Medical College	Canton
楊靜波	Yang Ching-p'o	PUMC Associate, Surgery, study leave abroad	Abroad
容啓榮	Yung, Winston W.	Technical Expert, Health Department, Municipality of Peking, study leave abroad	Abroad

1932

張慶松	Chang Ch'ing-sung	PUMC Instructor, Otolaryngology	Peking
陳希禮	Ch'en Hsi-li	PUMC resident, Ophthalmologist	Peking
江兆菊	Chiang Chao-chu	Technical expert, Central Field Health Station	Nanking
朱懋根	Chu Mao-ken	Kweiyang Provincial Hospital	Kweiyang
馮蕙熹	Feng Hui-hsi	Child Health Officer, Third Health Station	Peking
何碧輝	Ho Pi-hui	Central Hospital	Nanking
謝文蓮	Hsieh Wen-lien	National Medical College	Shanghai
許建良	Hsu Chien-liang	PUMC Instructor, Roentgenology	Peking

許 世 珣	Hsu Shih-hsun	Instructor, National Medical College	Shanghai
徐 蘇 恩	Hsu Su-en	Technical Expert, Central Field Health Station	Nanking
黃 懷 信	Huang Huai-hsin	Public Health Personnel Training Division, National Health Administration	Nanking
林 飛 卿	Lin Fei-ch'ing	Central University Medical School	Nanking
林 崧	Lin Sung	PUMC Instructor, Obstetrics and Gynecology	Peking
羅 宗 賢	Luo Tsung-hsien	PUMC Associate, Ophthalmology	Peking
史 永 貞	Shih Yung-chen	Not practicing	Shanghai
蘇 祖 斐	Su Tsu-fei	Head, Department of Pediatrics, Hsiang-Ya Medical College, study leave abroad	Changsha
湯 潤 德	T'ang Jun-teh	PUMC Assistant, Pediatrics	Peking
汪 培 娟	Wang P'ei-wo	PUMC Assistant, Obstetrics and Gynecology	Peking
嚴 鏡 清	Yen Ching-ch'ing	Lecturer, National Medical College	Peking
顏 春 輝	Yen Ch'un-hui	PUMC Assistant, Bacteriology, study leave abroad	Abroad
袁 印 光	Yuan Yin-kuang	Church General Hospital	Wuchang

1933

陳 國 楨	Ch'en Kuo-chen	PUMC Assistant, Medicine	Peking
周 壽 愷	Chou Shou-k'ai	PUMC Assistant, Medicine	Peking
瞿 承 方	Ch'u Ch'eng-fang	Central Hospital, Nanking, study leave abroad	Abroad
方 先 之	Fang Hsien-chih	PUMC Instructor, Surgery	Peking
徐 星 盦	Hsu Hsing-an	Kiangsi Provincial Hospital	Nanchang
徐 蔭 祥	Hsu Yin-hsiang	PUMC Instructor, Otolaryngology	Peking
黃 家 駟	Huang Chia-ssu	Red Cross Hospital	Shanghai
黃 克 維	Huang K'eh-wei	Central Hospital, Nanking, study leave abroad	Abroad
柯 應 夔	K'o Ying-k'uei	PUMC Assistant, Obstetrics and Gynecology	Peking
李 鴻 迥	Li Hung-chiung	PUMC Assistant, Dermatology and Syphilology	Peking
彭 達 謀	P'eng Tah-mou	Director, Urban Health Station, Nanking, study leave abroad	Abroad
司 徒 展	Szutu Chan	PUMC Instructor, Surgery	Peking
鄧 家 棟	Teng Chia-tung	PUMC Assistant, Medicine	Peking
汪 紹 訓	Wang Shao-hsun	PUMC Assistant, Roentgenology	Peking
王 耀 雲	Wang Yueh-yun	Metropolitan Hospital	Peking
魏 淑 貞	Wei Shu-chen	PUMC Assistant, Public Health	Peking
吳 瑞 萍	Wu Jui-p'ing	PUMC Assistant, Pediatrics	Peking

PUMC Graduates, 1934–1943

1934

張發初　Chang Fa-ch'u
趙淑英　Chao Shu-ying
趙以成　Chao Yi-ch'eng
陳梅伯　Ch'en Mei-po
程育和　Ch'eng Yu-ho
周金黃　Chou Chin-huang
周裕德　Chou, Willard Y.T.
樊長松　Fan Ch'ang-sung
樊海珊　Fan Hai-shan
范日新　Fan Jih-hsin
徐繼和　Hsu Chi-ho
許英魁　Hsu Ying-k'uei
黃禎祥　Huang Chen-hsiang
谷鏡玉　Ku Yun-yu
李鴻儒　Li Hung-ju
馬月青　Ma Yueh-ch'ing
墨樹屏　Moe, S.P. Paul
沈有泉　Shen Yu-ch'uan
童　村　T'ung Ts'un
王季午　Wang Chi-wu
汪凱熙　Wang K'ai-hsi
吳繼文　Wu Chi-wen

吳世鐸　Wu Shih-doh
楊建邦　Yang Chien-pang
俞煥文　Yu Huan-wen

1935

張光璧　Chang, K.P. Stephen
黃仁若　Huang, J.J. Theodore
林愛群　Lin, Hazel
馬家驥　Ma, Thomas C.G.
馬萬森　Ma Wan-sen
蘇啓楨　Su Ch'i-chen
宋　杰　Sung Chieh
曹松年　Ts'ao Sung-nien
王世濬　Wang Shih-chun
葉恭紹　Yeh Kung-shao

1936

陳本貞　Ch'en Pen-chen
朱文思　Chu Wen-ssu
范樂成　Fan Yueh-ch'eng
馮應琨　Feng Ying-k'un
熊汝成　Hsiung Ju-ch'eng
許天祿　Hsu T'ien-lu

SOURCE: Ferguson, *CMB and PUMC*, pp. 247–249 and PUMC *Annual Announcement*, 1934–1940.

黃翠梅 Huang Ts'ui-mei
李壁夏 Li Pi-hsia
梁炳沂 Liang Ping-yee
陸瑞蘋 Lu Jui-p'ing
聶重恩 Nieh Chung-en
王鴻文 Wang Hung-wen
楊月英 Yang Yueh-ying
郁采蘩 Yu Ts'ai-fan
余新恩 Yui, John

1937
陳景雲 Ch'en Ching-yun
朱貴卿 Chu, Irving
馮玉珊 Feng Yu-shan
何觀清 Ho, Eutrope A.
徐湘蓮 Hsu Hsiang-lien
黃淑筠 Huang Shu-yun
顧培玲 Ku P'ei-chia
李慶傑 Li Ch'ing-chieh
劉家琦 Liu Gia-chi
柳慎耳 Liu Shen-erh
劉緯通 Liu Wei-t'ung
盧觀全 Lu Kwan-ch'uan
歐陽旭明 Ouyang, George
卞學鑑 Pian Hsueh-chien
孫慧民 Sun Hui-min
鄧金鎣 Teng Chin-hsien
文忠傑 Wen Chung-chieh
楊文達 Yang Wen-tah
熊榮超 Young, Edward

1938
章安瀾 Chang An-lan
張峨 Chang E
陳國清 Ch'en Kuo-ch'ing
陳得林 Ch'en Te-lin
陳務民 Ch'en Wu-ming
鄭德悅 Cheng Te-yueh
趙伯喜 Cheu, Stephen Hay
賈偉廉 Chia Wei-lien
周金華 Chou, Edward C.H.
朱義達 Chu I-tah
方連瑜 Fang Lien-yu
謝維銘 Hsieh Wei-ming
許蕙娟 Hsu Hwei-chuan
李宗漢 Li Tsung-han
梁紹造 Liang Shao-chao
林必錦 Lin Pi-chin
劉慶東 Liu Ch'ing-tung
盧青山 Lu Ch'ing-shan
潘世儀 P'an Shih-yi

蕭起鶴 Siao Chi-hoah
司徒亮 Szutu Liang
譚仲彰 T'an Chung-chang
杜持禮 Tu Chih-li
汪心汾 Wang Hsin-fen
王師揆 Wong Shi-kwei
伍芳貞 Wu Fang-chen

1939
超錫祉 Chao Hsi-chih
陳錫謀 Ch'en Hsi-mou
陳明齋 Ch'en Ming-chai
蔣豫圖 Chiang Yu-t'u
朱宗堯 Chu Tsung-yao
許漢光 Hsu Han-kuang
管漢屏 Kwan Han-p'ing
雷愛德 Lei Ai-te, Edward
李季明 Li Gi-ming
林榮東 Ling Yung-tung
劉永 Liu Yong
宋漢英 Soong Han-ying
係明 Sun Ming, Franklin
湯春生 T'ang Chwen-seng
王正儀 Wang Cheng-i
王中方 Wang Chung-fang
王潤添 Wang Jun-t'ien
俞靄峰 Yu Ai-feng
虞頌庭 Yu Sung-t'ing

1940
張曉樓 Chang Hsiao-lou
張乃初 Chang Nai-chu
周華康 Chow Hua-k'ang
范國聲 Fan Kuo-sung
馮傳漢 Feng Ch'uan-han
薛慶煜 Hsueh Ch'ing-yu
高景星 Kao Ching-hsing
顧啓華 Koo Chee-hwa
李雨蒼 Lee Yu-chong, George
李慧芳 Li Hui-fang
林俊卿 Lin Tsuin-ch'ing
凌熾明 Ling Chih-ming
劉紹武 Liu Shao-wu
沈天爵 Shen T'ien-chueh
蘇英 Su Ying
田友道 T'ien Yu-tao
曾憲九 Tseng Hsien-chiu
王光超 Wang Kuang-ch'ao
王石泉 Wang Shih-tsuan
嚴仁英 Yen Jen-ying
郁知非 Yoh Tse-fei

1941

博儒陀	Bock, Rudolph
張學德	Chang Hsioh-teh
張天民	Chang Tien-min
陳國熙	Ch'en Kuo-hsi
陳有平	Ch'en Yu-p'ing
陳郁顯	Chin, Henry
屈鴻翰	Ch'u Hung-han
方永祿	Fang Yung-lu
韓康玲	Han K'ang-ling
何天騏	Ho T'ien-ch'i
徐慶豐	Hsu Ch'ing-feng
胡懋華	Hu Mao-hua
黃楠	Huang Nan
李溫仁	Li Wen-jen
馬永江	Ma Yung-chiang, Joseph
宋志仁	Sung Chih-jen
宋魯	Sung Lu
鄧慶曾	Teng Ch'ing-tseng
蔡如升	Ts'ai Ju-sheng
王德延	Wang Te-yen

1942

張茝芬	Chang Chih-fen
張希賢	Chang Hsi-hsien
陳敏	Ch'en Min
朱亮威	Chu Liang-wei
馮致英	Feng Chih-ying
傅正愷	Fu Cheng-k'ai
徐兆駿	Hsu Chao-chun
黃國安	Huang Kuo-an
黃萃庭	Huang Ts'ui-t'ing
康映蕖	K'ang Ying-chu

谷鈺之	Ku Yu-chih
郭嘉理	Kuo, Kelly C.
李月蓮	Li Yueh-lien
凌兆熊	Ling Chao-hsiung
劉文清	Liu Wen-ch'ing
石棨年	Shih Ch'i-nien
須毓壽	Su Yuh-chou
曾昭懿	Tseng Chao-i
王文彬	Wang Wen-pin
王禹孫	Wang Yu-sun
吳階平	Wu Chieh-p'ing

*1943**

張安	Chang An
陳伯潘	Ch'en Po-shen
陳文珍	Ch'en Wen-tseng
陳耀翰	Ch'en Yueh-han
金奎	Chin K'uei
朱洪蔭	Chu Hung-yin
鍾榮根	Chung Yung-ken
范琪	Fan Ch'i
馮保群	Feng Pao-ch'un
徐秉正	Hsu Ping-cheng
黃梓川	Huang Tzu-ch'uan
黃宛	Hwang Wan
闞冠卿	K'an Kuan-ch'ing, Kenneth
高潤泉	Kao Jun-ch'uan
李果珍	Lee Gwoh-chen
林華堂	Lin Hua-t'ang
陸惟善	Lu Wei-shan
宋鴻釗	Soong Hung-chao
陶榮錦	T'ao Jung-chin
吳天阜	Wu T'ien-fu, Laurence
葉蕙芳	Yeh Hui-fang

*These degrees were granted after World War II, when requirements had been satisfied.

Bibliography

MANUSCRIPT COLLECTIONS

American Red Cross Archives. American Red Cross National Headquarters. Washington, D.C. [RCA]

Simon Flexner Papers. American Philosophical Association Library. Philadelphia, Pennsylvania. [SFP]

Roger Greene Papers. Houghton Library, Harvard University. Cambridge, Massachusetts. [RGP]

Victor Heiser Papers. American Philosophical Association Library. Philadelphia, Pennsylvania. [VHP]

Edward Hume Papers. Missionary Research Library. New York City.

Nelson Johnson Papers. Library of Congress. Washington, D.C. [NJP]

National Archives. Washington, D.C. [NA]

Presbyterian Church in the United States Archives. Historical Foundation. Montreat, North Carolina.

Rockefeller Family Archives. New York City. [RFA]

Rockefeller Foundation Archives (including the China Medical Board Collection and the PUMC Papers). Rockefeller Archive Center, Hillcrest, Pocantico Hills, North Tarrytown, New York. [FA]

William Welch Papers. William Welch Library. The Johns Hopkins University School of Medicine. Baltimore, Maryland. [WWP]

In addition to the public collections, I am grateful to the following individuals for allowing me to utilize papers in their possession: Mrs. John Grant, Washington, D.C.; the late Dr. Marshall C. Balfour, Chapel

Hill, North Carolina; Miss Mary Ferguson, Sandy Spring, Maryland; Dr. Harold Loucks, Kennett Square, Pennsylvania.

INTERVIEWS

Marshall C. Balfour,
    February 15–16, 1972, Chapel Hill, North Carolina.
M. Searle Bates,
    October 11, 1971, New York City.
Chang Yao-teh,
    October 23, 1972, Washington, D.C.
Bacon F. Chow,
    October 1, 1971, Baltimore, Maryland.
Francis R. Dieuaide,
    March 30, 1972, New York City.
Nicholson J. Eastman,
    November 14, 1971, Baltimore, Maryland.
Mary E. Ferguson,
    November 22, 1971, Sandy Spring, Maryland; July 20, 1972, Washington, D.C.; and various other times.
Raymond B. Fosdick,
    July 27, 1970, Newtown, Connecticut.
L. Carrington Goodrich,
    October 15, 1971, New York City.
Franklin Ho,
    July 22, 1970, New York City.
Harold H. Loucks,
    November 14, 1971, Baltimore, Maryland.
John D. Rockefeller, III,
    June 13, 1973, New York City.
Isidore Snapper,
    October 14, 1971, New York City.
Andrew Warren,
    February 16, 1972, Chapel Hill, North Carolina.
Gerald F. Winfield,
    September 30, 1971, Rosslyn, Virginia.
Daisy Yen Wu,
    July 13, 1972, New York City.
Yuan I-chin,
    October 12, 1971; March 30, 1972, New York City.

BOOKS AND ARTICLES

This is a selective listing; it includes a sampling of the less technical published articles by the major participants in this book, and other articles and books directly related to the history of PUMC or Western medical edu-

cation and public health in China. For detailed references, including citations from manuscript sources, see the footnotes. For a more comprehensive bibliography, which includes general works on the Rockefellers, philanthropic foundations, American medical education, and Republican China, see the author's Ph.D. dissertation, "The Rockefeller Foundation in
China: Philanthropy, Public Health, and Peking Union Medical College,"
Stanford University, 1973.

ABMAC [American Bureau for Medical Aid to China] *Bulletin*, 1941–1945,
     1959, 1969, New York.
The American Bureau for Medical Aid to China, Inc., "Conference on the
     Present Medical Situation in China, June 15, 1946," New York City.
     Mimeographed copy located at the National Library of Medicine, Be-
     thesda, Maryland.
*Addresses and Papers, Dedication Ceremonies and Medical Conference,
     Peking Union Medical College, September 15–22, 1921.* Concord, N.H.:
     Rumford Press, 1922.
Adolph, Paul, *Surgery Speaks to China.* Philadelphia: China Inland Mis-
     sion, 1945.
Association for the Advancement of Public Health in China. *Memorandum
     on the Need for a Public Health Organization in China, Presented
     to the British Boxer Indemnity Commission.* Peking: 1926.
Atterbury, Marguerite. "A Study of Some Phases of Chinese American Co-
     Operation in Promoting China's Agricultural Extension." Ph.D. Dis-
     sertation, Columbia University Teachers College, 1961.
Aub, Joseph C., and Ruth K. Hapgood. *Pioneer in Modern Medicine,
     David Linn Edsall of Harvard.* Boston: Harvard Medical Alumni As-
     sociation, 1970.
Ayers, William. *Chang Chih-tung and Educational Reform in China.* Cam-
     bridge, Mass.: Harvard University Press, 1971.
Balme, Harold. *China and Modern Medicine: A Study in Medical Mission-
     ary Development.* London: United Council for Missionary Education,
     1921.
Bennett, Adrian A. *John Fryer: The Introduction of Western Science and
     Technology into Nineteenth Century China.* Cambridge, Mass.: Har-
     vard University Press, 1967.
Bernheim, Bertram M. *The Story of the Johns Hopkins.* New York: Mc-
     Graw-Hill, 1948.
Biggerstaff, Knight. *The Earliest Modern Government Schools in China.*
     London: Kennikat Press, 1972.
Black, Davidson, "Peking Union Medical College Department of Anatomy."
     Methods and Problems of Medical Education, First Series, 1924. New
     York: The Rockefeller Foundation, 1924.
Boorman, Howard, ed. *Biographical Dictionary of Republican China.* 4
     vols. New York: Columbia University Press, 1968.
Bowers, John Z. "The Founding of Peking Union Medical College: Policies

and Personalities," Parts I and II, *Bulletin of the History of Medicine* 45 (1971): 305–321, 409–429.

———. *Medical Education in Japan: From Chinese Medicine to Western Medicine*. New York: Harper and Row, 1965.

———. *Western Medicine in a Chinese Palace: Peking Union Medical College, 1917–1951*. New York: Macy Foundation, 1971.

———, and Elizabeth F. Purcell. *Medicine and Society in China*. New York: Macy Foundation, 1974.

Brown, E. Richard. "Public Health in Imperialism: Early Rockefeller Programs at Home and Abroad." *American Journal of Public Health* 66 (1976): 897–903.

Burton, Ernest D. "Journal and Record of Interviews and Observations, University of Chicago, Oriental Education Investigation, 1909." Typed mimeographed copy located at the Missionary Research Library, New York.

———, and Thomas C. Chamberlin. "Report of the Oriental Commission of the University of Chicago, Part VI, China, December, 1909." Typed mimeographed copy located at the Missionary Research Library, New York.

Campbell, Marguerite E. "Peking Union Medical College Libraries." *Methods and Problems of Medical Education*. Sixth Series, 1926. New York: The Rockefeller Foundation, 1927.

Cannon, Walter B. *The Way of an Investigator; A Scientist's Experience in Medical Research*. New York: Hafner, 1965.

Carter, W. S. "The First Five Years of the Peking Union Medical College." *China Medical Journal* 40 (1926): 726–743.

Chang Kwei. *Studies on Hookworm Disease in Szechwan Province, West China*. Baltimore: Johns Hopkins Press, 1949.

Chang Tsze-shen, Daniel G. Lai, and Hsi Ju-chu. "A Note on the Infant Mortality Rate in Kao-chiao, Shanghai." *Chinese Medical Journal* 50 (1936): 581–582.

Chao Yi-ch'eng. "Neurology, Neurosurgery, and Psychiatry in New China." *Chinese Medical Journal* 84 (1965): 714–742.

Chen, Lawrence M. "Public Health in National Reconstruction." 1937, Nanking. Nanking Council of International Affairs, Bulletin No. 3.

Chen, Theodore H. E. *Thought Reform of the Chinese Intellectuals*. Hong Kong: University of Hong Kong Press, 1960.

Chen, William Y. "Medicine and Public Health." *China Quarterly* 6 (1961): 153–160.

Ch'en Chih-ch'ien. "The Development of Systematic Training in Rural Public Health Work in China." *Milbank Memorial Fund Quarterly Bulletin* 14 (1936): 370–387.

———. "An Experiment in Health Education in Chinese Country Schools." *Milbank Memorial Fund Quarterly Bulletin* 12 (1934): 232–247.

———. "A Practical Survey of Rural Health." *Chinese Medical Journal* 47 (1933): 680–688.

————. "A Proposed Basic Medical Curriculum." *Chinese Medical Journal* 49 (1935): 861–867.

————. "Public Health in Rural Reconstruction at Ting Hsien." *Milbank Memorial Fund Quarterly Bulletin* 12 (1934): 370–378.

————. "The Rural Public Health Experiment in Ting Hsien, China." *Milbank Memorial Fund Quarterly Bulletin* 14 (1936): 66–80.

————. "Scientific Medicine as Applied in Ting Hsien." *Milbank Memorial Fund Quarterly Bulletin* 11 (1933): 97–129.

————. "Some Problems of Medical Organization in Rural China." *Chinese Medical Journal* 51 (1937): 803–814.

————. "State Medicine and Medical Education." *Chinese Medical Journal* 49 (1935): 951–954.

————. "Ting Hsien and the Public Health Movement in China." *Milbank Memorial Fund Quarterly Bulletin* 15 (1937): 380–390.

Cheng Chu-yuan. *Scientific and Engineering Manpower in Communist China, 1949–1963*. Washington, D.C.: National Science Foundation, 1965.

The China Christian Educational Association. *Bulletin*. 1924–1936. Shanghai.

China Medical Commission of the Rockefeller Foundation. *Medicine in China*. New York: University of Chicago Press, 1914.

China Ministry of Information. *China Handbook, 1937–1943*. New York: Macmillan, 1943.

The China Weekly Review. 1931–1937. Shanghai.

The China Year Book. 1920–1937. Tientsin.

"China's Khruschev Resurrected PUMC to Advance Revisionist Line in Education." *China's Medicine* 12 (1967): 890–892.

The Chinese Medical Directory. 1930, 1932, 1934, 1936, 1940. Shanghai.

The Chinese Students' Monthly. 1917–1929. Evanston, Illinois.

Chow Tse-tsung. *The May Fourth Movement: Intellectual Revolution in Modern China*. Cambridge, Mass.: Harvard University Press, 1964.

Chu Chang-keng. "The Revised Medical Curricula." *Chinese Medical Journal* 49 (1935): 837–846.

————. "The Training of Personnel for State Medicine." *Chinese Medical Journal* 51 (1937): 373–380.

Chu Fu-t'ang. "Accomplishments in Child Health Since Liberation." *Chinese Medical Journal* 79 (1959): 384–397.

Chu Hsi-ju and Daniel G. Lai. "Distribution of Modern-Trained Physicians in China." *Chinese Medical Journal* 49 (1935): 542–552.

Chung Huei-lan. "A Resume of Kala-azar Work in China." *Chinese Medical Journal* 71 (1953): 421–464.

Cohen, Warren I. *The Chinese Connection; Roger S. Greene, Thomas W. Lamont, George E. Sokolsky and American-East Asian Relations*. New York: Columbia University Press, 1978.

"Control of Kala-azar in China, Report Submitted by the Kala-azar Prevention Conference held at the National Institute of Health, from November 15 to 18, 1946." *Chinese Medical Journal* 67 (1949): 24–46.

Corner, George. *A History of the Rockefeller Institute, 1901–1953.* New York: The Rockefeller Institute Press, 1964.

Cort, William W., J. B. Grant, and N. R. Stoll. *Researches on Hookworm in China.* Baltimore: Johns Hopkins Press, 1926.

Croizier, Ralph C. *Traditional Medicine in Modern China; Science, Nationalism, and the Tensions of Cultural Change.* Cambridge, Mass.: Harvard University Press, 1968.

Cruickshank, Ernest W. H. "Peking Union Medical College, Department of Physiology." *Methods and Problems of Medical Education,* Fifth Series, 1926. New York: The Rockefeller Foundation, 1926.

Current Background. 1951–1965. U.S. Consulate, Hong Kong.

Curti, Merle. *American Philanthropy Abroad.* New Brunswick, N.J.: Rutgers University Press, 1963.

Dieuaide, Francis R. "Medical Education and the Curriculum at the Peiping Union Medical College." *Chinese Medical Journal* 48 (1934): 1017–1045.

———. "Medical Education and Some Recent Experiments." *National Medical Journal of China* 17 (1931): 283–301.

Directory of Selected Scientific Institutions in Mainland China. Stanford: Hoover Institution Press, 1970.

Dyer, Brian R. "Methods Developed at the Central Field Health Station for the Training of Sanitation Personnel." *Chinese Medical Journal* 50 (1936): 76–81.

Edwards, Dwight W. *Yenching University.* New York: United Board for Christian Higher Education in Asia, 1959.

Eliot, Charles W. *Some Roads Toward Peace, A Report to the Trustees of the Carnegie Endowment on Observations Made in China and Japan in 1912.* Washington, D.C.: The Carnegie Endowment, 1913.

Faber, Knud. *Report on Medical Schools in China.* Geneva: League of Nations Health Organization, 1931.

Fang Hsien-chih, Ku Yun-wu, and Shang T'ien-yu. "The Integration of Modern and Traditional Chinese Medicine in the Treatment of Fractures." *Chinese Medical Journal* 82 (1963): 493–504.

Fang I-chi. "Public Health." *The China Christian Year Book, 1932–1933.* Shanghai: Christian Literature Society, 1934, pp. 429–444.

———, and Li T'ing-an. "School Health in the Peiping Special Health Area." *China Medical Journal* 43 (1929): 697–706.

Fang Shih-san [Shisan C.]. "On Bacteriological Warfare." *Chinese Medical Journal* 70 (1952): 329–332.

Faust, Ernest Carroll. "The Future for Parasitology in China." *China Medical Journal* 42 (1928): 180–187.

Feng Lan-chou, Mao Shou-pai, and Liu Erh-hsing. "Research on Parasitic Diseases in New China." *Chinese Medical Journal* 80 (1960): 1–20.

Feng Ying-k'un. "Neurology in New China." *Chinese Medical Journal* 79 (1959): 398–408.

Ferguson, Mary E. *China Medical Board and Peking Union Medical Col-*

lege, A Chronicle of Fruitful Collaboration, 1914–1951. New York: China Medical Board of New York, Inc., 1970.

———. "Peking Union Medical College and China Medical Board, An Account of Administrative Relationships, 1915–1950." Unpublished manuscript in the possession of the China Medical Board of New York, and the author, Sandy Spring, Maryland.

The First Report of the Central Field Health Station. Shanghai: North China Daily News and Herald, Ltd., 1934.

Fleming, Donald H. *William H. Welch and the Rise of Modern Medicine.* Boston: Little, Brown, and Co., 1954.

Flexner, Abraham. *An Autobiography.* New York: Simon and Schuster, 1960.

———. *Medical Education in the United States.* New York: Carnegie Foundation, 1910.

Flexner, Simon and James Thomas Flexner. *William Henry Welch and the Heroic Age of American Medicine.* New York: Dover, 1941.

Fosdick, Raymond B. *John D. Rockefeller, Jr., A Portrait.* New York: Harper and Brothers, 1956.

———. *The Story of the Rockefeller Foundation.* New York: Harper and Brothers, 1952.

Fox, Theodore F. "The New China: Some Medical Impressions." *Lancet,* November 9, 1957, pp. 935–939; November 16, 1957, pp. 995–999; November 23, 1957, pp. 1053–1057.

Furth, Charlotte. *Ting Wen-chiang: Science and China's New Culture.* Cambridge, Mass.: Harvard University Press, 1970.

Gamble, Sidney. *Ting Hsien: A North China Rural Community.* Stanford: Stanford University Press, 1968.

Garrett, Shirley S. *Social Reformers in Urban China; The Chinese Y.M.C.A., 1895–1926.* Cambridge, Mass.: Harvard University Press, 1970.

Gates, Frederick T. "The Memoirs of Frederick T. Gates." *American Heritage* 6 (1955): 71–86.

Gould, Sydney, ed. *Sciences in Communist China.* Washington, D.C.: American Association for the Advancement of Science, 1961.

Grant, James D. "An Analysis of the Objectives, Techniques, and Accomplishments of Dr. John B. Grant in Establishing the First Health Station of Peking, China." College term-paper, Harvard University, April, 1973.

Grant, John B. "Department of Public Health and Preventive Medicine, Peking Union Medical College." *Methods and Problems of Medical Education.* Fourteenth Series, 1929. New York: The Rockefeller Foundation, 1929.

———. "The Faber Report on Medical Schools in China and After." *The Chinese Medical Journal* 49 (1935): 934–937.

———. "Public Health and Medical Events During 1927 and 1928." *The China Year Book, 1929–1930,* pp. 111–113.

———. "Public Health and Medical Events During 1929 and 1930." *The China Year Book, 1931,* pp. 119–129.

————. "Public Health and Medical Events During 1931." *The China Year Book, 1931–1932*, pp. 150–167.

————. "Public Health and Medical Events During 1932." *The China Year Book, 1933*, pp. 171–190.

————. "Public Health and Medical Events During 1933." *The China Year Book, 1934*, pp. 192–211.

————. "The Public Health Movement in China, 1922–1923." *China Mission Year Book, 1924*, pp. 358–363.

————. "Public Health Work in China." *China Medical Journal* 37 (1923): 677–678.

————. "State Medicine—A Logical Policy for China." *National Medical Journal of China* 14 (1928): 65–80.

————, and I. C. Fang. "Causes of Death for China; an Abridged Classification," *China Medical Journal* 43 (1929): 604–607.

————, and P. Z. King. "Tentative Appraisal Form for Health Work in Large Cities in China." *National Medical Journal of China* 14 (1928): 81–99.

————, and T. M. P'eng. "Survey of Urban Public Health Practice in China." *Chinese Medical Journal* 48 (1934): 1074–1079.

————, T. F. Huang, and S. C. Hsu. "A Preliminary Note on Classification of Causes of Death in China." *National Medical Journal of China* 13 (1927): 1–23.

Greene, Roger S. "The China Medical Board." *China Mission Year Book, 1917*, pp. 430–437.

————. "The China Medical Board, 1918–1919." *China Mission Year Book, 1919*, pp. 184–189.

————. "The China Medical Board of the Rockefeller Foundation." *China Mission Year Book, 1916*, pp. 320–323.

————. "General Considerations for Medical Curriculum Requirements in China." *Chinese Medical Journal* 49 (1935): 59–62.

————. "Medical Education in China." *Chinese Students' Monthly* 17 (1922): 653–658.

————. "Medical Needs of the Chinese." *Chinese Recorder* 49 (1918): 224–230.

————. "Public Health and the Training of Doctors and Nurses in China." *International Review of Missions* 14 (1925): 482–498.

————. "The Work of the China Medical Board in 1917–1918." *China Mission Year Book, 1918*, pp. 202–207.

————. "The Work of the China Medical Board, Rockefeller Foundation." *China Medical Journal* 31 (1917): 191–202.

Grieder, Jerome B. *Hu Shih and the Chinese Renaissance, Liberalism in the Chinese Revolution, 1917–1937*. Cambridge, Mass.: Harvard University Press, 1970.

Grmek, M. D., ed. *Serving the Cause of Public Health: Selected Papers of Andrija Stampar*. Zagreb: Andrija Stampar School of Public Health, 1966.

Gunn, Selskar M. "China and the Rockefeller Foundation," Shanghai,

1934. Unpublished manuscript located in the Hoover Library, Stanford, California.

Hayford, Charles W. "Rural Reconstruction in China: Y. C. Yen and the Mass Education Movement." Ph.D. Dissertation, Harvard University, 1973.

Heiser, Victor. *An American Doctor's Odyssey*. New York: W. W. Norton, 1936.

Hidy, Ralph W., and Muriel E. Hidy. *Pioneering in Big Business; History of Standard Oil Company (New Jersey), 1882–1911*. New York: Harper and Brothers, 1955.

Hoeppli, Reinhard. "The Epidemiology of Kala-azar in China." *Chinese Medical Journal* 57 (1940): 364–372.

Hood, Dora. *Davidson Black: A Biography*. Toronto: University of Toronto Press, 1964.

Horn, Joshua S. *Away With All Pests: An English Surgeon in People's China, 1954–1969*. New York: Modern Reader, 1969.

Hou, T. C., et al. "Achievements in the Fight Against Parasitic Diseases in New China." *Chinese Medical Journal* 79 (1959): 493–520.

Houghton, Henry S. "Tendencies of Medical Education." *China Medical Journal* 40 (1926): 956–969.

————. "Work of the Peking Union Medical College." *China Mission Year Book, 1924*, pp. 363–366.

Hsu, Francis L. K. *Religion, Science and Human Crises: A Study of China in Transition and Its Implications for the West*. London: Routledge and K. Paul, 1952.

Hsu, S. C., and T. H. Wang. "A Study of Infant Mortality in Nanking." *Chinese Medical Journal* 50 (1936): 573–580.

Hu Ch'uan-k'uei, et al. "The Control of Venereal Diseases in New China." *Chinese Medical Journal* 71 (1953): 248–258.

Hu Cheng-hsiang. "A Decade of Progress in Morphologic Pathology." *Chinese Medical Journal* 79 (1959): 409–422.

Hu Hou-ki. "The New Department of Health, Port of Shanghai and Woosung." *China Medical Journal* 41 (1927): 429–438.

Huang Chia-ssu. "Our Medical Team in the Countryside." *Chinese Medical Journal* 84 (1965): 800–803.

————, et al. "Surgery in New China." *Chinese Medical Journal* 79 (1959): 253–283.

Huang, H. H., and T. H. Wang. "A Survey of the Maternity and Child Health Work in Nanking." *Chinese Medical Journal* 50 (1936): 554–561.

Huang Kun-yen. "Control of Communicable Diseases in China." Unpublished paper presented at the Annual Meeting of the American Public Health Association, Atlantic City, New Jersey, November 15, 1972.

Huang Tse-fang. "Communicable Disease Information in China." *National Medical Journal of China* 13 (1927): 92–108.

————. "Developing a Railway Health Service." *Chinese Medical Journal* 49 (1935): 973–989.

―――. "The Development of Health Centres." *Chinese Medical Journal* 56 (1939): 546–560.

Huard, Pierre and Ming Wong. *Chinese Medicine.* New York: McGraw-Hill, 1965.

Hume, Edward H. *Doctors East and Doctors West: An American Physician's Life in China.* New York: Norton, 1946.

―――. "On Certain Trends in Medicine Today." *People's Tribune* 24 (1 August 1933): 153–158.

―――. "Relationships in Medicine Between China and the Western World." *China Medical Journal* 39 (1925), pp. 185–198.

Israel, John. *Student Nationalism in China, 1927–1937.* Stanford: Stanford University Press, 1966.

Johnson, Chalmers A. *Communist Policies Toward the Intellectual Class.* Hong Kong: Union Research Institute, 1959.

Kates, George N. *The Years That Were Fat: Peking, 1933–1940.* New York: Harper and Brothers, 1952.

King, P. Z. [Chin Pao-Shan]. "Health Services in New China." *People's China* 24 (16 December 1953): 14.

―――. "U.S. Imperialists Meet Double Defeat in Their Bacterial Warfare." *Chinese Medical Journal,* Supplement 70 (1952): 47–49.

Klein, Donald W., and Anne B. Clark, eds. *Biographical Dictionary of Chinese Communism, 1921–1965.* 2 vols. Cambridge, Mass.: Harvard University Press, 1971.

Kleinman, Arthur, et al., eds. *Medicine in Chinese Cultures: Comparative Studies of Health Care in Chinese and Other Societies.* Washington, D.C.: Department of Health, Education and Welfare, 1975.

Knowles, John B., ed. *Hospitals, Doctors, and the Public Interest.* Cambridge, Mass.: Harvard University Press, 1966.

―――. "The Quantity and Quality of Medical Manpower: A Review of Medicine's Current Efforts." *Journal of Medical Education* 44 (1969): 81–115.

Kuo Tze-hsiung. "Technical Co-Operation Between China and Geneva." *Information Bulletin No. 6.* Nanking: Nanking Council on International Affairs, 1936.

Kwok, D. W. Y. *Scientism in Chinese Thought.* New Haven, Conn.: Yale University Press, 1965.

Lampton, David M. *The Politics of Medicine in China: The Policy Process, 1949–1977.* Boulder, Colorado: Westview Press, 1977.

―――. "Public Health and Politics in China's Past Two Decades." *Health Service Reports* 87 (1972): 895–904.

―――. "Health Policy During the Great Leap Forward." *China Quarterly* 60 (1974): 668–698.

Latourette, Kenneth Scott. *A History of Christian Missions in China.* New York: Macmillan, 1929.

League of Nations. *Annual Report of the Health Organization for 1930.* Geneva: League of Nations, 1931.

League of Nations' Mission of Educational Experts. *The Reorganization of Education in China*. Paris: League of Nations' Institute of Intellectual Co-Operation, 1932.

Leathers, W. S. "The Integration of the Teaching of Preventive and Clinical Medicine." *Journal of the Association of American Medical Colleges* 14 (1939): 21–25.

Lee, Robert. "The Rural Reconstruction Movement." *Papers on China*. Cambridge, Mass.: East Asian Research Center, Harvard University 4 (1950): 160–198.

Lee, T'ao. "Some Statistics on Medical Schools in China for 1932–1933." *Chinese Medical Journal* 47 (1933): 1029–1039.

———. "Some Statistics on Medical Schools in China for the Year 1933–1934." *Chinese Medical Journal* 49 (1935): 894–902.

Lennox, W. G. "The Distribution of Medical School Graduates in China." *Chinese Medical Journal* 46 (1932): 404–411.

Li T'ing-an. "The Campaign Against Tuberculosis." *Chinese Medical Journal* 48 (1934): 301–303.

———. *Chung-wai i-hsueh shih kai-lun* [A general discussion of Chinese and foreign medical history]. Chungking, 1944.

———. "A Public Health Report on Canton, China." *National Medical Journal of China* 11 (1925): 324–375.

———. "Summary Report on Rural Public Health Practice in China." *Chinese Medical Journal* 48 (1934): 1086–1090.

Lim Kha-t'i [Lin Ch'iao-chih]. "Mass Survey for Cancer of Cervix Uteri in China." *Chinese Medical Journal* 81 (1962): 705–712.

———. "Obstetrics and Gynecology in the Past Ten Years." *Chinese Medical Journal* 79 (1959): 375–383.

Lim, Robert K. S. "Presidential Address." *National Medical Journal of China* 16 (1930): 117–121.

———, and C. C. Ch'en, "State Medicine." *Chinese Medical Journal* 51 (1937): 781–796.

Liu Jui-heng. "Central Field Health Station, Nanking." *Chinese Medical Journal* 50 (1936): 1855–1856.

———. "The Central Field Health Station as a Training Center for Public Health Workers." *Chinese Medical Journal* 49 (1935): 942–945.

———. "The Chinese Ministry of Health." *National Medical Journal of China* 15 (1929): 145–148.

———. "National Health Organization." *China Christian Year Book, 1936–1937*. pp. 336–355.

———. "Some Phases of Public Health Work in China." *Chinese Medical Journal* 48 (1934): 70–73.

Lu Hsün. *Ah Q and Others, Selected Stories of Lu Hsün*. New York: Columbia University Press, 1941.

Lutz, Jessie G. *China and the Christian Colleges, 1850–1950*. Ithaca, N.Y.: Cornell University Press, 1971.

Lyman, Richard S. et al., eds. *Social and Psychological Studies in Neuropsychiatry in China*. Tientsin: PUMC, 1939.

McCartney, James L. *Chinese Military Medicine*. Washington, D.C.: U.S. Government Printing Office, 1927.

MacFarquhar, Roderick. *The Hundred Flowers*. London: Stevens and Sons, 1960.

Manson-Bahr, Philip. *Manson's Tropical Diseases*. 16th edition. London: Balliere, Tindall, and Cassell, Ltd., 1966.

Markowitz, Gerald E., and David Karl Rosner. "Doctors in Crisis: A Study of the Use of Medical Education Reform to Establish Modern Professional Elitism in Medicine." *American Quarterly* 25 (1973): 83–107.

Maxwell, J. Preston. "Peking Union Medical College, Department of Obstetrics and Gynecology." *Methods and Problems of Medical Education*, First Series, 1924. New York: The Rockefeller Foundation, 1924, pp. 139–146.

May, Ernest R., and James C. Thomson. *American-East Asian Relations: A Survey*. Cambridge, Mass.: Harvard University Press, 1972.

Morgan, L. G. *The Teaching of Science to the Chinese*. Hong Kong: Kelly and Walsh, 1933.

Nathan, Carl. *Plague Prevention and Politics in Manchuria, 1910–1931*. Cambridge, Mass.: East Asian Research Center, 1967.

National Epidemic Prevention Bureau. *A Report, Being a Review of Its Activities From Its Foundation in March 1919 to June 1934*. Peiping: 1934.

National Public Health Activities: A Pictorial Survey. Nanking: Wei sheng shu, 1934.

Necheles, Heinrich. "Psychology of Chinese Students in the Light of Medical Education." *China Medical Journal* 42 (1928): 747–750.

Needham, Joseph. *Clerks and Craftsmen in China and the West*. Cambridge, England: Cambridge University Press, 1970.

Nevins, Allan. *Study in Power: John D. Rockefeller, Industrialist and Philanthropist*. 2 vols. New York: Charles Scribner's Sons, 1953.

"The New Rockefeller Hospital in Peking." *National Medical Journal of China* 5 (1919): 213–227.

New York Times. August–September 1921, New York.

Newsholme, Arthur. *The Evolution of Preventive Medicine*. Baltimore: Williams and Wilkins, 1927.

Orleans, Leo A. "Medical Education and Manpower in Communist China." *Comparative Education Review* 13 (1969): 20–42.

———. *Professional Manpower and Education in Communist China*. Washington, D.C.: National Science Foundation, 1961.

Paauw, Douglas. "Chinese National Expenditures During the Nanking Period." *Far Eastern Quarterly* 12 (November 1952): 3–26.

Parker, Franklin. "Abraham Flexner (1866–1959) and Medical Education." *Journal of Medical Education* 36 (1961): 709–716.

Peake, Cyrus. *Nationalism and Education in Modern China*. New York: Columbia University Press, 1932.

Peck, Graham. *Two Kinds of Time*. Boston: Houghton Mifflin, 1967.

Peiping Chronicle. 1932–1935, Peking.

Peking Union Medical College. *Annual Announcement*. 1918–1940, Peking.

———. *Bibliography of the Publications from the Laboratories and Clinics of the Peking Union Medical College and Hospital*. 3 vols: 1915–1925, 1925–1935, 1935–1940. Peking: PUMC Press.

———. *The Unison*. 1924, 1928, 1932. Peking: PUMC Press.

Peking Union Medical College Hospital. *Report of the Superintendent, 1930*. Peking: PUMC Press, 1931.

Penfield, Wilder. *The Difficult Art of Giving: The Epic of Alan Gregg*. Boston: Little, Brown, and Co., 1967.

———. "Oriental Renaissance in Education and Medicine." *Science* 20 September 1963, pp. 1153–1160.

P'eng, T. M. "A System of Medical and Allied Education at the National Defense Medical Center, Taipei, Taiwan." *Journal of Medical Education* 37 (1962): 463–472.

Peter, W. W. *Broadcasting Health in China*. Shanghai: Presbyterian Mission Press, 1926.

Pruitt, Ida. "Medical Social Workers: Their Work and Training." *Chinese Medical Journal* 49 (1935): 909–916.

Purcell, Victor. *Problems of Chinese Education*. London: K. Paul, Trench, Trubner and Co., 1936.

Quinn, Joseph R., ed. *Medicine and Public Health in the People's Republic of China*. Washington, D.C.: Department of Health, Education and Welfare, 1972.

Rajchman, Ludwig. "Report to the League of Nations, May 25, 1926." *National Medical Journal of China* 13 (1927): 288–292.

Read, Bernard E. "Chinese Materia Medica: A Review of Some of the Work of the Last Decade." *Chinese Medical Journal* 53 (1938): 353–362.

———. *Materia Medica: Tables and Notes*. 9th Edition. Peiping: Leader Press, 1931.

———. "Peking Union Medical College: Department of Pharmacology." *Methods and Problems of Medical Education*. Third Series. New York: The Rockefeller Foundation, 1925.

———, and J. C. Liu. "A Review of the Scientific Work Done on the Chinese Materia Medica." *National Medical Journal of China* 14 (1928): 312–320.

Reeves, Thomas C., ed. *Foundations Under Fire*. Ithaca, N.Y.: Cornell University Press, 1970.

Reeves, William, Jr. "Sino-American Co-Operation in Medicine: The Origins of Hsiang-Ya (1902–1914)." In *Papers on China* 14. Cambridge, Mass.: East Asian Research Center, 1960.

"The Reminiscences of Doctor John B. Grant." Columbia University Oral History Research Project conducted by Dr. Saul Benison, 1961.

Robertson, O. H. "Peking Union Medical College, Department of Medicine." *Methods and Problems of Medical Education*. Eighth Series. New York: The Rockefeller Foundation, 1927.

Robinson, G. Canby. *Adventures in Medical Education*. Cambridge, Mass.: Harvard University Press, 1957.

The Rockefeller Foundation. *Annual Report*. 1914–1951, New York.

———. *The President's Review*. 1917–1928, 1935–1950. New York.

Rockefeller, John D. *Random Reminiscences of Men and Events*. New York: Doubleday, 1937.

Rockefeller, John D., Jr. "Brotherhood of Men and Nations." No publishing information, 1918.

———. "Remarks of the Retiring Chairman, April 3, 1940." New York: The Rockefeller Foundation, 1940.

Round the World for Birth Control with Margaret Sanger and Edith How-Martyn. London: Birth Control Information Center, 1936.

"A Rural Health Experiment in China." *Milbank Memorial Fund Quarterly Bulletin* 8 (October 1930): 97–107.

Scott, James Cameron. *Health and Agriculture in China*. London: Faber and Faber, Ltd., 1952.

Seipp, Conrad, ed. *Health Care for the Community: Selected Papers of Dr. John B. Grant*. Baltimore: Johns Hopkins Press, 1966.

Shen Chi-ying. "The Cost of Various Types of Medical Services at the Peiping Health Demonstration Station." *Chinese Medical Journal* 47 (1933): 605–608.

Sheridan, James E. *Chinese Warlord: The Career of Feng Yü-hsiang*. Stanford: Stanford University Press, 1966.

Shryock, Richard H. *The Development of Modern Medicine*. New York: Alfred A. Knopf, 1947.

———. *The Unique Influence of the Johns Hopkins University on American Medicine*. Copenhagen: Ejnar Munksgaard, Ltd., 1953.

Sidel, Victor. "The Barefoot Doctors of the People's Republic of China." *New England Journal of Medicine*. 15 June 1972, pp. 1292–1300.

Smedley, Agnes. *Stories of the Wounded: An Appeal for Orthopedic Centers of the Chinese Red Cross*. No publishing information, 1941.

Smith, Robert Gillen. "History of the Attempt of the United States Army Medical Department to Improve the Effectiveness of the Chinese Army Medical Service, 1941–1945." Ph.D. Dissertation, Columbia University, 1950.

Snapper, Isidore. *Chinese Lessons to Western Medicine: A Contribution to Geographical Medicine from the Clinics of Peiping Union Medical College*. 2nd edition. New York: Crume and Stratton, 1965.

Snow, Edgar. *Red China Today: The Other Side of the River*. New York: Random House, 1971.

Spence, Jonathan. *To Change China: Western Advisers in China, 1620–1960*. Boston: Little, Brown, and Co., 1969.

Stevens, Rosemary. *American Medicine and the Public Interest*. New Haven, Conn.: Yale University Press, 1971.

Survey of the China Mainland Press. 1951–1965, U.S. Consulate, Hong Kong.

Sze Sze-ming. *China's Health Problems*. Washington, D.C.: The China Medical Association, 1943.

Tandler, J. "Medical Protection and Medical Education in China." *People's Tribune* N.S. 8 (1935): 383–399.

Tao, S. M. "Medical Education of Chinese Women." *Chinese Medical Journal* 47 (1933): 1010–1028.

Taylor, Adrian S. "Peking Union Medical College Department of Surgery." *Methods and Problems of Medical Education*. Third Series, 1925. New York: The Rockefeller Foundation, 1925.

"Technical Co-Operation with Certain Governments: China." *Quarterly Bulletin of the Health Organization, League of Nations* 1 (1932): 403–412.

"Technical Co-Operation with Certain Governments: China." *Quarterly Bulletin of the Health Organization, League of Nations* 2 (1933): 505–512.

Thomson, James C. *While China Faced West; American Reformers in Nationalist China, 1928–1937*. Cambridge, Mass.: Harvard University Press, 1969.

"The Ting Hsien Experiment." *Chinese Medical Journal* 47 (1933): 610.

Tsai Fang-chin. "American Standards of 'Good Medical Care' per 100,000 Population and their Comparison with the Present Medical Facilities in the First Health Area, Peiping." *Transactions of the Ninth Congress, Far Eastern Association of Tropical Medicine*. Nanking: National Health Association, 1935.

Tseng, Lily. "Midwifery." *China Medical Journal* 44 (1930): 431–445.

Twiss, George R. "Science Education in China." *The China Mission Year Book, 1924*, pp. 283–287.

Van Slyke, Lyman P. "Liang Sou-ming and the Rural Reconstruction Movement." *Journal of Asian Studies* 18 (1959): 457–474.

Varg, Paul. *Missionaries, Chinese and Diplomats: The American Protestant Missionary Movement in China, 1890–1952*. Princeton, N.J.: Princeton University Press, 1958.

Vincent, George E. "Medical Progress in China." *China Medical Journal* 34 (1920): 162–166.

Wang, Y.C. *Chinese Intellectuals and the West, 1872–1949*. Chapel Hill: University of North Carolina Press, 1966.

Wegman, Myron, Lin Tsung-yi and Elizabeth F. Purcell, eds. *Public Health in the People's Republic of China*. New York: Macy Foundation, 1973.

Welch, William H. *Addresses and Papers by William Henry Welch*. 3 vols. Baltimore: Johns Hopkins University Press, 1928.

West, Philip. "Yenching University and Chinese-American Relations, 1917–1937." Ph.D. Dissertation, Harvard University, 1971.

Who's Who in China. 1920, 1933. Shanghai.

Wong, K. Chimin and Wu Lien-teh. *History of Chinese Medicine*. Tientsin: Tientsin Press, 1932.

Worth, Robert M. "Health Trends in China Since the Great Leap Forward." *China Quarterly* 22 (1965): 181–190.

———. "Institution Building in the People's Republic of China: The Rural Health Center." *East-West Center Review* 1 (1965): 19–34.

Wu, Daisy Yen. *Wu Hsien, 1893–1959*. Boston: Privately published, 1960.

Wu Hsien. "Chinese Diet in the Light of Modern Knowledge of Nutrition." *Chinese Social and Political Science Review* 11 (1927): 56–81.

———. *Guide to Scientific Living*. Taipei: Academia Sinica, 1963.

———. [under pseudonym T'ao Ming], "Ting Hsien chien-wen tsa-lu," [Notes on Miscellaneous Experiences at Ting Hsien]. *Tu-li p'ing-lun* 4 (1932): 13–18.

———. "Yu yu-jen lun i-wu shu," [A Discourse with Friends on Medical Affairs]. *Tu-li p'ing-lun* 201 (1936): 39–42.

Wu Lien-teh. "Memorandum of Medical Education in China." *China Medical Journal* 28 (1914): 105–120.

———. *Plague Fighter: Autobiography of a Chinese Physician*. Cambridge, England: W. Heffer, 1959.

Yang, Marian. "Birth Control in Peiping: First Report of the Peiping Committee on Maternal Health." *Chinese Medical Journal* 48 (1934): 786–791.

———. "Child Health Work in the Peiping Special Health Area." *China Medical Journal* 43 (1929): 920–925.

———. "Control of Practising Midwives in China." *China Medical Journal* 44 (1930): 428–431.

———. "Letter to the Editor." *China Medical Journal* 42 (1928): 554.

———. "Midwifery Training in China." *China Medical Journal* 42 (1928): 768–775.

———, and H. H. Huang. "A Study of Still Births in 3974 Consecutive Deliveries in the First National Midwifery School Maternity Hospital." *Chinese Medical Journal* 49 (1935): 775–779.

———, and Yuan I-chin. "Report of an Investigation on Infant Mortality and Its Causes in Peiping." *Chinese Medical Journal* 47 (1933): 597–694.

Yao Hsun-yuan. "The First Year of the Rural Health Experiment in Ting Hsien, China." *Milbank Memorial Fund Quarterly Bulletin* 9 (July 1931): 61–77.

———. "Industrial Health Work in the Peiping Special Health Area." *China Medical Journal* 43 (1929): 379–387.

———. "Plan for Malaria Control in Yunnan." *Chinese Medical Journal* 56 (1939): 63–68.

———. "The Provincial Health Administration of Yunnan." *Chinese Medical Journal* 53 (1938): 577–583.

———. "The Second Year of the Rural Health Experiment in Ting Hsien, China." *Milbank Memorial Fund Quarterly Bulletin* 10 (January 1932): 55–66.

Yen Ching-ch'ing, and Liu Ch'ing-hsueh. "Death Rates in the City Districts of Peking." *Chinese Medical Journal* 78 (1959): 27–30.

Yen Fu-ching. "China's War-time Health Administration." *China Quarterly* 4 (1939): pp. 243–258.

———. "Economics of Medical Schools and Hospitals in China." *Chinese Medical Journal* 49 (1935): 887–893.

———. "The National Health Administration During War-Time." *The People's Tribune* 27 (1938): 45–48.

Yung, W. W. "Child Health Work in Peiping First Health Area, 1925–1935." *Chinese Medical Journal* 50 (1936): 562–572.

Index

ABMAC. *See* American Bureau for Medical Aid to China

Acadia College in Nova Scotia, 135

Acupuncture, 224, 225

Adaptation of Peking Union Medical College: Chinese architecture of PUMC, 7–8, 9; Chinese participation in administration, 57–62, 101–102 (*see also* Chinese leadership at PUMC); Communist criticism of, 211–215; curriculum modifications for, 15, 93–95, 99–103; denationalizing experience of students at, 115–116; graduates' adaptation to other Chinese institutions, 132; Henry Houghton's recommendations on, 103–105; need for recognized by John D. Rockefeller, Jr., 22, 48, 74; promotion of Chinese staff vs. Western control, 88–93; reforms required by the Nationalist government, 59–60, 99–101, 106; response of ordinary Chinese citizens to, 13–14; standards of vs. socioeconomic conditions in China, 46, 102, 103, 194–196, 203, 210, 211, 231; success of PUMC dependent on, 15–16, 47; transfer of Western research leadership to Chinese students, 120–125;

and Western efficiency in surgical missions by PUMC staff, 82–83; during World War II, 193–196

Adaptation of Western medicine to China, xix, 133; by John Grant, 6, 134, 140–141, 146, 148; by medical missionaries, 38; in rural China, 162–189 *passim*; William Welch's views of, 6, 7, 39–40

Administrative structure: and adaptation of PUMC to China, 57–63, 132; autonomy for PUMC, 52, 54–57, 62, 66; changes recommended by Henry Houghton, 103–105; Chinese advisory committee to PUMC, 57–58; Chinese leadership of all PUMC departments, 104; Chinese replacement of Western administrators, 58, 59, 106; Chinese representation in the PUMC Trustees, 22, 48, 58, 60–62, 64, 74, 76; conflict and controversy in, 62, 63; controversy about religion at PUMC, 66–69; duplication in board memberships, 50, 51, 63; endowment of PUMC via the China Medical Board, Inc., 55–57, 64; financial planning for PUMC, 53, 54, 63–64, 65 (*see also* Budget of Peking Union Medical College);

Designer:	Al Burkhardt
Compositor:	G & S Typesetters
Printer:	Thomson-Shore
Binder:	Thomson-Shore
Text:	VIP Primer
Display:	VIP Century Expanded Roman
Cloth:	Joanna Arrestox A 53500 Linen
Paper:	55 lb. P&S Offset Vellum A-50